# HOW
# ITALIAN FOOD
*Conquered*
# THE WORLD

## JOHN F. MARIANI

*Foreword by* LIDIA BASTIANICH

palgrave
macmillan

First published in 2011 by PALGRAVE MACMILLAN® in the United States—
a division of St. Martin's Press LLC, 175 Fifth Avenue, New York, NY 10010.

Where this book is distributed in the UK, Europe and the rest of the world, this is by
Palgrave Macmillan, a division of Macmillan Publishers Limited, registered in
England, company number 785998, of Houndmills, Basingstoke, Hampshire
RG21 6XS.

Palgrave Macmillan is the global academic imprint of the above companies and has
companies and representatives throughout the world.

Palgrave® and Macmillan® are registered trademarks in the United States, the United
Kingdom, Europe and other countries.

ISBN 978-0-230-10439-6

Library of Congress Cataloging-in-Publication Data
Mariani, John F.
   How Italian food conquered the world / John F. Mariani ; foreword by Lidia
Bastianich.
      p.   cm.
   ISBN 978-0-230-10439-6
   1. Cooking, Italian.   2. Cooking—Italy—History.   I. Title.
TX723.M328185   2011
641.5945—dc22

                                                              2010028193

A catalogue record of the book is available from the British Library.

Design by Greg Collins

First edition: March 2011

10  9  8  7  6  5  4  3  2  1

Printed in the United States of America.

# Contents

*Photos appear between pages 142 and 143.*

# Acknowledgments

I suspect that most historians never meet the people they write about, but I have been fortunate to interview and in many cases count as friends so many important figures who have contributed to the evolution of Italian food here and abroad over the last century. Many were the creators of dishes that became world famous, others opened restaurants that defined the style of a decade, others helped dispel stereotypical myths about Italian food and wines, and others were writers and editors who have helped in my research or published their own chronicles of world gastronomy.

I am, therefore, very grateful for the help I received—often over a plate of pasta with a good bottle of Italian wine—from these friends and associates:

Lidia and Joseph Bastianich, Russell Bellanca, Lucio Caputo, Marie-Bénédicte Chevet, Michael Chiarello, Arrigo Cipriani, Anna and Tony Cortese, Ryan D'Agostino, Nicky Di Chiara, Mary Ann Esposito, Pamela Fiori, Nicotra Fortunato, David Granger, David Greco, Pino Luongo, Sirio, Egidiana, Marco, and Mauro Maccioni, Laura Maioglio, Tony Mantuano, Augusto Marchini, Tony and Marisa May, Ferdinand Metz, Joe Miglucci, Stefano Ongaro, Roberto Ruggeri, Joe Scognamillo, Piero Selvaggio, Marilyn Sofia, Nick Sullivan, Henry Togna, Tony Vallone, Nick Valenti, Richard Vines, and Michael White.

This book was as much my agent Michael Psaltis's idea as mine, developed over a boozy lunch at an Italian trattoria, and it was further refined by my editor Alessandra Bastagli, whose insistence on focus and cogency made this what I hope is a good read as well as a thorough survey of gastronomic history.

As ever, my wife Galina was the one who, after I spent a long day writing and re-writing, made the prospect of a marvelous dinner one of the true perks of this project.

# Foreword

John Mariani's tale of Italian food and its culture is a revealing and very informative one. Beneath its cover, within the pages, lies a story of a people who, century after century, have sought to share a love of their food and culture and marry the two so effortlessly that the end result has not only captivated but "conquered the world."

After reading this tale of storied triumph, I found many answers to questions that I myself have asked along the way. Chapter after chapter, I found myself relating to these stories, encounters, and experiences very personally, intimately. Perhaps it is because my own story plays a part in the history of this magnificent culture that I can say this. I have lived and experienced firsthand much of what Mariani has researched and written about in this book.

In 1958, at the tender and impressionable age of 12, I found myself as a young immigrant in America. I was ready and eager to embrace my newfound home in a country that welcomed me with open arms. What I wanted was to be American—NOW! I couldn't master the language, learn the lyrics to the songs, or taste enough of the food fast enough. I wanted more America, and I wanted it now—yesterday! The first juicy taste of a grapefruit, the wiggly sensation of Jell-O, the squishy feeling of a PB&J sandwich—oh my goodness, first salty, then sweet—these were all experiences that made me ever-more American.

But back at home, we were Italian. The menu in our house consisted of a weekly meal of pasta e fagioli, polenta with brodetto di pesce on Friday nights, and homemade gnocchi on Sundays. As I began working in restaurants, mostly Italian restaurants, my palate was a stranger to the food being served. What was this food that I simply couldn't identify with, couldn't recognize? It was Italian-American! Spaghetti and meatballs, veal parmigiana, Caesar salad, and garlic bread with mounds of butter and garlic. Oh, how this food was then, and still is now, a much loved—rather, adored—cuisine. These Italian restaurants were full each night, but the food was not that of the Italy I knew.

It was then that I became obsessed with my Italian culture, with my heritage, and the foods of Italy—the food I grew up with, not the Italian food in America.

It soon became clear to me that I was blessed, for the renaissance of traditional Italian food was just beginning to happen in America. It was a very exciting time. But saying "traditional" means taking into consideration all of the twenty regions of Italy, with all of the subdivisions and microclimates. A tremendous amount of respect must be paid to the different borders and bodies of water, and to the culinary legacy of past occupations by other peoples—all of these aspects have helped ultimately to shape and flavor what is Italy today.

The culinary heritage of Italy is steeped in its products and their quality. There is an inherent respect for the seasonality of products and regional micro-climactic differences. This respect is also evident in the way that most Italians in Italy eat locally, using fresh, local products of their native region, prepared with the simplest of executions.

At the end of the day, all roads lead to Rome. Italian food is simply gratifying, effortlessly delicious, and nutritionally sound. The smells and flavors created are unparalleled, and once one has the raw ingredients, this cuisine is accessible to every cook and food-lover alike. It is safe to say that Americans have a love affair with Italy and its food and that they aspire to live the Italian style and eat the Italian way.

What I hear most often from the guests of my restaurants, readers of my cookbooks, and followers of my show, is that they not only love the foods of Italy, but they love what that food means to the Italians. It touches their hearts to see the importance of family and friends gathering around a table sharing and eating together. Italian food has certainly found its way onto our tables and into our hearts and, ultimately, has stopped at nothing short of conquering the world. I think that's pretty great.

*—Lidia Bastianich*

# Introduction

Go to a restaurant anywhere in the world today—even in Tokyo, Hong Kong, or Mumbai—and chances are you will see Italian dishes listed on the menu. There will inevitably be a pasta dish or two, perhaps cannelloni stuffed with foie gras and black truffles at a three-star Michelin restaurant in Paris. There might be a selection of Italian *salumi* and fresh *burrata* cheese offered at a gastro-pub in London. Pizzas seem to have become as requisite to a menu in New York as sirloin steak. Salads everywhere are now being dressed with extra virgin olive oil and a dash of balsamic vinegar. For dessert there will be housemade gelato and *panna cotta*. And the wine list will always carry Italian labels, probably even a few Super Tuscans.

On American television, celebrity chefs like Giada DeLaurentiis, Mario Batali, Lidia Bastianich, and Michael Chiarello promote the natural goodness and healthfulness of authentic Italian cooking. In the UK, star chef Jamie Oliver spread the gospel of Italian food on his six-part series *Jamie's Great Italian Escape*.

Until recently such interest in and ubiquity of Italian food and wine was unthinkable, and it would have been highly unusual to find Italian dishes on menus at non-Italian restaurants. The appearance of Prosciutto di Parma, Parmigiano Reggiano, aceto balsamico, arugula, radicchio, and imported pasta on a menu would have been a rare novelty as recently as the mid-1980s and in the not-so-distant past, the mere presence of garlic in a dish was regarded as emblematic of the unsophisticated taste of Italian cooks.

Indeed, while it is now indisputable that Italian food is among the most popular in the world, it was not very long ago that Italian food just about everywhere outside of Italy was regarded as little more than macaroni with red sauce, chicken parmigiana, pizza, and "dago red" wines. Before World War II, only a handful of major cities around the world had any Italian restaurants at all, and the menus were maddeningly similar—featuring mediocre ingredients—and the food was simply cheap and filling.

Later on, in the 1970s, food writers lumped Italian food with the other "ethnic foods"—Mexican, Chinese, and so on—while French food was always referred to as the international standard for "cuisine." The 1970 edition of France's culinary bible, *Larousse Gastronomique,* ignored Italian food almost entirely, listing but one Italian dish: *spaghetti à l'italienne,* with the instructions to boil *nouilles* (noodles) and pour on a *sauce tomate avec herbes* (tomato sauce with herbs).

Then, starting in the 1980s, Italian food—more often than not Italian-*American* food—became not only the most popular in the world but also among the most fashionable. Today, it would be impossible to dine at a Michelin-starred restaurant in Paris and *not* find cannelloni, ravioli, and gnocchi on the menus—though it is likely they might be stuffed with foie gras and truffles, not meat and cheese.

Today, there is hardly a non-ethnic restaurant in America that does not have an array of Italian dishes, from flatbread pizzas to arugula salads, from *carpaccios* to *panna cottas. Salumi* and *salsicce* have become the norm at new restaurants, as have *focaccia* and fennel bread. And, according to numerous industry surveys, Italian food is the most popular food in America—even more popular than American food. The *Michelin Guide,* which once shrugged off Italian restaurants as mere diversions, now awards its top, three-star ratings to six *ristoranti* in Italy. Many of the most popular restaurants in Tokyo are now Italian, and there are chic trattorias in Mayfair, Belgravia, and Knightsbridge.

This culinary popularity has carried over to Italian wines, which were once deemed undrinkable but are now judged among the best in the world, with wines like Tuscany's Sassicaia and Solaia winning "Wine of the Year" awards from magazines such as *Wine Spectator.* Back in the 1970s, it would have been unthinkable to try to sell an Italian wine for $100 or more; now there are many bottles at that price or higher.

In addition to countless magazine and newspaper stories covering Italian cooking, wines, chefs, and restaurants, Italian cookbooks have become the biggest bestsellers and command the most space on bookstore shelves, with "celebrity" names on their spines; and on TV, the most popular food shows are almost always about Italian cooking.

In this book, we will explore how the regional cuisines of Campania, Emilia-Romagna, Tuscany, Abruzzo, and the sixteen other regions of Italy were wholly isolated until well into the twentieth century. It was the emigrants to America—overwhelmingly from the south—who created, through sheer necessity, an

Italian-American food culture that by the end of the twentieth century had become as distinctive as neoclassical architecture was in the eighteenth century, Pre-Raphaelite painting was in the nineteenth, and postmodern art was in the twentieth. And it is still evolving.

As an Italian-American familiar with hearing epithets like "garlic eater," "spaghetti bender," and "macaroni," I have, over the past four decades, been an attentive witness to the rise in status of Italian food from a low-class, coarse ethnic food to the most recognizable, stylish, and influential cuisine in the world.

How that happened has as much to do with changing ideas of ethnicity and a surging interest in wholesome ingredients as it is does with taste and fashion. And it is a story full of suffering, endurance, acceptance, and triumph well beyond the basic sustenance of people for whom food must nurture the soul as well as the body.

Many years ago, when I was in college, I brought home four friends unannounced, just as my mother was finishing a dinner of *spaghetti alla marinara* with my father. She said, "Sit down, sit down, I'll make you some spaghetti." My friends all protested she need not go to any bother. But she just shook her head and said, "Don't worry, there'll be enough. I'll just stretch the sauce a little. Now, tell your friends to wash their hands."

There always seems to be enough sauce to go around in Italian kitchens.

# Chapter 1

# A Plate of Soup
# Surrounded by Too Many Spoons

Simply put, there *was* no Italian food before there was an Italy. There was Tuscan food and Ligurian food and Sicilian food and Sardinian food, but for two thousand years there was no *Italian* food. Not until 1861, when most of its 20 regions were unified as a kingdom under Victor Emmanuel II, was there a country called Italy. Even then, city-states such as Venice and Rome (which was declared the new capital) and some of the papal states remained separate from the new country. Before 1861 and for a century afterward, what people ate in Rome had little to do with what they ate in Bari, and when Florentines dined, it was not on the same food and wine enjoyed by Neapolitans or Venetians. There was regional food, but for two thousand years there was no Italian food. Then as now, and especially in the kitchen, Italians resisted being thought of merely as Italians.

The name Italy had of course been used for millennia, referring to the dozens of highly diverse regions on the long finger of mountainous land that divides the Mediterranean in two. "I call Italy all that peninsula which is bounded by the Ionian Gulf and the Tyrrhenian Sea and, thirdly, by the Alps on the landward side," wrote the Greek historian Dionysius of Halicarnassus in the first century BC in his *Roman Antiquities.*[1] But he was speaking of Italy as he might of Asia or Africa rather than as a territory of indigenous people who regarded themselves as Italians. The Italian language, derived from Latin, is not even found in print earlier than the tenth century, and most people spoke only their local dialect, unintelligible to people in the next region, sometimes even in the next town, well into the twentieth century.

The story of Italy's myriad food cultures begins within the much wider context of the Mediterranean Basin and with the people who so relentlessly invaded the peninsula for more than two thousand years. With its rippling, ragged coastlines jutting out into the seas, its broad, fertile valleys, and hillsides ideal for viticulture, Italy was always ripe for trade and conquest. The Greeks settled in southern Italy and Sicily around 800 BC; the Gauls came to the northern Po Valley in the fifth century BC; soon afterward, Rome consolidated its power and began its march to empire, expanding its dominance over most of the known western world as far as Britain.

Then, beginning in the fifth century AD, successive barbarian tribes drove southward into Italy. The Visigoths sacked Rome in 410, and when the German general Odoacer declared himself King of Italy in 476, the Western Roman Empire came to its end. For the next thousand years every inch of Italy was fought over, divided, and restructured by successive invaders—Ostrogoths, Lombards, Byzantines, Franks, Normans, and Arabs, well into the fourteenth century, when the new northern Italian city-states struggled for hegemony, often through alliances with the papacy.

Sicily, valued as the bread basket of the Mediterranean because of its vast wheat fields, was controlled by the Greeks, Vandals, Ostrogoths, Byzantines, Arabs, Normans, and the Holy Roman Emperor in succession, before going into decline in the thirteenth century under inept French and Aragonese control. In 1713, Naples and Sardinia came under the rule of Austria, which also gained control over Tuscany and Venice; Corsica was sold by Genoa to France; finally, Napoleon invaded Italy in 1800, crowning his brother Joseph King of Naples.

It is little wonder, then, that Italy has been compared colloquially to a plate of soup surrounded by too many spoons. This varied political history is reflected in its culinary history, which reflects so many culinary influences. By the third century BC, Roman food culture had absorbed Greek cookery—a very simple diet of grains, vegetables, and fish—in only the most ancillary ways. The appetites of both wealthy Greeks and Romans favored sweet and sour flavors of honey and vinegar; one of the principle flavorings was fermented fish sauce, along with spices like coriander, cumin, and oregano. And well-to-do Romans valued the sweet wines of Greece over Italy's own wines.

The world's first known cookbook is Roman, entitled *Apicius*, after nobleman Marcus Gavius Apicius, or *De Re Coquinaria* (On the subject of cooking), which appeared during the first century AD. Probably compiled by Apicius's slave cooks for the slave cooks of other wealthy families, the recipes, nearly five hundred of them, provided little indication of measurements but gave a good idea of the lavish banquets mounted by men like Apicius. Dinners described by Apicius and early chroniclers like Cato, Pliny, Plautus, Plutarch, and especially Petronius in the "Trimalchio's Feast" section of his picaresque *Satyricon,* were as extravagant as any in history. There were tables piled high with exotica such as porpoise, dormice, coxcombs, ostriches, sows' wombs, cranes, flamingoes, and camels, all washed down with sweet, scented wine. The third-century emperor Heliogabalus once ordered six hundred ostriches to be slaughtered for pies to be served to his banquet guests and supposedly fattened vats of eels with the meat of Christians slain in the Coliseum. In most cases such gluttonous meals would be interrupted for guests to visit vomitoria in order to expel what they had eaten; then they would go back to the table and gorge for hours more.

In the cities there were taverns and food stalls, and in Rome, the attractions of the Coliseum, theater, prostitution, and thievery went hand in hand with gluttony, as fourth-century historian Ammianus Marcellinus wrote, describing the vices of the Romans: "Attracted by the smell of cooking and the shrill voices of the women, who scream from cockcrow like a flock of starving peacocks, they stand about the courts on tiptoe, biting their fingers and waiting for the dishes to cool. Others keep their gaze fixed on some revolting mess of meat till it is ready."[2]

But the common man of Rome and the rest of Italy lived on little more than bread, olives, a few vegetables such as chickpeas and broccoli, and, when available, meat. Landowning farmers enjoyed an additional bounty, especially eggs and fruits, perhaps even some animals for slaughter. The Roman legions marched down paved Roman roads on a diet of grains of oats, wheat, barley, and spelt, in the form of porridge and bread, along with a little meat. Everyone drank wine, usually cut with water. (By the end of the first century, aqueducts were providing Rome with 50 gallons of water per capita per day.)

Trade also brought different elements to the cuisine of the Italian peninsula. The seaside cities like Genoa, Venice, Naples, and Palermo grew wealthy both from importing and exporting food, especially spices. Wine and olive oil was shipped around the Mediterranean from Italian vineyards. In the interior of Italy inns lined the roads that were built throughout Italy to ensure the easy movement of merchants. By the time Rome had grown into an omnivorous empire, the universal taxation of conquered people and the import of spices from as far away as India brought untold wealth to the capital. Still, given their expense, such exotica as cinnamon, saffron, ginger, and coriander was available only to Rome's wealthiest citizens.

The disintegration of the empire in the fifth century led to the corruption of Roman law, the reversal of great advances in Roman agriculture and irrigation, and the closing off of well-established trade routes. Further, with the onset of the Dark Ages, most Europeans would endure five hundred years of food shortages and a diet that was barely sufficient to keep body and soul together, consisting mostly of grains and vegetables. Famines were frequent and long; chronic wars interrupted trade routes, and starving one's enemies by destroying foodstuffs or blockading whole cities was standard military policy.

The Black Death, or the bubonic plague, which probably began in China in the 1330s, reached Florence in 1348 and spread from there throughout the Western world, killing between one-third and two-thirds of the population. The vestiges of this epidemic did not entirely disappear from Europe until the nineteenth century. Towns were breeding grounds for disease, and food was also scarce in urban settings; for while they provided protection of food stores and granaries for its citizens, food was not produced there and merchants in town could sell only what was brought in from the country, and that was usually scarce. Almost all food, especially vegetables, was expensive for the peasants, with the exception of bread. Vegetable crops were dependent upon local farmers' ancient agricultural practices, which were unimproved for millennia, and crops were prone to failure.

Central markets were established within the city walls and became, after the church, the social center of the populace. Feast days, akin to the Roman idea of tamping down popular discontents with "bread and circuses" (minus the slaughter of Christians), were established by the church as a way both to maintain the people's link to their religion and to allow for a display of excess now and then, so that the extra expenditure on a little frying oil or honey was geared to a saint's holy day, and the killing of a pig was license to drink a little more wine than normal, as long as every part of the pig was eaten or preserved.

Otherwise, the church preached frugality *in extremis*. In the monasteries, monks had vegetable and herb gardens, but largely they depended on the local farms and towns to provide their sustenance, except for the mendicant orders, which depended entirely on begging. Not until the sixth century, when the Benedictines changed the rules for monks' diets, were they allowed to eat two meals a day; prior to that, monks subsisted on a single meal of porridge, dried biscuits, and little else. Still, only one meal was allowed on fast days, which could number at least two hundred per year.

As ever, the aristocratic courts had access to the best food and wine, and, except for the absence of slave girls, medieval banquets were not much less extravagant than those of ancient Rome. The rich, called the *popolo grasso* (fat
people), ate meat in great quantities, eschewed fish except on fast days, and
adored game dishes, so that the nursery rhyme about four-and-twenty black-
birds baked in a pie was not far from the kind of dainty dishes actually set before the king.

The *popolo grasso* were also the main consumers in the lucrative spice trade.
Spices, though extremely expensive, still made their way to European cities and
made the merchants who sold them rich. Venice and other Italian port cities
were strategically important at the onset of the Crusades in 1095, the original
aim of which was to free the Holy Land from the Muslims. The church's success in rousing the populace of Europe to arms was based on religion, but the
wars also offered cities, nobles, and merchants new opportunities for territo-
rial and mercantile expansion, while liberating the poor from their wretched
state in life. By the time the Crusades ended, with the Christians' abandonment
of Acre in 1291, Europe had gained access to Arab culture, science, and trade;
and since the papacy and Byzantine Empire had been weakened as the nobility and merchant class grew stronger, Italian city-states emerged as the new
great powers in the Mediterranean. Venice was the ultimate victor because the
city was under the protection of Byzantium and so well situated on the Adriatic. It also was closest to the spice sources and grew rich from its fishing trade
and held a monopoly on salt drawn from its own lagoons.

Into this late medieval world sailed Marco Polo, a Venetian who began a remarkable journey in 1271 to reach Kublai Khan's court in China. During his travels, Polo conducted business with and for Khan, visited Southeast Asia and India,
ruled the city of Yangchow for three years, and acted as an escort for the Khan of
Persia's wife. After fifteen thousand miles of travel over fourteen years, he returned to Venice in 1295 and immediately joined his city's struggle against the
port city of Genoa. After being captured, while he was imprisoned for two years,
he dictated a memoir of all he had seen on his travels to Asia, a narrative that
was to remain the principal account of the Orient for a Western audience until
well into the nineteenth century.

Despite its exaggerations and probable falsification of some events, Polo's descriptions of the magnificence of Chinese cities showed Europe still to be in the
shadows of the Dark Ages in art, science, architecture, warfare, and gastronomy.
He described vast fleets of trading ships bringing spices from the East Indies, and

the array of foods and aspects of cuisine that he encountered: exotic and familiar fruits, like bananas, vegetables, different cooking methods, tastes, refined sugar, eating places and three-story wine halls. He was astonished at the size and scope of the fish markets in Hangzhou, which brought seafood 25 miles upriver. Marco Polo could not believe that so much seafood could be sold in a single day.

He also described the passion the Chinese had for noodles, which he compared to the kind of vermicelli already enjoyed back in Italy. The long-discredited myth of Marco Polo's discovering noodles and bringing the idea back to Italy seems to have come from a misreading of one of the myriad corrupted texts that made up what came to be called *The Travels of Marco Polo*. By the same token, he also commented on the important role of rice in Chinese cuisine, a revelation that would have been far more surprising to Italians, because there was none being cultivated in Italy at that time.

Marco Polo's achievements were spectacular at a time when the world known to Europeans did not extend much beyond Persia in the east and certainly not beyond Portugal in the west. But far beyond dazzling his readers with his tales of adventure and challenging Europeans to learn from the Orient, Marco Polo stoked a raging appetite for foods and spices that could be found only in China, India, and the Indies. Indeed, the high price of spices such as cinnamon, saffron, and turmeric gives the lie to the absurd contention that medieval cooks doused their food with spices because the meat and fish were poor in quality. No one could afford to waste spices on bad meat or fish.

The prospect of unfathomable wealth—not political power, not the extending of the Christian religion—drove that appetite eastward. After Venice vanquished Genoa in the War of Chioggia in 1380, the way east would go through Venice, which acquired the name "La Serenissima." That is, until someone could somehow find a route sailing west.

Even before Marco Polo's return from the Orient in 1295, the project of finding a sea route to India for the sole purpose of obtaining spices had been undertaken by other determined merchants. Brothers Ugolino and Vadino Vivaldi left Genoa in 1291 with a ten-year plan to reach India by sailing westward and down the African coast. They never returned, and their fate is unknown.

In 1488, Portuguese nobleman Bartholomew Diaz actually rounded the tip of Africa but was prevented by a mutinous crew from pushing on to India. Finally, in 1498, Vasco da Gama, sailing from Lisbon, reached Calcutta, returning a year later, his hold heavy with Indian spices. His achievement paid off tremendously well for Portugal: within 25 years of his voyage, it had become Europe's principal conduit for Eastern spices and charged exorbitantly for them, effectively loosening Venice's hold on the spice trade.

Six years earlier, however, a Genoese sea captain named Christopher Columbus had sailed under the Spanish flag straight westward in search of the Indies but instead found a New World of unimaginable wealth—not rich with the sought-after spices of the Orient but far, far richer in foods that led to what became known as the Columbian Exchange. This reciprocity of trade, from Europe to the Americas and back, was truly a revolution. Food historian Felipe Fernández-Armesto has called it "a long-term structural shift in history [and] one of the biggest modifications ever inflicted by man on the rest of nature" as plants and animals that had developed in isolation for over two hundred million years were suddenly, as of the sixteenth century, "shifted around the world in a convergent pattern."[3] From the New World to the Old came amaranth grain, avocadoes, various beans, bell peppers, blueberries, cashews, chile peppers, cocoa, vanilla, corn, papayas, peanuts, pecans, pineapples, white and sweet potatoes, pumpkins, quinoa, and tomatoes. In turn, the Old World sent to the New apples, artichokes, asparagus, bananas, barley, black pepper, cabbage, carrots, coffee, lemons and limes, garlic, lettuce, oats, millet, olives, peaches, peas, rice, rye, soybeans, sugarcane, tea, and, perhaps most important, wheat.

Europeans also brought bees, chickens, cows, geese, horses, pigs, sheep, and water buffalo to the Americas. Spaniard Ponce de Léon introduced beef cattle to Florida in 1521 and his countryman Francesco Vásquez de Coronado brought them into southwestern America; the Spanish brought hogs to Florida in 1539. Within decades, the gastronomies of both hemispheres were mightily enriched and drastically altered; within three centuries many of the imported foods had become staples in areas where they had been completely unknown.

Italy eventually imported most of the foods from the Americas, both out of botanical interest and as welcome new forms of nutrition. Other foods, like the chile pepper, first introduced by the Portuguese to India, could be grown abundantly in southern Italian soil. It was appreciated for the intensity of flavor it provided to the usual bland diet of grains, vegetables, bread and porridge—even more than expensive black pepper from the East. Cocoa, at first, was a novelty only for those who could afford it. Eventually, new chocolate houses made it more widely available as a stimulating beverage, although the process of converting it into edible chocolate did not come until the nineteenth century. Vanilla, introduced to Europe from Mexico in the sixteenth century by Spanish explorer Hernando Cortez, helped fuel an appetite for ice cream and pastries.

Potatoes, first encountered in Colombia, were brought back by the Spanish in 1536. In Italy, their culinary value was recognized only after a Carmelite monk named Nicolò Doria brought the tuber to Genoa in 1585 and insisted it was perfectly edible. Still, despite its being widely adopted by the Germans, Irish, even the French, the potato was more or less ignored in Italy.

Tomatoes from South America, on the other hand, took firm root in southern Italy upon being introduced in the sixteenth century, although they at first had a reputation for being poisonous, if highly decorative. In 1544, botanist Piero Andrea Mattioli called them *pomi d'oro,* "golden apples," a name that stuck, becoming *pomodoro* in Italian. Still, the first known recipe for cooked tomatoes does not appear until 1705, in a Roman cookbook, and no tomato sauce recipe was published until 1797.

Native Americans had more than two hundred types of corn, another crop brought to Europe by Columbus. This import arrived from the Americas by a circuitous route, shipped along the eastern Mediterranean trade routes to Veneto, and was therefore erroneously labeled *granturco,* "Turkish grain." Corn took promising root in Italy, for while Italians did not eat the kernels on the cob (they considered it fit for animal fodder only) it made a fine, inexpensive flour that could be baked into bread or, more commonly, cooked into polenta (from Latin *pulmentum*), a porridge that could fill empty stomachs on a daily basis. Two hundred years later northern Italian attitudes had changed little towards the porridge, as described by Tuscan Angelo Pellegrini in his book *The Unprejudiced Palate* (1948) of growing up on a diet of little but polenta: "And so we ate it hot with cream cheese, or with turnip greens cooked and sprinkled with a miserly dash of olive oil, or with hot cracklings, and a thousand other lovely auxiliaries. . . . We sliced it and grilled it or fried the stuff with indifferent results. It was, it remained always and forever—*polenta,* a veritable plague, an evil from which no deliverance seemed possible."[4]

So widespread was the consumption of polenta among the poor in northern Italy that it led many to develop pellagra, a deficiency disease that the Mexicans had long before learned to avoid by adding lime to their corn, which released niacin, and by eating it with a wide variety of other nutrients. Goethe, traveling through Italy from 1776 to 1778, coming face to face with the scabrous disease, was horrified, writing that the Italians' diet of polenta "makes the bowels costive, especially in children and women, and their cachetic complexion is evidence of the damage they do to themselves."[5]

Clearly, the addition of foods like corn and potatoes brought from the Americas had begun to affect the diets of people all around the world; but it would take centuries before agricultural advances could meet the nutritional needs of a European population that had increased quickly in the sixteenth and seventeenth centuries, when the population of Genoa alone grew from two hundred thousand to four hundred thousand.

Oddly enough, as spices became more plentiful and cheaper in the eighteenth century, the taste for them began to decline, probably owing to a drop in their social cachet. Beef became more available than ever during the Renaissance. Servants enjoyed meat five times a week, and in hospitals patients ate a pound of beef three times a week. Veal was preferred to beef by the wealthy, but on the farms, oxen were used as work animals until they became too old, at which point they were fattened and slaughtered for food. In the cities, with only a minimum salary—ten to fifteen *soldi* a day—one could purchase three pounds of boneless beef, a quantity of protein sufficient for a whole week. Fish was much more expensive; as in northern Europe, in Italy cod was salted and dried, called *stoccafisso* or *baccalà*.[6]

In contrast to corn, rice, introduced by the Arabs into Sicily and northern Italy, had only modest success as an edible grain. It was used by the rich for risottos mixed with meat, seafood, vegetables, and fruits, and by the poor as still more porridge. Instead, Italians increasingly turned to more wheat-flour-based products, including boiled noodles.

It is possible that Italy adapted long strands of noodles from the Arabs, who called their noodles *itriyah,* an echo of which can be heard in Sicilian dialect as *tria.* In the geography book *Kitah-Rugiar* (1154), Al-Idrisi, an Arab who lived in Sicily, described making *itriyah* on a large scale in the Sicilian town of Trabia, which exported the finished product throughout the Mediterranean. Giambonino da Cremona in the thirteenth century collected eighty Arab recipes, including *sambusaj,* triangular cuts of dough encasing ground meat, like ravioli.

I use the English word "noodles" here (originally from German *nudel*) only because the word "pasta" (which comes from the Latin for "paste") was used in a more general sense to describe any food made with a paste or pastry, including *lasagne, maccheroni,* and so on. The flour for bread and durum semolina for pasta was often regulated; a Naples law of 1713 forbade wheat traders to grind their product in the mills reserved for durum wheat. The first instance found of the word "pasta" referring specifically to macaroni and vermicelli was in 1584, in a culinary treatise entitled *Lo Scalco,* written by Giovanbattista Rossetti, the head steward of Lucrezia d' Este, Duchess of Urbino, but the word was not yet in widespread usage.

The general word "macaroni" has coexisted with "vermicelli" (little worms) at least since the fourteenth century in Italian, while "spaghetti" (little strings) did not enter print until 1839, in a book on Neapolitan home cooking. The first printed reference to macaroni is by a Genoese named Ponzio Bastone, who in 1279 left as a bequest a *bariscella piena de macaronis* (a basket of macaroni) in his will, suggesting it was a food of some value. In *The Decameron,* written from 1351 to 1353, Boccaccio tells the tale of a land where there is a mountain made out of Parmesan cheese on which the people do nothing but eat macaroni all day. By the fifteenth century, some doctors were already warning about overindulgence in pasta.

In English print, the word "pasta" is not found until 1870 or "spaghetti" until 1885, although "macaroni" had been mentioned in English as early as 1590 and "vermicelli" by 1660. In Latin the word *laganum* described a dish composed of dough strips roasted on hot stones, not boiled in water. Yet the word seems to be a direct antecedent to *lasagne,* which specifically does denote noodles boiled in water, a dish described, though not by name, by Isadore of Seville in the seventh century.

By the eighteenth century, macaroni eating was so commonly associated with Italians that the word began to acquire other connotations. Italians used *maccheroni* or *maccherone* for a boorish person. The well-known line in the jaunty eighteenth-century American ditty "Yankee Doodle" about a fellow who "stuck a feather in his hat and called it macaroni" refers to a naïve Yankee rube affecting the style of a small tricorn hat of a kind worn by London dandies of the Macaroni Club, who enjoyed eating Italian macaroni.

Macaroni was certainly well-known enough to Europeans for novelist and gourmand Alexandre Dumas (*père*), to write in his *Grand Dictionnaire de cuisine* (1873), that "everyone is familiar with these long tubes of paste like hollow vermicelli."[7] Sicilians in particular became famous for their luxurious pastas, and each region of Italy began creating their own forms, shapes, and dishes, often commemorative, and suited to the kinds of specific sauces served with them. No one has ever come up with an official figure for the number of pasta shapes in Italy today, but it seems in excess of five hundred.[8]

Merely to suggest the breadth of the options when it comes to shapes, consider the *strangolapreti* ("priest chokers") gnocchi of Trentino Alto Adige *spaghetti alla ghitarra* cut on guitar-like strings and sauced with chilies in Abruzzo; the multi-layered *timballo* of macaroni in Campania; and *banditi* ("bandit's pasta") with fava beans and tomato in Basilicata.

At first, pasta making was laborious and time consuming, not readily practiced by the poor, until the first rudimentary pasta-making machines, called *ingegni,* appeared in the sixteenth century; by the end of the next century, machine-made macaroni and vermicelli were cheap enough to be affordable to everyone, becoming part of the daily meal among both rich and poor. Commercially made pasta became widespread in the eighteenth century, and by 1785, Naples had become the capital of noodle production, with 280 shops selling the product, the drying of which had been perfected at Torre Annunziata. Genoa also thrived on pasta production, and even though Paris tried to compete in the market, Italian-made pasta was considered far superior in quality.

Pasta's popularity began in the Middle Ages and flourished in the sixteenth century—this distinctive food had come to be identified with the people in all regions that made up the patchwork quilt of the Italian peninsula. The rich, especially in Naples and Sicily, might season their spaghetti with cinnamon and sugar. Wealthy Piedmontese, Tuscans, and Bolognese enriched their pasta with an abundance of eggs, even adding saffron from Abruzzo to color it, though more commonly it was served in soups or on top of another ingredient, such as meat—not as a first course on its own—or as a side dish.

Nineteenth-century aristocrats dined exclusively at each other's homes, where the chefs showcased their talents and their employers' generosity in extravagant meals that might go on for hours into the night. A classic menu item was the *timballo*—a gargantuan composition of several layers of short pasta tubes, spices, sauces, meats, eggs, and other ingredients molded into a tall cake-like form, which Giuseppe di Lampedusa describes in his novel *The Leopard* (1958), about mid-nineteenth-century Sicily: at a formal dinner in his summer palace, Don Fabrizio, Prince of Salina, eschews the northern fashion of beginning with soup in favor of presenting "monumental dishes of macaroni . . . worthy of the quivers of admiration they evoked. The burnished gold of the crusts, the fragrance of sugar and cinnamon they exuded, were but preludes to the delights released from the interior when the knife broke the crust; first came a smoke laden with aromas, then chicken livers, hard-boiled eggs, sliced ham, chicken, and truffles in masses of piping hot, glistening macaroni, to which the meat juice gave an exquisite hue of suéde." Lampedusa writes of how the guest organist at the dinner thanks God for such largesse, realizing that he and his wife could "exist for a month on the cost of one of these dishes."[9]

Nevertheless, and despite the availability of pasta, through the eighteenth and nineteenth centuries famine, pestilence, disease, wars, and demographic shifts made the lives of most Europeans dismal at best, and their subsistence diets had little taste at all at a time when salt and pepper were still scarce commodities and fish was nearly impossible to obtain except along the coasts and seas. Neapolitans were called "leaf eaters" because their diet consisted mainly of vegetables. Beggars still clogged city streets and country roads. Disease caused by malnutrition swept through towns from Pisa to Palermo. Even in Emilia, whose capital was nicknamed *Bologna la grassa* (fat Bologna), few people had much meat on their bones. As one chronicler wrote, the Emilian diet "bears a strong peasant stamp— simple, crude, rooted in barbarian traditions."[10]

Since the Middle Ages, the church, which collected alms for the poor while collecting tithes to build cathedrals, always responded to such deprivations by recommending fasting and intoning that the pangs of hunger on earth would be rewarded in heaven with riches that would make the Garden of Eden itself seem barren. Because wheat was expensive, until plantings in the Americas brought down the price, bread was usually made with barley, rye, and millet. As of 837 AD, at the Council of Aix, eggs were prohibited on fast days because they were an animal product, and in the fourteenth century, the church forbade eating butter during fast days, although dispensations could be bought from the church, one of the liturgical abuses that outraged Martin Luther.

Visitors to Italy in the eighteenth and nineteenth centuries found little to praise in what they ate, or were forced to eat. Inns tended to serve much the same food day in and day out, with little or no choice of dishes. Goethe, who cataloged nearly everything he came in contact with, adored Italy but never found much to say about his meals. Neither did the English poets Byron and Shelley, who lived in Italy but whose lack of interest in the region's insipid food was understandable. Essayist, poet, and translator Leigh Hunt, who spent 1821 and 1822 in Italy, was, like all northern Europeans, delighted by the abundance of fruit—at "a cheapness that made us laugh"—as well as milk in bottles. He noted that the consumption of olive oil was "immense," adding, "it is probably no mean exasperator of Italian bile," citing an Italian book on health as to the way olive oil "inflames the blood, disturbs the humors, irritates the fibres, and produces other effects very superfluous in a stimulating climate."[11]

But Hunt also wrote of his "growing acquaintance" with *maccheroni,* which he found the Italians put in soups, mixed with meat, butter, oil, and grated cheese. The Italian, "has a great abstract respect for fasting," he wrote, "but he struggles hard to be relieved from it."[12]

Charles Dickens, who spent a year in Italy from 1844 to 1845, had far less to say about the food than he did about torture instruments, mentioning only three meals consumed at inns and trattorias along his route from Genoa to Naples. Outside of Genoa he sampled *taglierini,* cockscombs and sheep's kidneys, and "small pieces of some unknown part of a calf" served with whitebait. Near Parma, dinner consisted of cabbage "boiled with a great deal of rice in a tureen full of water, and flavoured with cheese," some bits of pork fried with pig's kidneys, two red fowls and two "little red turkeys," a stew of garlic and truffles, and more. The third meal, which he calls "the usual dinner" he was getting used to, was a vegetable and rice soup in need of "plenty of grated cheese, lots of salt, and abundance of black pepper," stewed pigeon, half a fowl, a bit of roast beef "the size of a small French roll," a scrap of Parmesan cheese, and "five withered apples, all huddled together on a small plate, and crowding one upon the other, as if each were trying to save itself from the chance of being eaten."[13]

On heading south, Dickens was appalled at the poverty he found crossing the Neapolitan frontier at Fondi, seeing beggars rap their chins with their right hand to signal hunger.[14] The poor of the countryside and the small towns, in provinces cut off from the trade routes, remained ever dependent on the way one harvest followed another. The southern landowners claimed everything the peasants tilled; those who worked the land would be punished if they were caught eating white bread because it meant they had "stolen" the landlords' wheat from the harvest. To avoid this punishment, the peasants waited till the crops were harvested. To prepare the fields for the spring crop, the peasants burned the vestiges of the harvest, keeping some of the burnt (*arso*) grain for themselves to incorporate into their meager diet. They might then bring what was left to a local pasta-maker, just as they brought their dough to be baked in a baker's oven.

This state of numbing poverty, which had persisted since the Renaissance and through the Enlightenment and the Age of Revolution, would continue beyond the Unification of Italy. When American educator Booker T. Washington, a former slave, visited Sicily in 1910, he was astonished to find children laboring in mines like slaves. "The Negro is not the farthest down," he wrote. "The condition of the coloured farmer in the most backward parts of the Southern States in America, even when he has the least education and the least encouragement, is incomparably better than the condition and opportunities of the agricultural population of Sicily."[15]

The only relief from such hardship came on the saints' feast days called *sagre,* descended from Roman food festivals. Food was at the center of the festivals, like the chestnut *sagra* of Canale in Piedmont, the asparagus *sagra* of Bassano del Grappa in Vento, the *porchetta* suckling pig *sagra* of Lavezzola in Emilia Romagna, and the goose *sagra* of Mortara in Lombardy. These holidays constituted brief moments of jubilation and excess, even if that meant little more than a child receiving an orange to eat.[16]

France's gastronomy developed along provincial lines similar to that of Italy. The effect of Catherine de Medici, a Florentine whose mother was a French countess, on French cookery has been debated for centuries, ever since she married Henry II in 1533 and moved to France with her own cooks. Some recent historians have questioned just how much influence a fourteen-year-old girl could have brought to the French court. Henry, who cared little for his new wife, allowed her no influence in court, so it is possible that Catherine wielded hers in the kitchen. When Henry died, in 1559, Catherine assumed political powers that had been long denied to her as regent to her ten-year-old son, Charles IX. Catherine and Charles later became too busy slaughtering Protestant Huguenots to attend to the court kitchen.

It is probably closer to the truth to say that while Catherine did not "teach the French to cook," as Italians chefs have long and proudly contended, she did bring her chefs and Tuscan culinary ideas to France at a time when the courts of Europe had already established their gastronomies around luxury, embellishment, and, increasingly, structured rules and manners.

If such was the state of eating and drinking for the rich and poor, from the Renaissance through the eighteenth century, what might have been served and to whom at the restaurants in Italy during those centuries? The answer is that there weren't any restaurants. There were roadside inns and rudimentary wine taverns called *osterie,* or cooks' shops—most run by certified guild members—but the idea of going out to eat, of having one's own table, a menu, wine list, and someone to serve you was as foreign to Italians as to everyone else in Europe and America until the first half of the nineteenth century.

The restaurant was an invention of French *traiteurs* (whence comes the Italian word *trattoria* for a small eatery), guild members who specialized in specific techniques like roasting, grilling, soup making, and so on, which was eventually expanded to offering travelers a menu of dishes. Only after the French Revolution expelled the aristocracy's chefs from service did those brigades of cooks begin opening what came to be called restaurants—places to restore the traveler's body and spirit with good food and wine.

What was to become the foundation for "classic" culinary principles in the nineteenth century was set down by Marie Antoine Carême, known as the King of Chefs and the Chef of Kings, who compiled three volumes (of five, published from 1833 to 1835) of the encyclopedic *L'Art de la Cuisine Français aux dix-neuvième siècle,* in which he mentions "*macaroni d'Italie.*"

There had been many Italian cookbooks since the Renaissance, but most had been written specifically for aristocrats' kitchens, not independent chefs. Most important of these was a nine-hundred-page treatise by Bartolomeo Scappi, private cook to Pius V, a pontiff who, oddly enough, was ascetic in his diet and vengeful towards those who were not, once threatening to excommunicate anyone who tried to enrich the watery broth on which he subsisted. Scappi's 1570 book, entitled *Cooking Secrets of Pope Pius V,* included more than nine hundred recipes and had a very broad scope, from kitchen management to precise cooking procedures, which included his instruction that macaroni should be cooked "for as long as it takes to say three Pater Nosters." Scappi believed food should be presented beautifully, with color, even artifice, as when he describes fish to be molded into the shape of a goat's head. In any case, Scappi's was not a book for the ordinary cook, who was most likely illiterate and saw no wisdom in turning a piece of good fish into a goat's head.

In the United States, the "Gilded Age" (a term coined by Mark Twain and Charles Dudley Warner in their 1873 book of that title) was in full swing, as the new millionaires of the industrialized post–Civil War period were spending lavishly. But there was also a kind of Gilded Age occurring in those European capitals where new money and old aristocracy were reflected in the spectacular hotels of that era. Where once travelers stayed at boarding houses or inns, they were now able to check in to extravagantly decorated hotels with marble columns, gilded mirrors, vast staircases, velvet couches, and murals by some of the finest contemporary artists—appropriate settings for balls and banquets, weddings, and state dinners. By the end of the century, every European capital and resort city had its grand hotel.

Yet wherever these hotels might be located, inevitably the dining rooms and menus slavishly copied French style and cuisine. The Imperial in Vienna might serve an Austrian pastry or two, the Grand in St. Petersburg a Russian *coulibiac,* and Le Grand Hotel in Rome might include macaroni and vermicelli among their dishes. But the rest of the dishes, the wines, and the service were resolutely French. At a time when European aristocrats, American industrial titans, and London bankers had little interest in or knowledge of what constituted Italian or British or Russian food, French was the way to go. Thus, at Ristorante Covo in Milan, every dish on a 1906 menu was French: *consommé "Ésperance," loup de mer à la Russe, selle de veau "Nationale," macedoine de legumes à la crème, cailles rôties.* (To finish off, there was a small nod to Italy: *cassata Sicilienne.*) Dining in such grand hotels was a public display of one's wealth, power, and breeding, and increasingly, one's good taste.

After the Unification of Italy, in 1861, King Victor Emanuel II held a state dinner—the menu, even though it included Italian food, was written entirely in French, a conceit followed by the new restaurants in the big cities. Dassetto, a restaurant that opened in Rome in 1880 and became known for its fine cuisine, served pheasant, tournedos Rossini, and duck with orange sauce, all in the French manner. American restaurants such as Delmonico's in New York toed the French line. Overwhelmingly, of more than 3,500 recipes in *The Epicurean* (1898), by Delmonico's former chef Charles Ranhofer, the majority were derived from French recipes, and next to every American dish was a French translation in parentheses. Ranhofer did include several Italian dishes of the day, including gnocchi, macaroni "Neapolitan style," spaghetti, ravioli "à la Bellini," and risotto "with Piedmontese truffles," all with French translations.

In the large Italian cities, a certain number of *ristoranti* outside of hotels became fashionable in their own right, serving wealthy Italians and world travelers in the international style. Italy had for centuries been a major destination for artists, musicians, writers, and aristocracy, but in the mid-nineteenth century, more Americans and Europeans than ever before could afford to visit, and many of the old taverns, osterias, and trattorias were upgraded to the level of a true *ristorante*. In Rome, for example, Passetto began as a trattoria on the Piazza Tor Sanguigna in 1860, then moved and expanded as a full-fledged and fashionable restaurant on the Via Zanardelli.

Simple trattorias serving cheap food sprang up across the Tiber in Trastevere, as the ancient Roman district developed into the city's bohemian neighborhood. In the 1880s, in the meat-processing neighborhood called Testaccio, the workmen created a cookery called Quinto Quarto, referring to the undesirable "fifth quarter" of the animal they were allowed to keep for themselves—the offal, nerves, heads, and tails. A trattoria named Checchino, opened in Testaccio by the Mariani family in 1887, still serves those working-man's dishes, from *insalata di zampe,* an aspic made with nerves gleaned from calf's trotters, to various dishes made with *la pajata,* milk-fed lamb's intestines.

In 1860, Pacifico Piperno took over a building in the Jewish ghetto and opened a tavern where he served specialties of the Roman Jews, including spaghetti with salt cod, offal, and *carciofi alla giudea,* fried baby artichokes, "in the Jewish style"—a preparation that dates back two thousand years and was part of the springtime Passover Seder. At the turn of the century, Piperno became a restaurant, drawing a sophisticated crowd and new competitors to the neighborhood. In 1909, the artist and editor Romeo Marchetti established an annual artichoke dinner in spring, which for the next fifty years was attended as a mark of honor by luminaries in the arts, politics, and industry.

Venice was known for its *bacari,* little wine bars with inexpensive bites of food, and the fashionable *caffés* that had been part of the city's social life since 1683. In the *caffé* under the arcades of Piazza San Marco, visitors could enjoy an *ombra*— a drink taken in the hot afternoon within the shade (*ombra*) of St. Mark's bell tower. By 1775, at least two dozen *caffés* dotted St. Mark's Square alone. The Caffé Quadri claimed as guests Stendhal, Lord Byron, the elder Dumas, Wagner, and Marcel Proust.

After the La Fenice opera house opened in 1792, the already well-established Caffé San Fantin developed into Antico Martini *ristorante* and has been favored by artists and musicians ever since. In Milan, the spectacular Galleria Vittorio Emanuele II, built between 1865 and 1877 by Giuseppe Mengoni to honor the new king of the Unification, had space for a brewery and a popular coffee concert with orchestra and dancers. This operation was bought by Virgil Savini, who in 1884 turned it into a mix of cafés and restaurants, drawing those exiting the nearby Teatro alla Scala and Teatro Manzoni, including composers Verdi, Puccini, and Mascagni, conductor Arturo Toscanini, dancer Eleonora Duse, poet Gabriele D'Annunzio, and literary firebrand and founder of Futurism Filippo Tommaso Marinetti.

After Unification, Italy saw the slow but certain rise of its own middle class, and housewives had more consistent access to good, fresh products. These they used not in slavish imitation of French culinary models but to refine their own traditional regional dishes and to create new ones expressive of their evolving status. Most urban Italians, of course, ate at home, and with the rise of the middle class, many preferred to do so. By the last quarter of the nineteenth century, something that could be called *la cucina italiana* was beginning to coalesce. All it needed was someone to make sense of it all.

The man to do so was a Florentine silk trader, a bachelor named Pellegrino Artusi (1820–1911), who, upon retiring in his late sixties, spent his time traveling between his home in Florence and his seaside estate in Viareggio. For his amusement, he decided he would write a little cookbook based on his experiences and travels through Italy.

The research and writing pleasantly occupied his time, and he hoped his opus might have a readership outside his circle of friends. But when he submitted it to publishers, none believed enough people would be interested in such a collection of recipes. So, in 1891, dedicating his book to his cats, Biancani and Sibillone, he privately published *La Scienza in Cucina e L'arte di Mangiar Bene: Manuale Pratico per Le Famiglie* ("*The Science of Cooking and the Art of Eating Well: A Practical Manual for Families*"), printing just two thousand copies. He was going to need a lot more.

Artusi's book went on to become one of the two bestselling books in Italy of that or any other era, going through fourteen editions and selling an astounding 283,000 copies by 1910. *La Scienza in Cucina* was so successful because it was the first cookbook aimed at an emerging middle class and the first that treated of a cuisine that could truly be called Italian. It was also written in the Tuscan dialect then being adopted by educated people as the lingua franca of their new country. As a result, the housewives of Italy found in Artusi a guide not just on the running of a modern Italian kitchen but on how to read and speak Italian itself.[17]

Artusi's book was not written for aristocrats' kitchen staff, so he dismissed the overwrought, French-based *briconella* (frippery) of previous recipe books. When he did include a French dish, it was clearly because he thought it was a good one. He kept *béchamel* sauce, for example, but tweaked it to be more Italian, less complicated, and renamed it *balsamella*.

By the same token, since he was writing for and belonged to the upper class himself, Artusi snobbishly avoided dishes he felt had "a whiff of the folkloric" or those so regional as to be "limited to particular environments or social levels." He did not, however, ignore all regional dishes, though those from the south are few and far between in the book. Thus, the reader finds *tortellini alla bolognese, anolini alla parmigiana, tagliatelle all'uso di romagna, risotto alla milanese, maccheroni alla napoletana, ravioli alla genovese,* Triestian *presnitz,* and scores of other regional recipes. Not surprisingly, given Artusi's station, he gives only a very few recipes for polenta, which was so commonly associated with humbler kitchens.[18]

Another reason Artusi's book was so popular was that it embraced the kind of foods more and more Italians were eating, owing to their access to more diverse ingredients. The book covers fried artichokes, a specialty of Rome's Jewish populace, though he says they are also a Tuscan specialty; couscous, introduced to Italy by the Arabs, for which Artusi includes a recipe given to him by two Italian Jews; black risotto in the Florentine style; macaroni with sardines in the Sicilian style; and meatballs (*polpette*), which in Artusi's day were made "the size of an egg."

Of meatballs, he writes, "Don't think I'm pretentious enough to tell you how to make meatballs. This is a dish that everybody knows how to make, including absolute donkeys," a statement that indicates just how ubiquitous *polpette* were in the Italian kitchen. He does not, however, connect them with spaghetti, as in the Italian-American dish that became iconic in the early twentieth century.

Single chapters cover soups (including those for "days of abstinence"), starters, sauces (*salsa,* which denoted a condiment rather than pasta sauce, which was called *sugo*), eggs, fried dishes, entremets, stews, chilled dishes, greens and legumes, fish, and roasts. Desserts are divided into pastries and *torte e dolci al cucchiaio* (cakes and sweets to be eaten with a spoon), syrups, preserves, and ice creams, including sorbets.

Artusi also included sample seasonal menus for "an elegant dinner for each month of the year," which showed his disdain for the extravagance of courtly excess by trimming service to a mere seven or eight courses, beginning with soup, usually containing pasta, a simple appetizer like figs and prosciutto, a fish dish, entremets like stuffed zucchini, a roast, dessert, fruit, and cheese. While this may seem like a great deal of food, these menus were not being recommended for everyday meals, and, overall, the dishes are light, based on the seasons, and never elaborate. Artusi was a great believer in fresh, healthy food and disdained the richness and heaviness considered a virtue in the past. His fish and roasts are served simply, perhaps with a light sauce of the meat drippings.

In fact, there is much written in the book against overindulgence. He insisted that "those who do not do physical labor should eat more sparingly than those who do," and advised, "Unless you lead an active life, you should forgo the use of wine at lunch, because red wines are difficult to digest, while white wines, which contain more alcohol, cloud the mind." Most important, he lectures, "Guard yourself from gluttony." He also advocates exercise and temperance, warning that to be "overrun by wine [is] to commit a hideous sin."

Artusi did not always provide strict measurements for recipes, in the assumption that home cooks would have a grasp of such details, but he offered a great deal more than did most cookbook authors of his time. Thus, in a complex dish like calf's tongue in spicy sauce, Artusi instructs the reader to mince a six-inch stalk of celery and small carrot, a quarter cup of olive oil, two anchovies, seven tablespoons of "well-rinsed capers," a quarter cup of breadcrumbs sprinkled with "just a drop of vinegar," a piece of onion the size of a hazelnut, and "less than half a clove of garlic."

On the subject of garlic, Artusi recommended it, in moderation, but acknowledged its notorious reputation for its strong odor and its association with the lower classes. "The ancient Romans left garlic to the down and out," he writes, "while King Alfonse of Castile abhorred it to the point that he would punish anybody who dared appear at court with its odor on his breath." Artusi was familiar with long-held claims of garlic's medicinal and health benefits, repeating assertions that "it provides relief to those suffering from hysteria, promotes the secretion of urine, bolsters the stomach, aids in digestion, and, since it cures worms, is a preventive against endemic and epidemic diseases." He wags a finger at those who would banish it from their kitchens as a social stigma of the lower classes, insisting, "this fixation deprives them of tasty, wholesome food."

Perusing Artusi's book, one can only come away with the notion of how modern it seems and how remarkably it reflects what became the staples of twentieth-century Italian food on menus, not just in Italy but around the world. Look on any page and you will find dishes such as *minestrone, vitello tonnato,* fried zucchini, *baccalà,* chicken *alla cacciatora, bistecca alla fiorentina, saltimbocca,* risotto with cuttlefish, potato gnocchi, Tuscan *cacciucco* seafood stew, *zabaione, babà* with rum, and *zuppa inglese.* Not so surprising is his omission of Ligurian pesto

sauce, made from basil, garlic, and olive oil, since that condiment was of fairly recent vintage, having been first mentioned in a cookbook (*Vera cuciniera genovese*)
only as recently as 1863. He also includes a recipe for *pizza libretti* (little books
pizza), which he says a lady sent to him, insisting it was not to be called *schiac-
ciata* (squashed)—"because it should come out anything but flat." Indeed, the
puffy *pizza libretti* he describes bears no resemblance to what we know of as
Neapolitan *pizza alla margherita,* topped with mozzarella, tomato, and basil; instead, it is merely dough made with eggs, cognac, or meat broth, folded over, cut
into triangles, and fried in oil.

It is possible that Artusi may never have tasted or even heard of Neapolitan
pizza. In fact, *pizza alla margherita* was of very recent origin, created to celebrate
the new queen's visit to Naples in 1889. Its fame had not yet spread north from
Naples.

Artusi does include *sugo di carne,* a meat sauce simmered for five or six hours,
containing no tomato. And then there is but a single recipe for *sugo di pomodoro,*
but he seems dismissive of the whole idea, writing, "I will speak anon about
tomato *salsa,* which must be distinguished from tomato *sugo,* as the latter is simple, *i.e.,* made from tomatoes that are simply cooked and run through a food
mill. At the most, you may add a small rib of celery and a few leaves of parsley and
basil to tomato *sugo,* if you feel you must."

And that is all. He included no instructions, no recipe at all, for a sauce that
was soon to become the foundation of what would be known and beloved around
the world as Italian cooking.

Artusi's achievements in publishing *La Scienza in Cucina* were momentous for
Italy itself, though he was hardly aware of it at the time. He had found a reward-
ing way to live out his retirement years, and he was generous with his newfound
wealth. He donated his fortune to a home for the elderly, made dowries for poor
girls, and bequeathed the royalties from his book to his servants. Artusi died at
the age of 91, in 1911, a year after publishing the last edition of his famous cookbook, in which he wrote his own epitaph, at the end of a recipe for *gnocchi alla
romana:* "I hope you will like these as much as my guests have. If you do, toast me
if I'm alive, or say a Rest in Peace if I've gone to push up cabbages."

# Chapter 2

# The Great Escape

When my maternal great-grandmother, Maria Grazia, was a little girl in the Campanian town of Laurino, she worked for a wealthy *padrone*. One day, he beat her unconscious, and the local doctor threatened that if the girl died he would see to it that *il signore* would be prosecuted to the full extent of the law. Her infraction? She was a moment late in opening the door for a guest at the master's home.

Maria Grazia survived to remember that horror. Unfortunately, there were to be many other horrors in her youth, as there were in the lives of many Campanian peasants, and they had no reason to believe things would ever improve for their class in Italy. So when Maria's father arranged a marriage for her to a plasterer named Paulo Girolamo, who had already emigrated to America, the girl dutifully bade goodbye to family and friends. She was happy to leave Italy, never to return. She arrived at New York's Ellis Island in 1885, one of more than five million Italians who immigrated to the United States between 1880 and 1910—80 percent of whom were from southern Italy—seeking to escape *la miseria* of the Old Country.

The Unification of 1861 had given Italians a new national pride, albeit as a kingdom. But the country had managed only modest social reforms, and industrialization helped only marginally to improve conditions among the poor. Political alliances and wars served only to deepen the poverty and illiteracy that was still the norm throughout Italy, most indelibly for the people in the southern regions from Abruzzo and Molise down to Campania, Calabria, and Sicily. The medieval landlord system was still powerfully entrenched in those regions, suffocating any economic rise among the lower classes—a chronic situation called *il problema del mezzogiorno,* (the Southern problem) that described the social, economic, and psychological divide between the north and the south. Adding to the problem was a doubling of the population in the south between the time of Unification and the turn of the new century.

For the poor, immigration was next to impossible, but many less destitute Italians found work and a new life in London, where an emerging Anglo-Italian community was gradually establishing notable businesses in the food industry. As early as 1803, an "Italian Eating House" was opened by Venetian Joseph Moretti off Leicester Square; Piedmontese John Baptiste Pagliano, former cook to the Venetian ambassador, set up a very profitable catering business named Sablonière. Swiss Italian Carlo Gatti began selling ice cream in London in 1850 and within a generation had become a very wealthy man. In the rest of Great Britain, selling ice cream was a job largely associated with Italians.

By the middle of the century, Italian eateries in London were as modest as all others. Indeed, two guidebooks published for visitors to the Great Exhibition of 1851 did not mention a single restaurant above the tavern or chophouse level, recommending instead the hotel dining rooms, none of which were Italian.[1]

But it was the Americas, especially Argentina and the United States, that welcomed immigrants in waves after the Unification—first the Germans and Irish, then Russians, Poles, Czechs, and Scandinavians, and, starting in the 1880s, the Italians and Jews. Between 1880 and 1920, one out of every four U.S. immigrants was a Sicilian. Like my maternal great-grandmother from Campania and my paternal grandparents from Abruzzo, 97 percent of the Italians came through Ellis Island, where one of the first things they saw was a sign in several languages reading, NO CHARGE FOR MEALS HERE.

This was not the first period of Italian emigration to the United States. During the years when France controlled Louisiana, there had been an earlier, much smaller Italian migration to this state; immigrants from Liguria, Piedmont, and Lombardy (regions with close ties to France) came to settle in Louisiana. By 1850, Italians in New Orleans numbered 915; about a hundred more than lived in New York at the time. After the Civil War, Italians came to New Orleans in large numbers—sixteen thousand between 1880 and 1914—principally from Palermo, many of whom worked on Louisiana's sugar and cotton farms and were recruited by Louisiana growers, who shipped cotton back to Europe on ships from Sicily carrying citrus fruits.

In 1898, the New Orleans paper the *Daily Picayune* described a new arrival under the headline "Another Batch of Surly Sicilians," whose "chorus of excited yells, queries, exclamations, calls in high-pitched vernacular . . . was positively deafening. And the gyrations of arms, heads, and the bodily contortions which, strangely, seemed to be indispensable with the exchange of greetings among some of the Latin races, were enough to cause any sedate and practical onlooker to fear that a limb or two of the most vehement of the excited performers would suddenly be severed and fly off."[2]

The newcomers were accepted as foreign workers, not new Americans, and when yellow fever broke out in New Orleans in 1902 and 1905, the Italians, living in French Quarter tenements, were blamed for the spread of the disease.

These "surly Sicilians" would work the farmlands without argument. Married couples would even share the labor—which would have been a rarity back in Sicily—and plantation owners had to make accommodations for them, as well as for their families, whose young sons and daughters would also work the fields. In those days, the pay for the harvest season was a dollar a day, with an allowance for lodging and a small garden plot. Plantation stores began stocking spaghetti, macaroni, olives, and sardines, and by 1900, about 7 percent of the grocery stores in New Orleans were owned by Italians, who now numbered about six thousand; by 1910 Italians made up 80 percent of the population of the French Quarter.

As has always been the case in American immigration, the food business provided the easiest access to ownership and entry into American society, as long as the immigrant learned enough English. In New Orleans, Italians came to run most of the groceries, bakeries, peanut vending businesses, ice cream shops, and fruit stands. The city's oldest fruit stand was opened in 1852 by the Pareti Brothers, from Sicily. The Italians also succeeded in taking over the strawberry industry in Tangipahoa Parish, outside of New Orleans. They began as migrant workers and then eventually learned to turn strawberries into a far more profitable crop than cotton, which they then abandoned. By the late 1880s, an average of two carloads of strawberries arrived from Tangipahoa Parish daily, and by 1911, the crop sold for more than $1.1 million.

Meanwhile, a Ligurian named Angelo Socola arrived in New Orleans in 1849 at the age of 18, and worked his way up to become an importer of Italian and

Mexican products. After getting a college education, he developed a high-yield rice strain that flourished in the region. He went on to develop steam-powered threshing mills and became known internationally as the father of Louisiana's rice industry. Along the way, he also founded the People's Bank of Louisiana.

Having learned the craft of making ice cream in Palermo, Angelo Brocato emigrated to the United States, worked on a sugar plantation, and saved enough money to open his own namesake ice cream shop in New Orleans's French Quarter; by 1905, he was able to open a sit-down parlor that mimicked the elegant ones he remembered in Palermo. In 1908, Francesco Prestia started the White Rose Ice Cream Company, using horse-drawn wagons to sell his wares.

These immigrants also opened restaurants serving an amalgam of Creole and Italian dishes. Local restaurateur Madame Elizabeth Kettenring Dutreuil Begué, a Bavarian who opened the restaurant Begué's (now Tujague's) in the French Quarter in the 1860s, wrote a short chapter on macaroni in her book *Madame Begué and Her Recipes: Old Creole Cookery* (1900), noting,

> Macaroni is a general article of food in New Orleans among the rich and poor. It is very cheap, and is a most excellent dish. We have in New Orleans large Macaroni factories, where not only Macaroni is made by Italians, but the twin sisters of Macaroni, Spaghetti and Vermicelli, are also manufactured fresh daily. While there is no city in the United States in which Macaroni is cooked in real Italian style but New Orleans, which has long been a favored point of migration for the sons of sunny Italy, the Creole cooks have modified and improved upon the Italian methods, so that Macaroni à la Creole is just as famous a dish as Macaroni à l'italienne, and by many considered superior.[3]

A large number of Italian immigrants also settled on the West Coast. By the end of the nineteenth century, 80 percent of California's immigrant community was northern Italian—largely Ligurians or Genoese—and by 1905, there were approximately sixty thousand Italians in San Francisco. Plying the waters in their traditional Genoese *felucce*, shallow boats that could face up to the local high seas, with trawling nets called *paranzelle*, they founded Fisherman's Wharf market and were largely responsible for driving the Greeks and Slovaks from the industry. Others located to Monterey to work in the canning industry, as depicted in John Steinbeck's 1945 novel *Cannery Row.* Many others were involved in mining and in the fishing industry along the coast, from Eureka and Martinez down to Monterey and San Diego. By 1910, Italians controlled 80 percent of the fishing industry in California. Always hardworking and eager to take on agricultural jobs, the Italians settled easily in the fertile farmlands of Napa, Sonoma, and Mendocino, while others found a cornucopia of fruits and vegetables waiting to be farmed, an industry they had dominated in the Central Valley by the 1880s.

Naturally, they also became involved in California's olive farms. Growing olives in California dated back to the failed efforts of Spanish Franciscan monks of the eighteenth century to plant trees in Mission San Diego de Alcalá. Later plantings grew into a million trees by 1910, most in the San Joaquin and Sacramento Valleys, but the young olive oil industry could not compete with lower-priced cottonseed oil, which was often mixed with lard and olive oil, exported from New Orleans to Europe, then shipped back again with an olive oil label on it. Pure olive oil from Europe was also cheaper, and the California olive industry foundered.

Olives were not economically viable in California until an Oakland woman named Freda Ehmann learned how to pickle and ship them in kegs to eastern hotels and restaurants. Frederic T. Boeletti, a professor at the University of California, improved on this idea around 1900 by canning the olives. He put the state's olive industry on a firm footing, and Italians were well positioned to take advantage of it.

In 1906, an immigrant from the tiny Adriatic island of Vis named Paul Mariani decided to better his life and to follow the girl he loved, Victoria Svelich, to America. He made it to San Francisco, where his plan to get into the fishing industry was thwarted by the city's 1906 earthquake.

He relocated to Cupertino to farm, but in his first year rain completely destroyed his crop. Swearing to pay back the growers who had gotten him started, he bought their fruit then sold it for them. He soon developed the first mechanized prune dehydrator, which was to become the standard of the industry, and his business thrived. His promise to everyone was, "My bond is my word. I don't need a contract. If I shake your hand, it's a deal."[4]

With little formal education himself, Mariani insisted his children would have the best, so his son Paul Jr. obtained a Master's degree from the University of California at Davis in horticulture, fruit technology, and business administration. In 1952, the company pioneered the sale of dehydrated fruit in a visible package that allowed consumers to see the quality of the product. Later they developed the gusseted zipper-lock bag. Ever resourceful, when rain threatened to kill all the cherry crops in the region, Paul Jr. managed somehow to rent U.S. Air Force helicopters to fly over the field and blow the water off the berries.

Canning was not only an important industry for Italians in California; it made important ingredients available across borders and oceans. By the middle of the nineteenth century, canned foods had become a novelty for the middle class that could afford them. During the Crimean War and the U.S. Civil War, improvements were made in canning technology, but the process was perfected by a Piedmontese named Francesco Cirio, who in 1856 founded his company, eventually called Società Anonima di Esportazione Agricola Francesco Cirio, in Turin. This company soon had subsidiaries in Milan, Naples, Berlin, Brussels, London, and Paris, with two thousand railway cars for transporting its products, which starting in 1875 included the sweet, flavorful tomatoes of San Marzano, near Naples. This industrial event coincided with the emigration of southern Italians to America, making tomatoes as available on this side of the Atlantic as on the other.

When those supplies dried up during the German blockade of the Atlantic sea lanes in World War I, three northern Italian immigrant families who had settled in White Plains, New York, grew rich by canning tomato paste. One of those families soon discovered that the climate and soil of California was as conducive to producing excellent tomato crops as any territory in Italy, so they moved to San Jose to found the Bel Canto Foods canning company, establishing their tomato brand under the name Contadina, an Italian word for a female farmer, a picture of which appeared on the label. By the mid-1930s, they were processing and shipping two hundred thousand tons of tomatoes across the United States.

In Gilroy, California, two Calabrian families, the Filices and Perrellis, bought the burned-down Bisceglia Brothers Cannery, and by 1920 were producing 350,000 cases of canned tomatoes and fruit. They later moved the expanded company to Richmond and became one of the country's leading canners. The company also invented a machine to remove the pits from cling peaches, which helped revolutionize the industry, setting up the Filper Corporation to produce the machine worldwide.

Immigrant enterprises in California grew from circumstance and necessity. After working in the chocolate industry in Uruguay and Peru, Ligurian immigrant Domenico Ghirardelli moved to California in 1849 to try his fortunes in mining during the Gold Rush, giving it up to open a tent store in Stockton to sell supplies and confections to fellow miners. Success there enabled him to open both a store and hotel in San Francisco, and in 1852, he founded Ghirardely & Girard (later Mrs. Ghirardelli & Co., then the Ghirardelli Chocolate Company). In 1865 he observed that hanging a bag of chocolate in a warm room caused the cocoa butter to drip out, the residue of which could be processed into ground chocolate. This technique came to be called the Broma process and eventually became the standard of the chocolate industry.

Attuned early on to the power of advertising, Ghirardelli hired some of the best artists and advertising experts to make the company name and logo known throughout the West, even putting collectible motion picture star cards in every package of milk chocolates. Upon retiring in 1892 Ghirardelli left the company to his three sons, who divested all but the chocolate part of the business. By 1923, the Ghirardelli name was emblazoned on its cocoa building in 15-foot-high illuminated letters, a sign that would become as iconic to visitors passing through the Golden Gate as was the Statue of Liberty in New York Harbor.

The living and working conditions in the west may have been better than in the eastern cities, but bigotry against Italians ran high everywhere. In 1910, Italians were the lowest-paid workers in America—including African Americans—making an average of $10.50 a week, compared with the average American worker's $14.37. The manipulation of people who did not speak English was easy and effective, so it should not be entirely surprising to learn that approximately half of the Italian immigrants in the United States—more than any other ethnic group— returned to their native country, some almost immediately. Some returned to fight in World War I, and others returned to Italy only after they had made enough money—and some had even made fortunes. These last were proud returning sons and daughters who amazed their old friends in the old towns. As Tuscan-born Angelo Pellegrini wrote in his book *The Unprejudiced Palate*, all the townsfolk were impressed with the returnees' fine clothes but also with their tales "of wheat fields so vast that no fast train could traverse them in a single day; of meats and sweets and fine clothes so universally enjoyed that it was impossible to distinguish the rich from the poor," insisting that no American "ever eats an entire sandwich; he always throws away the fringe of crust."[5]

The problem for the southern Italian *contadini* who emigrated to the east coast of America was that they had largely come from a strictly agricultural background, yet found themselves in urban ghettos upon arriving in the New World, usually living under wretched conditions in tenement neighborhoods where they had little opportunity even to learn English. It was difficult for the immigrants to understand even each other, their Italian neighbors, who spoke in regional dialects, not Italian.

These enclaves, which came to be called Little Italys, were compact neighborhoods, squalid and prone to diseases. The men would take whatever jobs were offered to them and were sometimes transported hours out of town to pick apples or dig ditches. Yet jobs they were, and there was money to bring home at the end of the day.

In Boston, the Italians settled in the North End; in Providence, they followed the Irish to Federal Hill, the entry point of which is still marked by a sculpture of *la pigna,* a pineapple, the traditional American symbol of hospitality and abundance; in St. Louis, they came to work the clay mines and smelters and took root at the crest of what became known as the Hill. In San Francisco, it was in North Beach, next to Chinatown and Fisherman's Wharf, where so many of the Italians worked. The area around Taylor Street was Chicago's Little Italy, mostly populated by Sicilians, while Tuscans migrated to a neighborhood on the South Side, called the Heart of Italy. The Italians moved to South Philadelphia; Murray Hill in Cleveland; east of the Inner Harbor in Baltimore. In Canada, Little Italys developed in Montréal on Saint Laurent Boulevard; in Ottawa in Centretown West; and, in the 1930s, in Vancouver's Strathcona District.

But New York's Italian immigrant community dwarfed all the others—a mix of Calabrians, Campanians, Abruzzese, Barese, Pugliese, and Sicilians, who had to learn first to live together, then to live among *americani.* By 1900, there were 220,000 Italians in New York; ten years later, the number swelled to 545,000. By 1930, Italian immigrants represented 17 percent of the city's population.

After emigrating from Abruzzo to New York in 1910 at the age of 16 to work as a railway yards laborer, Pascal D'Angelo, called the "pick and shovel poet," wrote in his autobiography that in Italy a peasant had to turn over four-fifths of whatever he grew to his landlord: "This was possible up to a short while ago. But today such a thing is absolutely impossible since no peasant would agree to it unless his head were not functioning normally. And what is it that saves the man and keeps him from being ground under the hard power of necessity? The New World! Previously, there was no escape; but now there is."[6]

Italians moved into the Lower East Side, East Harlem, Red Hook in Brooklyn, the Bronx, and, most of all, into the grid area south of Greenwich Village and north of Chinatown. Pushcarts and horse-drawn wagons rolled through the narrow streets, full of bread, fish, even ice cream, because a relatively easy way for any immigrant to begin a new life in the city was to sell food, principally to his own people.[7]

The Germans and Eastern Europeans had their *Schlächterfleischen* butchers and bakeries, the Jews had their delicatessens and kosher butchers, and the Italians had groceries, pastry and bread shops, live poultry markets, and pasta stores. As early as 1848, a Frenchman named Antoine Zerega had opened the first commercial pasta plant in the United States in Brooklyn. By the 1930s, Brooklyn and Queens had eight major macaroni plants operating. In 1929, there were 550 pasta factories in the United States (second only to Italy itself; France was third, then Argentina), and they were actually exporting more than the United States imported.

By 1938, there were more than ten thousand Italian-run groceries in America. There was good trade in importing canned and bottled goods from Italy. Photos, posters, and food labels of the time show cans of imported tomatoes right alongside boxes of macaroni made in the United States and cans of Carnation evaporated milk. The grocers made their own salami and sausages, bakers reproduced the shapes and styles of Italian regional breads, and though the mozzarella could not be made from the milk of water buffaloes as in the Old Country, the immigrants learned to make cheeses from American cows' milk. The first Italian cheese shop was Alleva Dairy, opened in New York's Little Italy in 1892, by Pino Alleva, from Benevento in Campania. Basilicata cheesemaker Savino Di Palo immigrated to New York in 1910 and opened a *latteria* dairy. Eventually he brought his family to America to help run the business, which then catered largely to the neighborhood. Gennaro Ottomanelli emigrated in 1900 from Bari to Greenwich Village to push a cart through the streets selling sausages. He returned to Italy to learn butchery and came back to New York to open a full-fledged butcher shop called Ottomanelli Brothers, where he distinguished himself from competitors by specializing in fresh game.

The immigrants clung fast to their culinary roots, and a turn-of-the-century social worker reported of Italian families, "Not yet Americanized, still eating Italian food."[8] Even far from the eastern cities, in small communities where Italians settled, their diet closely resembled that enjoyed in good times back in the Old Country. In one ten-block Italian-American neighborhood called Greenbush in Madison, Wisconsin, the daily diet included polenta, vegetable soups, wild greens, eel, dried codfish, offal, baby lamb, *cassata* cake, and Italian cookies. The men made their own wines, which they called Marsala.[9]

Italian immigrants' wines were usually made from zinfandel grapes, most of which were shipped in from California, but some came from New York, where the Hudson Valley Wine Company was established in 1907 by a retired Wall Street banker named Alexander Bolognesi. The grapes were crushed and fermented into cheap bulk wine that came to be known, at least as early as 1906, by both its happy American imbibers and bigoted detractors as "dago red." During Prohibition, many Italians took advantage of the dispensation that wine grapes could be sold for home use as well as for sacramental wine intended to be used at Mass.

Italian immigrants everywhere ate fairly well and quite nutritiously, while spending less than a quarter of their income on food, whereas back in Italy they had been spending up to 75 percent. My great-grandparents Maria Grazia and Paul Girolomo never really believed that the streets of New York were paved with gold, but they did find them lined with markets selling reasonably priced food. Their daughter, my grandmother Alvina, born in East Harlem, spoke of how her father would have a veal chop and a shot of grappa every morning before going off to work as a plasterer, and no one in his family ever went to bed hungry. My aunt Marilyn recounts how she and her three sisters would always come home from school to have a good lunch, while the non-Italian children ate the food dished out in the school cafeteria. Still, being of a generation that was already feeling more American than Italian, the Girolamo children yearned for the kind of soft white loaf sandwich bread they saw American children eating and disdained the coarser whole wheat bread that was the norm in Italy.

The immigrants' access to everything that had once been available only to the rich or on a special holy day—the big platters of pasta; tender beef, lamb, pork, and even veal; a chicken that had not grown old and tough; and wonderful sweets and candies—not only improved their diet but increased their new sense of being Italian Americans. Many proudly put on weight and the men patted their stomachs as a sign of the *abbondanza* of their new country.

This abundance was celebrated with all due reverence and reverie toward the patron saints in street festivals like San Gennaro in New York's Little Italy, begun in 1926. Then, it lasted one day; now, in its ninth decade, it lasts for 11 days and is a

major tourist attraction, drawing three million visitors each year. Occurring usually in the last two weeks of September, the festival begins with a procession carrying the statue of San Gennaro—whose blood is said miraculously to liquefy back
in the cathedral in Naples—from Mulberry Street to Canal, north of Chinatown,
and to the Most Precious Blood Church. The sacred is vibrantly blended with the
profane, with fireworks, parading Italian bands, street corner singers, and stands set
up on the streets to sell what have became traditional festival foods: sausage and
peppers, pizza, pasta, heroes, and fried, sugared fritters called *zeppole* (see page 41
for recipe). Games of chance abound, puppet shows with the centuries-old commedia dell' arte figures Punch and Judy play throughout the day, clowns appear
out of nowhere, jugglers and fire eaters add to the noise and music, and the air is
perfumed with competing aromas of onions, garlic, meats, and sweets.

In America, the former *contadini*, who might have had a small plot of rented
land back in the Old Country, reveled in having their own gardens, even in the
back of tenements or on flat rooftops, where they could plant a pear tree or raise
basil, flat parsley, and oregano. Mexican chile peppers replaced Calabrese *peperoncino*. They would wrap fig trees in canvas to protect them from New York win-
ters. During the depression of the 1890s the city of Detroit allowed gardeners to
grow food in vacant lots, an idea that spread to 20 other cities by 1896, and Italians took full advantage by growing plots of tomatoes, eggplants, and peppers. In
rural settlements, the women would cook down the tomatoes into a pulp, strain
out the seeds and skin, then set the pulp on wooden boards to dry into a concentrated paste that was put into crocks and covered with olive oil. In cities, the
process was done much the same way, only on fire escapes and roofs.

Such abundance had the effect of throwing the Italian housewife and mother
into an entirely new role. In the Old Country, her job was to produce a family,
then to see that it had enough to eat; in America, she was now expected to prove
herself a *good* cook, capable of making a wide array of dishes, even delicacies.

My paternal grandfather, Michelangelo Mariani, and his wife, Rubina, had not
been quite as poor in Italy as so many of their fellow immigrants. They came
from Vasto, a hillside town above the Adriatic in Abruzzo, and Rubina's family
had been involved in the clothing business. But America offered far more opportunity for them, and eventually Michelangelo opened his own small shop in
the Bronx, making wire sock stretchers, while Rubina, who never learned to love
America and refused to learn English, stayed home and cooked the kind of dishes
she had eaten back in Vasto for her family in America. The portions just got bigger. Her domain was the kitchen, and before consenting to allow my mother,

Renée Sofia, to marry her son, my father, Eligio, she insisted the hapless young woman learn how to cook all her son's favorite dishes.

Those dishes included macaroni, lasagna, gnocchi, and polenta—the last out of a certain nostalgia, for in the minds of the immigrants, polenta was still the monotonous food of the poor. These dishes were served almost always with one kind of tomato sauce or another. There was a simple one of garlic, oil, and tomatoes called marinara, supposedly because it was made quickly, as soon as the mariners' wives spotted their husbands' returning fishing boats in the distance (see page 42 for recipe). Pasta *alla marinara,* which might be combined with golf-ball-size meatballs, was a staple of those southern Italian immigrants who had lived along the coast in Italy.

Marinara, chunky with tomato, and other, smoother tomato sauces, became the all-purpose "red sauce" by which Italians would always become known both in and out of their communities. Yet for decades, marinara was still not found much in southern Italian cookbooks or on menus. It is not among the two thousand recipes in *La Cucina: The Regional Cooking of Italy* (2009) compiled by the Accademia Italiana della Cucina. Nor is there a listing for marinara in *The Oxford Companion to Italian Food* (2007).

The earliest instance I have found of the use of the word in American popular culture was in the 1930 movie *Rain or Shine,* directed by Sicilian-born immigrant Frank Capra, when a character refers to spaghetti "with some marinara sauce." By 1939, a New York restaurant guide recommended, rather offhandedly, a "Mixed Fish Soup Marinara Sauce" (40 cents) at Del Pezzo restaurant on West 47th Street, suggesting the term was by then somewhat familiar to readers. There was also meat sauce—in Italy it would be called a *sugo di carne*—in which garlic would be sautéed in oil, then removed; meat, either ground or as a hunk of beef, would be browned, and then tomatoes, onions, *peperoncino,* and herbs, especially oregano, would be added, cooked for hours till the meat broke down and the sauce thickened, full of flavor. It differs significantly from the well-known Bolognese *ragù,* which has plenty of vegetables and ground meats but either no or very little tomato or just a tablespoon or two of tomato paste; in any case, *ragù* was a rich family's dish, not for peasants. In America it was often just referred to as gravy or, because it was most commonly served on Sundays after Mass, Sunday gravy.

In 1937, one enterprising immigrant importer, Giovanni Cantisano, and his wife, Assunta, began putting their tomato sauce into Mason jars in their Rochester, New York, basement. They sold it to neighborhood stores, then expanded through the United States under the label Ragù. They later sold the company to Cheeseborough Ponds, which by 1973, the year Giovanni died, sold $100 million of the product.

In his memoir, *An Italian Grows in Brooklyn* (1978), ad agency owner and restaurateur Jerry Della Femina told how, while growing up in the 1930s, "there were no restaurants in my neighborhood. We didn't go out to eat. We ate either at our house, or cousin Ronnie's, or Uncle Dom's, or whatever. My grandmother would start making her meat sauce at seven in the morning on Sunday and within five or six hours that smell would be all through the house, covering everything—clothing, furniture, appliances—and then it would go out the front door and into the streets, to mix with the aroma of neighboring meat sauces."[10]

Film director Martin Scorsese has said of those red sauces, "The Italians of my parents' generation are held together by the notion of family. That is why the pasta sauce is so sacred to the Italian family."[11] To Americans, the sauce became the very symbol of what was Italian food.

Amazingly, there is no record of Italians enjoying tomato sauce with pasta before the middle of the nineteenth century, although, as Pellegrino Artusi suggested, it was becoming very popular, especially in the cooking of the south—Abruzzo, Molise, the Marches, Basilicata, Puglia, Campania, Calabria, and Sicily—the very regions from which the immigrants had come in such large numbers. In 1870, novelist and gourmand Alexandre Dumas (*père*), in his *Grand Dictionnaire de cuisine,* provided a recipe, from a woman curiously named Mme. Ristori, for a "beef sauce" made with three pounds of rump beef and six tomatoes, garlic, onions, and paprika, covered with consommé, and boiled for three hours. The sauce is then layered with macaroni and ham pulp, and sprinkled with Parmesan cheese. It is not baked; instead, Dumas instructs the reader to "pour a glass of ice water on top and serve as a pottage," further noting that "in Naples, the glass of water is obligatory." Aside from that last inexplicable step, the sauce could pass for an Italian meat *ragù* or *sugo.*[12]

The French culinary term *à l'italienne* was commonly used in chefs' cookbooks to describe either a dish made with macaroni or vermicelli, usually served with butter and cheese, or as a *gratin,* as in the recipes for gnocchi, lasagna, macaroni, ravioli, and even polenta included by Georges Auguste Escoffier in his *Le Guide Culinaire* (four editions, 1902–1921). Escoffier does include a "*sauce italienne,*" which calls for "tomato-flavored Demi-glace," pureed mushrooms, and diced ham simmered for five to six minutes and mixed with tarragon, chervil, and parsley, to be used in "the preparation of many small entrées."[13]

So, too, in *Madame Begué and Her Recipes,* "Spaghetti à l'Italienne" is made only with butter, flour, and Parmesan cheese, while "Macaroni à la Sauce Tomate" uses a sauce made from tomatoes, butter, garlic, thyme, bay leaf, sherry, flour, and cayenne pepper, which is not far from the kind of tomato sauces Italians made. The addition of butter and flour indicates the Creole principle of always starting with a roux, which Italians never used in their tomato sauces; Begué also recommended cooking the macaroni 20 to 25 minutes, which would be at least 10 minutes past the tender "al dente" stage Italians find ideal.[14]

Thus, while southern Italians increasingly enjoyed pasta with tomato sauce, it was in the United States where it became a ubiquitous Italian-*American* food, the first of many that would seem inextricable from any discussion of Italian cooking. Not only was it served with pasta, but it also was the sauce that was lavished on their meat, chicken stews, and seafood. They spread it on eggplant, used it as a dipping condiment for fried foods, and poured it on sausage and peppers. They cooked big meatballs in it. And it was the sauce that made a pizza a pizza *alla margherita.*

Outside of Italy, these and so many other "red sauce" dishes that filled the repertoire of the Italian-American cook were, ironically, to become far more commonly associated with a general idea of Italian food than the actual regional cuisine of Italy. Not that there were many Italian restaurants anywhere outside of the United States and Argentina before World War II, but those that existed were far more firmly in the Italian-American style than they were devoted to the cookery of Liguria, Umbria, Piedmont, or even Pellegrino Artusi's Tuscany.

## ZEPPOLE

These long fritters are a staple of Italian street fairs and are named *zeppole* because of their "zeppelin"-like shape.

*5 tablespoons unsalted butter*
*Pinch of salt*
*2 tablespoons sugar*
*1 cup all-purpose flour*
*4 large eggs*
*Vegetable oil, for frying*
*¹/₂ cup confectioners' sugar*
*¹/₄ teaspoon ground cinnamon*

1.  In a saucepan, combine the butter, salt, and sugar with 1 cup water, and bring to a boil. Remove from the heat, and add all the flour at once. Stir vigorously to blend well. The mixture will form a dough. Return the pan to the burner, turn the heat to medium, and stir the dough for another minute. Remove from the heat.
2.  Add the eggs, one at a time, to the flour mixture, beating well with a hand-held mixer until incorporated.
3.  In a medium-size saucepan or skillet, pour the oil to a depth of 1 inch, and heat it to 375°F. Take two teaspoons and dip them into the hot oil to coat. Then, with one spoon, scoop out a walnut-size piece of dough and carefully drop it into the hot oil, helping to scrape it off with the other spoon. Quickly repeat, dropping in more scoops of dough. Fry for about 6 minutes, until the zeppole have are nicely browned. Drain on paper towels.
    Repeat with the remaining dough, keeping the oil at 375°F.
4.  Mix the confectioners' sugar and cinnamon together and place in a sifter. Sift the cinnamon sugar over the zeppole.

Makes about 18 zeppole.

## MARINARA SAUCE

While most Italians north of Rome rarely used tomatoes in their sauces, Italian-American immigrants from the South made the simple tomato sauce called marinara into a staple of their cooking, usually using canned tomatoes imported from Italy.

*$1/2$ cup extra-virgin olive oil*
*5 garlic cloves, crushed*
*Two 28-ounce cans Italian-style tomatoes, with juices, crushed or chopped*
*3–4 leaves of fresh chopped parsley*

1.  In a large saucepan, heat the olive oil over medium-low heat, then add garlic and cook until lightly browned. (The garlic cloves may be left in the sauce or removed.)
2.  Add the tomatoes and parsley, salt and pepper to taste, and bring to a boil. Reduce to a simmer and cook for 20 minutes.

Use over pasta or as a condiment and sauce.

# Chapter 3

# Feeding the *Americani*

Italian immigrants may have catered primarily to their own neighbors, who were familiar with the food, but very soon the cafés and pastry shops began to be popular with other ethnic groups. Going to Little Italy became a city diversion, like going to Chinatown. Visitors accustomed to American apple pie, German strudel, and Jewish babka could go to an Italian café to sip dark espresso coffee with a lemon peel on the saucer and nibble on sugar-dusted, ricotta-stuffed cannoli and anise-flavored cookies with names like *biscotti* (twice baked), *ossi dei morti* (dead man's bones), *baci di dama* (lady's kisses), and *brutti ma buoni* (ugly but good).

Italian pastries almost glowed with color—the red, white, and green of Italy's new flag—while others were filled with pastry cream or custard and lavished with dark chocolate. Cookies full of hazelnuts and cakes riddled with candied fruit, once made only on feast days, were now always in the shop windows. In summer there would be freshly made citrus ices served in pleated paper cups from a cart pushed by the "hokey-pokey man," a name derived from the vendor's sing-song come-on, "*O, che poco!*"—"Oh, how little!"

Such sweets would have been a rare indulgence for most in the Old Country; in America they were a frequent treat. One of the earliest New York ice cream parlors to open, in the 1820s, was the fanciful Palmo's Garden, whose immigrant owner Ferdinand Palmo fitted it out with gilded columns, huge mirrors, and an Italian band. In 1892, opera impresario Antonio Ferrara opened a confections parlor under his name on Grand Street, where he could entertain his musician friends. Veniero's on East 11th Street began as a billiard parlor in 1894 that sold a little candy and coffee, evolving into an enormously successful pastry shop that created the cake for Franklin D. Roosevelt's inauguration.

Such cafés and pastry shops were small indulgences for the Italians in America. None but a handful had any experience eating in or running a restaurant, nor was there usually any excess money to spend on such frivolities as dining out. With the food so good at home, there was little reason to eat out anyway. The few Italian restaurants that existed in the mid-nineteenth century in New York were usually owned by northern Italians. One, Riccadonna, was well known as a place where a four-course meal cost 30 cents (a modest sum then), and a grand feast of seven courses with wine was a pricey $1.25.

The Neapolitan immigrants did bring their favorite street food to America—the pizza, which they ate with the crust folded over, as a kind of sandwich or snack. Records indicate that the first true pizzeria—although that term for a place selling pizza was not then used—in Italy was established in 1780, when Pietro Colicchio opened Pietro . . . e basta così (Peter . . . and that's enough) in Salita Sant'Anna di Palazzo in Naples. He later gave ownership to Enrico Brandi, who changed the name to Pizzeria Brandi and in turn gave it to his daughter Maria Giovanna Brandi, who would marry the man who had made pizza famous, Raffaele Esposito. (Pizzeria Brandi is still in existence.)

The local popularity of pizza as a street food of strictly Neapolitan origin made the arrival in 1889 of the new queen of Italy a reason to promote the city's native foods. Esposito commemorated her visit by naming a pizza after her, *pizza alla Margherita,* made in the three colors of the new Italian national flag—red tomatoes, white mozzarella, and green basil—which she diplomatically declared her favorite. The *pizza alla Margherita* became suddenly fashionable in Naples, though nowhere else in Italy—the word *pizzeria* did not even appear in Italian print till 1918—but the idea came to America via the Neapolitans who settled in the eastern cities.

The first known pizzeria to open in the United States was G. Lombardi's in 1905 on Spring Street in New York. At first a grocery, the store began to sell pizzas to the immigrants, specifically Neapolitans who craved it and for whom it was impossible to make in their home kitchens. From there, pizza's popularity grew rapidly, at first in and then beyond the Italian-American neighborhoods. By the 1930s, most of the Italian neighborhoods in eastern seaboard cities had pizzerias, many just taverns, others freestanding.

Given the low cost of its ingredients, pizza became more widespread than it was in Naples, and the toppings grew quickly in number, often with a regional twist, like the white clam pizza created at Pepe's Pizza, which opened in New Haven in 1925. Chicago-style deep-dish pizza, cooked in a black iron skillet, was the creation of Ike Sewell and Ric Ricardo of Pizzeria Uno in Chicago in 1943. The thickness of the dough and the lavish use of disparate ingredients typified the Midwestern idea that making a dish larger is always better.

A postwar boon to pizza makers occurred when GI Ira Nevin returned from Italy to New Rochelle, New York, and combined his family's expertise in oven repair with his newfound love of the pizzas he had had in Naples to came up with the Baker's Pride gas-fired ceramic deck pizza oven. Prior to that, pizzas were baked in hand-built, brick-lined ovens fired by coal.

In the eastern cities, pizzas were still considered simple, cheap, filling fare, especially to be enjoyed on a Friday night, when Catholics were still forbidden to eat meat, with a beer or bottle of cheap red wine. By the 1950s, take-out made sales soar, so that special cardboard boxes were created for the purpose, usually imprinted with a roly-poly, mustachioed Italian *pizzaiolo* tweaking his cheek and saying "Hot and Fresh!" or "You've Tried All the Rest, Now Try the Best!"

Largely, though, most Americans at that time had never heard of pizza. "If someone suggests a 'pizza pie' after the theater, don't think it is going to be a wedge of apple," wrote New York *Herald Tribune* food columnist Clementine Paddleford in 1939. "It is going to be the surprise of your life, . . . a nice stunt to surprise the visiting relatives, who will be heading East soon for the World's Fair. They come to be surprised, and pizza, pronounced 'peet-za,' will do the job brown."[1]

After the war, Americans began to recognize pizza as fast food right along with hamburgers, hot dogs, and French fries, so that by 1953, crooner Dean Martin (born Dino Paul Crocetti to Abruzzese immigrants in Steubenville, Ohio) had a huge hit with the song "That's Amore," by Harry Warren (born Salvatore Antonio Guaragna) and Jack Brooks, crooning "When the moon hits your eye like a bigga pizza pie/ That's amore!" Although Martin thought the song was ridiculous and did not want to record it, he debuted it in the movie *The Caddy* and the single went to number two on the Billboard charts.

The Americans liked such silly gimmick songs because Italians, more than any other ethnic group, seemed to correspond to favorite stereotypes of them as pizza-loving, pasta-eating, happy sensualists. By 1955, a character in the hit TV comedy show *The Honeymooners* could make a joke about low-calorie pizza and get a big laugh from the American audience.

The first frozen pizza was marketed by Celentano Brothers in 1957. A few years later Rose and Jim Totino, owners of one of the first pizzerias in Minneapolis, came out with their own brand of frozen pizza, which by the late 1960s was the top-selling frozen pizza in the United States. It was bought out in 1975 by Pillsbury for $20 million.

The Italians also loved their hero sandwiches, long, sliced loaves of seeded Italian bread stuffed with mozzarella, provolone, ham, lettuce, peppers, and other foods, even meatballs or breaded chicken. The "hero" in question was the person man enough to devour one of the huge sandwiches, which also went by regional names like grinder, spuky, wedge, and, especially in Philadelphia and New Jersey, hoagie. Back in the 1930s, a version called the Italian beef sandwich appeared in Chicago, a hero made with slices of beef and its juices, topped with sweet peppers. In New England it might be called a submarine or sub, a name coined by grocer Benedetto Capaldo to commemorate the submarine base in Groton, Connecticut, where he had his store.

In 1965, a 17-year-old high school graduate in Bridgeport, Connecticut, named Fred DeLuca was trying to figure out how he would pay for college with a summer job that paid only $1.25 an hour. At a backyard barbecue that summer, a family friend, Dr. Peter Buck, suggested he open a submarine sandwich shop and wrote out an investment check for $1,000. That first shop evolved into Subway sandwich shops, with 16 units opened around the state by 1974. Three decades later, the franchised chain had more than thirty thousand stores in 92 countries.

Philadelphia was the birthplace of another variant of the hero, the Philly cheesesteak, concocted by Pat and Harry Olivieri of Pat's Restaurant as a slender loaf topped thinly sliced beef and American-style cheese. In New Orleans, a Sicilian-American variant of the hero sandwich is the muffuletta, made on a large round seeded loaf and containing salami, cheese, ham, garlic, and a mixture called olive salad, a hefty item created at the city's Central Grocery (see page 59 for recipe).

Italian immigrants were delighted that Americans occasionally enjoyed their street foods—all adaptations of southern Italian antecedents—but having worked as cooks and waiters in others' eateries and restaurants, a few believed they could move beyond pizza and grocery sandwiches into the restaurant business. In fact, the trade-up from pizzeria to full-fledged restaurant had a real psychological significance for those who had worked hard but still enjoyed no better regard from their customers than being called garlic-eaters who ran "pizza joints."

A restaurant was an improvement in social status, even if the first of them were extremely humble eateries. Mario's opened on Arthur Avenue in the Bronx in

1919 as a pizzeria with a take-out window. It grew to be a famous restaurant that counted as regulars the New York Yankees, politicians seeking the Bronx vote, sports figures like Muhammad Ali, and movie stars like Paul Newman. At a certain point in its history, Mario's stopped serving pizzas at dinner unless patrons also ordered another dish.

For all these humble struggles towards respectability, it had been a sea captain named Giovanni Del-Monico who had opened the very first true restaurant featuring foreign cuisine in America, which he proudly named Delmonico's—a "Restaurant Français." Here customers sat at their own table, covered with linens, were offered a printed menu and wine list, and had access to a private dining room, just like the new restaurants in Paris.

Del-Monico (the original family spelling) was from Ticino in northern Italy, which was long controlled then finally annexed as a canton by Switzerland. He became the captain of a schooner but sought to settle on land, so he set up a small wine shop near New York's Battery and sold his product to the quickly developing merchant class at the foot of Manhattan. The store did not fare well, and he returned to Switzerland to gather fraternal and financial support from his brother Pietro Antonio Del-Monico, then a confectioner in Berne. With seed money, they sailed for New York and opened a European-style pastry shop on William Street, where they sold high-quality pastries for a penny, and coffee and brandies for six cents, along with Cuban cigars. The money was collected by Peter's wife at a time when a woman cashier was considered an amazing novelty.

By 1830, the brothers (who had removed the hyphen from their name) took over the entire building, importing more family members along with Parisian chefs to run their new restaurant concept. Prior to this time, meals in America and pretty much everywhere in the western world were taken at taverns, eating houses, or boarding houses, where patrons ate whatever the proprietors served to everyone on any given day. Delmonico's first menu listed its dishes in both French and English in facing columns, including *Potage au vermicelli* next to "vermicelli soup." The Delmonico brothers, who now included Lorenzo, bought property in Williamsburg, Long Island, (later Brooklyn) and raised chickens for their eggs, cattle for their meats, and gardens for their fruits and vegetables—they used the best ingredients available.

In 1835, fire swept through lower Manhattan, destroying the restaurant, a disaster that nonetheless allowed them to expand their own vision of what a restaurant could be; in 1837, they opened a three-and-a-half story building on South William Street with Pompeian marble columns at the front door, glowing gaslight, rich mahogany and crystal, gleaming mirrors, fine silverware, and crisp white tablecloths. Waiters dressed in dark jackets and aprons, and there were fine wines from California and New York State, some with Italian names on their labels—sixteen thousand bottles, all stored a hundred feet below the restaurant. The new restaurant cost a staggering $100,000. But by then New York had three hundred thousand inhabitants, and many of them could afford to dine at "Del's." Many more would dream about it. Everyone had heard of it.

Giovanni—now John—died in 1842, and Lorenzo, who had earned the nickname Lorenzo the Great, took over a rapidly expanding business of hotels and restaurants. He pioneered the so-called hotel European plan, whereby the payment of room and board was separate from the food bill. Guests ordered only what they wished to eat, à la carte, not from a fixed price menu. He was also canny enough to know that inviting the press for preview dinners would result in headline stories the next day.

The Delmonicos kept moving uptown, to Madison Square, as the city's business grew north, along the way acquiring from the Maison Dorée restaurant the illustrious chef Charles Ranhofer, who created many of Delmonico's best-known dishes, like lobster à la Newburg, baked Alaska, and the Delmonico steak. When Charles Dickens came to a celebratory dinner in his honor in 1868, Ranhofer created dishes named after literary and national figures, including *crème d'asperges à la Dumas, côtelettes de grouse à la Fenimore Cooper,* and *agneau farci à la Walter Scott.*

The last of the Delmonicos' restaurants, at Fifth Avenue and 44th Street, opened in 1897, was the most opulent and modern of them all, with electric lights, Tiffany china, a full orchestra, a glorious palm court, vast banquet spaces, and a "bride's room," reserved for privacy. In fact, among all its other innovations, Delmonico's was the first restaurant to allow women to dine alone, in 1868, albeit in a private dining room. Previously, women were permitted to dine in restaurants only with their husbands. Delmonico's also made history—in 1861 Samuel F. B. Morse sent the first cablegram across the Atlantic from the restaurant; 40 minutes later, the answer came back to the wild applause of 350 assembled guests.

The restaurants survived fires, the Civil War, major depressions, and World War I, but, as fashions and dining habits changed, Delmonico's did not, and the last of the family-owned restaurants closed in 1923, with the onset of Prohibition.

In the late nineteenth century, many of immigrants found employment as cooks and waiters in these and other palatial restaurants, like Delmonico's, Rector's, and Louis Sherry's, where the chef might be French or German, but the kitchen crew was largely Italian. In fact, the kitchen staff at the elegant St. Regis Hotel, opened in 1906, was composed entirely of Italians. It was inevitable, then, that Italian Americans would open their own restaurants, not just pizzerias.

Delmonico's was obviously a standard few Italian immigrants could afford, and they were aware that there was no market for Italian food beyond the usual soups of macaroni and vermicelli. The first Italian eateries, aside from pizzerias, started serving food out of grocery stores or were boarding houses that served meals. Mamma was the cook, Pappa ran the front, and the children brought out the food.

The first Italian restaurants in New York began to open before the turn of the century, way downtown, in Little Italy, and in the "Bohemian" section of Greenwich Village, a neighborhood that is still full of Italian eateries today. These attracted the artists and poets, none of whom had any money to spend on lavish meals, so that a plate of spaghetti and a bottle of Chianti in a straw-wrapped bottle was enough to make an evening merry. One of the earliest Italian places to open in the United States was Caffé Moretti, probably in the 1850s, decades before the waves of *immigranti* arrived. Stefano Moretti put his cheap eatery in a basement in New York's financial district, and, according to William Grimes in *Appetite City: A Culinary History of New York* (2009), built his business "on the plainest of fare, nothing more than huge bowls of boiled spaghetti in 'beef gravy' with Parmesan cheese,"[2] a dish that was cause of much amusement among American patrons, who had not a clue how to eat the stuff. Note, too, that it was not served with tomato sauce but beef gravy.

By the turn of the century, similar, modest *ristoranti* were being established in cities like New York, Boston, New Haven, and Providence, as well as in San Francisco. Joe Guffanti's, described by the *New York Times* in 1900 as a "Dingy Place in Seventh Avenue," was entered through the saloon's back door; the dining room held six to eight tables, and the clientele consisted of Italians "of the more prosperous class . . . almost always well dressed. Then there are business men of the neighborhood who like Joe's food better than what they can get at home; men-about-town, whose appetites have grown satiated with the elaborate viands of restaurants more 'swell'; reporters, detectives, actors, and a variety of other wanderers for whom the odor of Signor Guffanti's soup has a pleasant charm."[3] When Italian clothes designer Ermenegildo Zegna wanted to do business in New York in the 1930s, he took all the Italian tailors out to dinner at Guffanti's, with the Italian Consul as guest of honor.

Guffanti had come to America as a child and prospered well enough in the restaurant business to sail triumphantly back to Italy to visit with his mother and old friends but returned distraught after a single day in his hometown. He told his customers when he got back, "You see, it was like this. I thought I'd have a mighty fine time, but when I got home the guys around there knew I was an American by the cut of my trousers. So they pulled my leg and tried to work bunko games on me and played hell with me generally. I couldn't stay in the country—couldn't stand it—that was all there was to it. No, Sir! I'll never go back again. An American can't stand it over there. There's no use in his trying. New York is the only place for a decent man to live in."

The restaurants of the 1920s usually were decorated in the same style—the tiled floors, tin ceilings, simple chairs and tables, and red-checkered tablecloths common to simple eateries. They were also, at least initially, very cheap, in the same way that Jewish, Chinese, Spanish, and Mexican restaurants were at the time. Fifty cents or less could buy a hungry man an entire meal. In 1927, Chicago's Italian Village restaurant served enormous portions and spaghetti with meatballs was only 40 cents. Even as late as 1930, a New York Italian restaurant named Lucca was advertising, "All You Can Eat for Fifty Cents," which included antipasto, soup, spaghetti or ravioli, meat, something called "fried cream," and a tray of pastries and ice cream.

Italian restaurants usually grew from a more informal eatery to a full-fledged restaurant. For example, Vincent's Clam Bar in New York's Little Italy started out in 1904 as just that, a sidewalk clam bar overseen by Giuseppe and Carmela Siano. It eventually became a small restaurant they named after their son, Vincent.

Angelo Del Monte and "Papa" Marianetti opened a restaurant in San Francisco's North Beach neighborhood in 1886 that they called Fior d'Italia, which claimed, erroneously, to be "the Oldest Italian Restaurant in America." Originally it had been set up set up just to serve the clients of a bordello in the building. That structure burned down in 1893, and another was destroyed in the 1906 earthquake, so the family operated out of a tent for a year, feeding the newly homeless from "great kettles of soup." "The Fior" was in a new building by 1907 and grew as their business attracted more non-Italians than just the locals of North Beach. In successive locations, the restaurant grew to 750 seats, serving 1,500 people a day. (Today it is located on Mason Street, its banquet rooms decorated with murals of Assisi, Tuscany, and Umbria.)

With very few exceptions, almost all Italian restaurants in the east were opened by southern Italians who based their menus on their own family food, not on restaurants in the Old Country restaurant—of which most immigrants would have no knowledge. For this reason the Italian restaurant in America was not a replica of any in Italy but a whole new kind of eating place, where one was as likely to find platters of pork chops with vinegar peppers and sirloin steaks as spaghetti and meatballs, most of them lavished in garlic-rich "red sauce," which soon became synonymous with the Italian-American restaurant itself.

Dishes that would once have been considered only for a feast day, such as veal, swordfish, lasagna, and cheesecake, became an everyday indulgence on new Italian-American restaurant menus. Portions were larger, there was plenty of meat and sausages, and everyone ordered rich desserts such as spumoni ice cream, zabaglione, and cannoli filled with pastry cream. Cheesecake, made with ricotta (French- or Jewish-style cheesecakes were made with farmer's or cream cheese) was mostly unknown back in Italy but became ubiquitous in Italian-American restaurants, often brought in from a local pastry shop. Dinner ended with a drip-pot of espresso, served with lemon peel, which was added to take away the bitterness of the inferior coffee they used and which became a garnish customers expected to see. Often a bottle of cheap anise-flavored liqueur like Sambuca would be set on the table, compliments of the house.

New dishes were adapted and elaborated on from old ideas, often named for towns the cooks emigrated from. One will not find on any menu in Italy dishes called "veal Sorrentino," which denoted there was eggplant in the dish; "clams alla Posilippo," named after the district in Naples where so many immigrants came from; and "filet of sole alla Livornese"; yet these dishes have become standard items on every old-fashioned Italian-American restaurant. Although true *scampi*, a Venetian dialect name for a Mediterranean prawn, were not available in American markets, Italian-American cooks used shrimp and called a dish of them sautéed in garlic, butter, lemon juice, and white wine "shrimp scampi."

In other cases, dishes were created in honor of famous Italians, as in "turkey alla Tetrazzini," a dish of baked spaghetti and turkey, named after the reigning Italian soprano of the early twentieth century, Luisa Tetrazzini, and spaghetti alla Caruso, with chicken livers and tomato, after tenor Enrico Caruso (see page 60 for recipe). It is amazing how quickly such dishes were adapted as standards on Italian-American menus; one 1930s New York restaurant guide remarked that the city was "full of Italian restaurants—good, bad, and indifferent—all serving the same courses of minestrone, spaghetti, ravioli, scaloppine and tortoni." So entrenched were such dishes on Italian-American menus that on visiting New York, a Sicilian named Niccolò de Quattrociocchi reported in his memoirs that he'd dined at an Italian restaurant "where I was introduced to two very fine, traditional American specialties called 'spaghetti with meatballs,' and 'cotoletta parmigiana,'" which he thought were "just for fun called Italian," but added, "as a matter of fact, I found them both extremely satisfying and I think someone in Italy should invent them for the Italians over there."[4]

Two well-known New York restaurant guides, published a decade apart—*Dining Out in New York,* by G. Selmer Fougner of the New York *Sun* (1939), and *Knife and Fork in New York,* by Lawton MacKall (1948)—differed little in their reports on Italian menus of the day. Fougner credits Louis Zucca of Zucca's on West 49th Street with creating a dish called "Chicken cutlet Milanese" ($1.00), but most of the Italian entries in the guides list little more than ravioli, gnocchi, spaghetti, and chicken cacciatore, along with the recommendation for a "good Chianti."[5]

MacKall's write-ups are longer and more detailed, and he includes a 13-page chapter called "Antipasto to Zabaglione," but the restaurants included do not differ much in menu from Fougner's descriptions. Vesuvio, in the Theater District, served "eggplant Parmesan, asizzle with melted cheese and tomatoes" and saltimbocca; Gino's, on Lexington Avenue, served chicken Tetrazzini and "a la Gino (with garlic sauce)"; and patrons of Sorrento, on West 49th Street, were greeted by the owner, Gaetano, who suggested the clams a la Posilipo and Italian sausage with peppers and Pizzaiola sauce. Of Peter's Back Yard, opened in 1906 on West Tenth Street, MacKall writes that it was "known to the literary Bohemia of those days as Galotti's. . . . Tone of the place is still that of an era when Edna St. Vincent Millay was penning love lyrics, Eugene O'Neill was writing one-acters, and Sinclair Lewis was plugging a book called *Main Street.*"[6]

Little by little, finer, more expensive dishes were added—though no Italian restaurant dared to charge what a French one would for more or less the same dish. Filet mignon abounded, and pricey lobster fra diavolo in a hot tomato sauce had become popular by the end of the 1940s.

Both guides mention the flourishing Enrico & Paglieri, opened in 1908, on West 11th Street. Fougner said the eight-course dinner was $1.25 in 1939. The specialty here was chicken: "The late Enrico Fasani told me he had seen

14,000,000 chickens fulfill their destiny," wrote MacKall, who noted that guests could watch them turn slowly on the rotisserie behind kitchen windows.[7]

There were menus with some regional variations, especially in New Orleans, where the Creole influence was absorbed by every kind of cookery. Mosca's, on the city's west bank, was opened by immigrants Provino Mosca and his wife, Lisa, from San Benedetto del Tronto in Marche. They owned a restaurant in Chicago then relocated to Louisiana in 1946, when their son Johnny returned from army service in Italy, where he had been injured in combat and reassigned to wait on luminaries like Winston Churchill, General Charles de Gaulle, and Marshall Tito.

The little roadside restaurant, originally called Williswood, had a large number of late-night patrons from the local gambling halls of the era and thrived; when those halls were closed down in the late 1940s, the family increased its local business by offering a more extensive menu of Italian dishes laced with Creole seasonings. They used Gulf crab, oysters, and shrimp to good effect and served their specialty, spaghetti Bordelaise, which was like traditional spaghetti with garlic and oil, but at Mosca's was made with plenty of butter, which had nothing to do with a classic French bordelaise made from demiglace, red wine, marrow, shallots, and herbs.

The misnamed barbecued shrimp, which is not barbecued at all but baked with abundant amounts of butter, garlic, thyme, Worcestershire sauce, and bottled hot sauce, was a creation of Pascal's Manale restaurant, formerly called Frank Manale's, when it opened in New Orleans' Uptown District in 1913. Frank Manale's nephew Pascal Radosta bought it and tacked on his first name.

In San Francisco, Ligurian immigrants created a seafood stew called cioppino, made with the local Pacific seafood, especially crabs, the name an echo of *ciuppin,* a Genoese term for a similar dish back home.

Perhaps the most famous of all American salads was an accident: Over the July Fourth weekend in 1924, Italian immigrant Caesar Cardini found his restaurant, Caesar's Place, in Tijuana, Mexico, packed with a crowd of Californians, including many Hollywood movie stars, who had come across the border to drink and gamble at the racetrack there. Running low on food, Cardini scrambled to concoct a salad as a main course, made from Romaine lettuce, olive oil, croutons, Worcestershire sauce, and Parmesan cheese, tossed, then carefully arranged on a plate. Cardini told his guests to have fun and eat it with their fingers. Thus was born the Caesar salad, which became such a success with Americans that Cardini later patented and packaged the dressing. The salad was once voted by the

International Society of Epicures in Paris as the "greatest recipe to originate from the Americas in fifty years."

A number of Italian-owned restaurants began as speakeasies with the onset of Prohibition in 1920, many of them—of thousands in New York—once legal taverns run by Italians. Prohibition crippled the fine dining rooms around the United States: Boston's Locke-Ober Café had to seal up its wine cellar; and the new Waldorf-Astoria Hotel opened in 1931 with no bar or storage facilities for wine, beer, or liquor. As one wag of the day put it, people would rather eat sawdust off the floor and have a drink than dine at a fancy restaurant without booze. This offered a great opportunity for immigrant groups to cater to a new audience, and that audience began to become familiar with a few cheap Italian dishes and bottles of "dago red" wine, which were often served in the establishments hidden away in downtown neighborhoods like Little Italy, Greenwich Village, and the Lower East Side.

One of the best-known speakeasies was run by Italian immigrants John Ganzi and Pio Bozzi, from Parma, up on New York's Second Avenue, with a clientele of raffish local newspapermen, who needed to eat almost as much as they needed to drink. The owners started serving food and in 1926 opened the Palm as a restaurant. (Its name came from the municipal license bureau's mistranslating the name of owners' hometown.) The place was low-lighted, with dark corners, tables hidden away, and sawdust on the floors, and the only decoration in the place was on the walls, artist's cartoons and caricatures of regular patrons and New York celebrities. In those early days, the kitchen served basic Italian food, not steaks and chops, so that whenever a customer ordered a steak, Ganzi ran up Second Avenue to a nearby butcher shop, bought a steak, and cooked it back at the Palm. Soon it developed a reputation for its steaks, as did a slew of other Italian-run eateries along East 45th Street, called Steakhouse Row, around the corner from the Palm. There was Christ Cella, originally a speakeasy opened in 1923, serving liquor in coffee cups from a basement kitchen; Colombo's, located in a former Chinese laundry; Pietro's, opened by Pietro Donnini; Joe & Rose's, which started as a grocery in 1915, then became a speakeasy, then a steakhouse; and Bruno's Pen & Pencil. These and others set the mold for the Italian-American steakhouse and for the New York steakhouse—both terms were used by restaurateurs around the United States to bolster their image.

After Prohibition many Italian restaurants of the 1930s expanded their menus and premises to enormous sizes. Multitiered, with a warren of private and banquet dining rooms, decked out with facsimiles of baroque Italian sculpture and paintings of the owner's father and mother, as well as photos of famous customers, the Italian-American restaurant became a place where everyone came for a good time, plenty of food, low prices, and maybe some music by a strolling trio of guitar, violin, and accordion. In 1927, Alfredo Capitanini opened the Italian Village in Chicago, which from the start catered to performers from the Lyric Opera and other city artists. As the restaurant grew, it acquired a Hollywood-like stage-set décor that evoked a rustic Italian village, complete with cart wheels, murals of Venice's Rialto, and Italian statuary.

The appearance of true restaurants above the pizzeria and trattoria level was indicative of the appreciation by Americans of Italian-American cooking and reflected the rise in social status of Italian-American entrepreneurs, their restaurants among the most fashionable of their time. But except for one or two Italian restaurants in London and Buenos Aires, few cities outside of Italy or America had Italian restaurants of any kind, and fewer still would ever be called fashionable.

Barbetta, in New York, was one of the few fine dining Italian restaurants of the era, set in a very elegant townhouse. It was opened by Sebastiano Maioglio in 1906 on West 39th Street and moved in 1925 to West 46th Street, and to this day is visited by famous musicians, opera singers, and Broadway stars. Its menu was one of the few in the city that did not serve strictly Italian-American or Neapolitan food; Maioglio was proudly from Piedmont and proudly served dishes such as *fonduta* and *agnolotti* from his homeland.

But the apotheosis of the big-hearted, carnival-like Italian-American restaurant of the first half of the twentieth century was Mamma Leone's, originally opened in 1906 in a little room above a wine cellar at the back of the Metropolitan Opera, later moved to much larger premises on West 48th Street in 1914, playing host to everyone from comedian Will Rogers to entertainer George M. Cohan. At Mamma Leone's, Mamma was always there, dressed in black, overseeing every aspect of her domain. The nude statues of Venus were mildly scandalous, the baroque dining rooms—more like feed halls—full of color, light, and noise. You sat down with your family and were presented with big baskets of Italian bread and a huge wedge of cheese. Platters of celery and olives followed, then garlic bread, massive portions of lasagna, gnocchi, meatballs and macaroni, juicy pork chops, filets, veal steaming with marinara sauce and melted cheese, and fried calamari. There was music in the air, and the waiters spoke in sing-song broken English, laughing heartily at everything the Americans joked about and promising the ladies there were no calories in the cheesecake.

Mamma Leone's was one of the first theme restaurants—its theme was that of an Italian-American fantasy that had absolutely no basis in reality back in the Old Country, where the majority of Italians were still economically deprived of the pleasure of going out to dinner. For most Americans, the experience of dining at an Italian restaurant like Mamma Leone's was one of the cheaper forms of entertainment available, especially during the Great Depression.

In Los Angeles, Italians had ventured into the restaurant business by the 1920s, catering mostly to a Hollywood crowd that favored fried chicken eateries and Continental nightclubs such as Sebastian's Cotton Club, Roscoe "Fatty" Arbuckle's Plantation, and the Cocoanut Grove. Of the successful restaurants run by Italian immigrants, some served Italian food, others did not. One of the best-known was the Paris Inn, which was taken over and expanded by Umberto Rovere, who boasted he had once been a "grand opera baritone" as well as a waiter, a boxer, a wrestling promoter, and a vaudeville performer. In 1930, at a cost of $100,000, Rovere and chef I. Pedroni remodeled the restaurant to seat as many as five hundred people and added a new décor complete with French flags and an Eiffel Tower mural. Rovere also came up with the idea of singing waiters—a first, and a natural for Hollywood—which caught on later in other cities. The Paris Inn even had its own radio show.

Chef Joseph Musso, who was married to Rovere's sister, joined with Firmin "Frank" Toulet to open Musso and Frank Grill (originally, in 1919, Frank's Café), with a huge menu of steaks, chops, and mostly American food with some European touches. It immediately drew the Hollywood crowd because it was downtown and near the movie studios.

Alexander Perino came from a winemaking family of 12 children in Brusnengo, Italy, emigrating in 1915 to New York, where he worked at Delmonico's and the Plaza Hotel, washing dishes and waiting tables. Finally, in 1925, he moved to Los Angeles, where he worked at the Victor Hugo Restaurant and the Biltmore Hotel. (He was fired after dropping a tray of tea and crumpets.) But he had been saving his money, and in 1932, he opened the posh, pink-and-peach painted

Perino's, on Wilshire, which for decades was considered one of the finest restaurants in Hollywood.

Perino's served pastries from a solid silver cart, pink roses adorned each table, and the waiters wore white gloves. Perino was manic about his ingredients, having his greens grown for him on the Palos Verdes Peninsula by a Japanese American farmer. He charged accordingly—dinner was $1.25, very expensive for the time—and served a menu of Continental specialties like steak Diane, chicken quenelles, and pumpernickel cheese toast. The chef who kept the kitchen in top form for 37 years was Attilio Balzano.

Legends abounded about Perino's glittering clientele—Charlie Chaplin handed out $10 bills to panhandlers outside, Cole Porter wrote songs on the menus, and opera bass Ezio Pinza declared Perino's gnocchi better than any he had had in Italy. Regulars included everyone from movie stars such as Cary Grant and Elizabeth Taylor to mobsters such as Benjamin "Bugsy" Siegel to presidents Franklin Roosevelt and Richard Nixon. When Perino's finally closed for good, in 1986, after fires and relocations, the *Los Angles Times* called it "the last of the legendary eateries from Hollywood's Golden Age" and ranked it with Chasen's, Sardi's, and the Brown Derby.

Another Italian immigrant seeking his fortune in the Los Angeles restaurant business was named Romeo Salta (born Romeo Saltalamacchia in 1904 in Taranto), a former cook on the Italian submarine fleet, then a *garzone di cucina* (kitchen boy) on the luxury liners *Conte Verde* and a *piccolo* (busboy) on the *Conte Biancamano*. After one crossing to New York in 1929, Salta disembarked and never went back, taking waiter jobs and moving west until he got to Los Angeles, where he worked at two of the more notable Continental-style restaurants of the period, the Trocadero and Vendôme.

On his days off, he went in search of what he had not yet been able to find: a restaurant serving the kind of food he had known in Italy. The Italian restaurants he did find were cheap, the menus always had overcooked spaghetti and meatballs, and the jukeboxes blared. Saving his money, Salta took a lease on an old drugstore and opened a place he called Chianti because he knew all Americans were familiar with the name of the wine. The restaurant was at first anything but elegant. There was sawdust on the floors and the décor was rudimentary, but his cooking was as he wanted it to be, which meant that he had to charge higher-than-usual prices.

Business did not boom and he had no money for publicity in a town that ran on it. Fortunately, one evening he was visited by the powerful newspaper columnist Ed Sullivan, who went on to praise his food in his column, "Little Old New York," catapulting Salta and Chianti into the public eye. Success was assured overnight. Hollywood stars like Errol Flynn, Bing Crosby, and Lucille Ball came to dine, and Angelenos were introduced to new dishes like *spaghettini alla carbonara, risotto alla Milanese,* and *torta di mascarpone.*

Despite Salta's efforts in Los Angeles to upgrade Americans' appetite for Old World Italian food, the dominance of the Italian-American style, rooted in Campanian, Abruzzese, Calabrian, and Sicilian provincial cookery, was ubiquitous in the United States by the late 1930s. As a result, Italian cuisine during that period never received anything like the respect accorded French cuisine, even though the ingredients used in French kitchens were no better than in Italian kitchens and it was very likely that a French meal was being cooked by an Italian back in the kitchen. An Italian-American restaurateur would have to have been suicidal to charge the same price for veal *scaloppine* as a French restaurateur did, even if the latter served half the amount of veal.

As much as they had come to love the food, Americans would still refer to Italian restaurants as "that Italian joint," "that spaghetti house," "that Italian dive," or a place that served "good guinea food." Back in Italy, such characterizations were unknown, and most Italians had never set foot in a restaurant of any kind. But food was to play a major part in the resurgence of Italy as a world power in the 1930s, and that required changes in the ways Italian ate and drank as they marched onto the world's stage.

## MUFFULETTA

Of the many Italian-American sandwiches called heroes and grinders and subs, only the muffuletta had Sicilian origins, though it was created as a "po' boy" sandwich at the Central Grocery (where it is still made) in New Orleans in 1906 by Salvatore Lupo.

*Two 7-inch muffuletta rolls, or 1 round Italian bread with sesame seeds*
*4 teaspoons extra-virgin olive oil*
*4 ounces domestic ham, thinly sliced*
*4 ounces Genoa salami, thinly sliced*
*4 ounces provolone cheese, thinly sliced*
*4 ounces mortadella, thinly sliced*
*4 to 6 tablespoons prepared olive salad made from a mixture of olives and bottled Italian pickled vegetables*

1.  Slice the rolls or bread in half horizontally. Brush both sides with the olive oil. Layer the sliced fillings on the bottom pieces, top with the olive salad, and cover with the top pieces of the bread.
2.  Cut each sandwich into 2 or 4 pieces.

Serves 2–4.

## SPAGHETTI ALLA CARUSO

Named after the world-famous tenor Enrico Caruso (although one chronicler claims the dish originated from New York's Caruso restaurant chain), spaghetti alla Caruso was extremely popular on restaurant menus by the 1950s.

*1 tablespoon salt*
*12 ounces spaghetti*
*¹/₄ cup olive oil*
*1 medium yellow onion, finely chopped*
*6 garlic cloves, chopped*
*9 to 10 ounces chicken livers, coarsely chopped*
*10 ounces tomatoes, peeled, seeded, and coarsely chopped*
*2 tablespoons balsamic vinegar*

1. Bring 4 quarts water to a boil in a large pot. Add the salt and the spaghetti, and cook until al dente.
2. Meanwhile, heat a large saucepan over low heat and add the olive oil. Add the onion and cook, until it begins to turn golden. Add the garlic and cook, stirring, for 2 to 3 minutes more. Using a slotted spoon, remove the garlic and onion from the sauce pan and set aside.
3. Add the chicken livers to the saucepan, and sauté until they lose their color and become slightly seared on the outside, 4 to 6 minutes.
4. Return the garlic and onion to the pan, add the tomatoes and salt and pepper to taste, then add the balsamic vinegar. Cook until the liver is cooked through and the tomatoes have disintegrated into the sauce, about 5 minutes.
5. Drain the pasta and serve it immediately with the sauce.

Serves 4.

## Chapter 4

# The New Way of the Old World

As a child, Benito Amilcare Andrea Mussolini could easily empathize with those of his countrymen who left Italy for the Americas. The oldest of three children, he was born into poverty in 1883 in Romagna—his father was a blacksmith, his mother an elementary school teacher. Like much of Italy, Romagna had for centuries been ravaged by invaders from every direction, so that the people learned to be violent, goaded to and tantalized by anarchy. Mussolini's father gave his son three revolutionary names—after Mexican Benito Juárez and two Italian socialists, Amilcare Cipriani and Andrea Costa. Mussolini grew up a violent boy, open to his father's jeremiads against the social order as they watched caravans of starving, unemployed *giornalieri* (day workers) trudging through his town of Predappio.

What might have happened had the Mussolinis emigrated to America is not impossible to imagine. Benito might have joined an anarchist movement, like Sacco and Vanzetti did, or, if he found America a more benevolent place, perhaps he would have become a New York union boss or politician. Instead, the thick-chested, rock-jawed Benito stayed in Italy, escaped military service by exiling himself to Switzerland, returned to Italy to edit Socialist newspapers, joined the army to fight in World War I, and emerged as a leader of the new Fascist party.

That Mussolini ultimately brought Italy to ruin after his alliance with Adolf Hitler is evident from the way his own people brought him to justice—he and his mistress were shot and their bloodied bodies were hung by the ankles in a public square in Milan.

As dictator, Mussolini knew he could effect radical social change with a wave of his hand, even if it came down hard on his opponents' necks. He feared that in the early part of the twentieth century Italy's birthrate was not high enough to counter the opposing populations of France, Germany, and Great Britain, so he swore to raise Italy's population of 40 million people to 60 million within a single generation. He placed a tax on bachelors, and women were encouraged to have as many children as possible, with the promise that the state would take care of them all. Il Duce delivered free meals for the poor and medical assistance, and made admirable attempts to wipe out widespread tuberculosis.

There was severe rationing throughout the war—lasting until 1948—and after the Germans had requisitioned the country's largest pasta factory, Barilla, in Parma, black market pasta factories proliferated. To improve nutrition, Mussolini had waged the "battle for wheat," beginning in 1925, knowing that an increasing population would need the Italian staples of bread and pasta. For a long time, Italy had been importing most of its wheat from other nations, and during World War I the German navy tried to stop shipments of wheat from the Americas. Thus, using tremendous manpower resources that helped cut unemployment, Mussolini reclaimed fallow land and drained marshes for farming, also ridding those areas of malaria.

By 1929, there were 1,600 pasta makers in Italy, the largest producer of pasta in the world. (The United States was second.) Ironically, much of the industrialization of Italian agriculture in the early twentieth century was the result of landowners being forced to buy machinery in order to replace the cheap labor of the *contadini* who had emigrated to America.

The battle for wheat, if not wholly won, was among Mussolini's few achievements during his 20-year dictatorship. Another was the final breakdown of the medieval feudal system, giving both men and women more economic freedom. He backed a branch of the Fascist party called Rural Housewives, which in the 1930s had three million women members, whose zealotry showed even in their recipes for dishes like a "patriotic omelet" of eggs, greens, and tomatoes—the colors of the Italian flag.

In 1933, a book appeared called *Living Well in Difficult Times: How Women Face Up to Economic Crisis,* by Fernanda Momigliano. The title was well chosen, for the worldwide Depression was bearing down as hard on Italy as anywhere else, and later, with the onset of World War II, feeding families would only get much harder. Momigliano's next book, *Eating Italian* (1936), was an attempt to include more regional distinctions, including the cookery of the Italian Jews. (Momigliano, as a Jew herself, came close to capture and deportation by the Germans during the war.)

Il Duce, who prided himself on an ascetic diet (though he developed a gastric ulcer that restricted him to little but milk and fruit), also allied himself with one of the most eccentric literary men of the twentieth century, Filippo Tommaso Marinetti (born Emilio Angelo Carlo Marinetti), the author of countless poems, plays, and diatribes, and, most notably, the "Futurist Manifesto" of 1909, wherein he advocated an art of violence, cruelty, and injustice, in which everything of the past was to be destroyed and abolished—except war. This Marinetti glorified as the pleasure of rioting for the common people. He even wished to destroy the very thing that was keeping Italians alive: In 1932 he published a manifesto on cookery, *La Cucina Futurista,* in which he denounced pasta as a "gastronomic fetish of the Italians" that was making Italian men "stolid, leaden hunks, dull and insensitive. They need to be more in tune with the Italian female, who is a slender, spiraling transparency of passion, tenderness, light, strong will, impulsiveness, and heroic tenacity."[1] When the mayor of Naples declared that *vermicelli il pomodoro* was the food of the angels, Marinetti retorted that if it were true, it only confirmed his belief that paradise must be boring.

In place of pasta, Marinetti wanted to substitute absurd, wholly decadent combinations of foods, like pineapple with sardines and salami with cologne, and "Alaska salmon baked in the rays of the sun with a Martian sauce." He would spray perfumes into a dark dining room, and have diners stroke velvet, red silk, and sandpaper with their left hand while listening to the recorded sound of a loud airplane engine.

He challenged cooks to make "sculpted food," like the food depicted by Futurist painter Luigi Colombo—a rissole with minced veal, stuffed and roasted with 11 kinds of cooked vegetables, then placed on the plate and crowned with thick honey and supported at its base with a ring of sausage set on three spherical pieces of browned chicken—the kind of dish that might well appeal to twenty-first century "molecular" chefs, as would Marinetti's urging the chemical industry to come up with pills, powders, albumen compounds, synthetic fats, and vitamins to replace food. Kitchens were to be equipped with ozonizers, ultraviolet lamps, electrolyzers, colloid blenders, and distillers.

Mussolini must have admired Marinetti's call for a stronger, leaner Italian male, but the radical manifestos and shifting political loyalties eventually made Marinetti and his Futurists bothersome to Il Duce. The Fascists "pet Marinetti

up to a certain point, and as stealthily as possible," wrote Futurist Corrado Govoni in 1933, "and [then] they refuse recognition to Futurism and massacre the
Futurists."[2]

Damned by some as an anarchist and derided by others as a buffoon,
Marinetti loved nothing more than to enrage his detractors, goading audiences
at his theater troupe's live performances to throw vegetables at them. Anti-
women, anti-Catholic (although later he claimed Jesus was a Futurist) and pro-
Fascism, he served in the Italo-Abyssinian war and World War II, dying in 1944
of heart failure.

Mussolini's hubris also extended to the high seas in his decision to compete with
other nations' great ocean liners and to win the Blue Riband speed record for a
Transatlantic crossing, long held by the German ships *Bremen* and *Europa*. Mussolini proceeded to merge Italy's three existing shipping companies into one, to
be called the Italian Line, and began building two new vessels in Genoa's Ansaldo
shipyards. In 1928, Italy's largest vessel was the 32,000-ton *Augustus*, but this
would be dwarfed in the 1930s by the new *Rex*, at 51,000 tons, 880 feet in length,
and running at 28 knots. On August 1, 1931, King Victor Emmanuel III and
Queen Elena attended the launch of the *Rex*, which proudly sported the colors
of the Italian flag on its two funnels.

In August 1933, *Rex* did win the Blue Riband, with a speed of four days and
13 hours (beaten two years later by France's *Normandie*). *Rex*'s outdoor swimming pools were among the most beautiful of any of the ocean liners', and sand-
topped *lidos* were created to make American passengers believe that on *Rex*, "the
Riviera comes to meet you."[3]

Its sister ship, constructed simultaneously, was the smaller but even more luxurious 48,000-ton *Conte di Savoia*. Yet because the line's passengers were to be
principally non-Italians, the menus consisted of only a very few Italian items, like
ravioli with Bolognese sauce and minestrone "*casalinga*"; instead, most offerings
were in the established international style—jellied chicken bouillon, poached fish
with Hollandaise sauce, *vol-au-vent financière*, and a choice of three sauces—
*ravigote*, mayonnaise, and "French."[4]

The glory of the Italian Line was even used as a tie-in to the Fascistic architecture of the Italian pavilion at the 1939 New York World's Fair. Within the
pavilion's walls was a huge restaurant designed to mimic the look of the Italian

ships, complete with nude statuary that was quite eye-opening for American visitors at the time. Here one could feast on all manner of dishes not often found on the typical Italian-American menus of the day—*saltimbocca, agnolotti,* and *fonduta* with shavings of white Alba truffles, all complemented by fine wines like Barbera and Barolo poured by genteel Italian waiters who could have been Hollywood movie stars.

Although Mussolini was revered by many Italian Americans, his alliance with Hitler immediately evoked the comedic wrath of American popular culture, which portrayed Der Führer as a raging, carpet-chewing maniac and Il Duce as a fat, fatuous buffoon. The best depiction of these caricatures is in Charlie Chaplin's 1940 film *The Great Dictator,* when the two leaders—Adenoid Hynkel, Dictator of Tomania (Chaplin) and Benzino Napaloni, Dictator of Bacteria (Jack Oakie) threaten each other with a spaghetti-throwing fight.

Mussolini himself had once said, "Everybody dies the death that corresponds to his character."[5] This proved prophetic: In the end, his bloodied body hung upside down in a public square. Italy rejoiced at his downfall, but by that time he had driven the country into a state of ruin far worse than conditions before he came to power. And Italians were starving again.

Before the war, *ristoranti* were still of minor importance and meant more to tourists than locals. The deluxe hotels in Italian cities featured an amalgam of French and Italian favorites dressed up to look like a fantasia of baroque and neo-classical décor. The French dishes were always and everywhere prepared according to strict, classic recipes, but Italian dishes, without such a foundation, would differ from restaurant to restaurant, cook to cook.

Of course, those with money to eat out paid no attention to Marinetti's or Mussolini's harangues. In 1931, the new Touring Club Italiano published a 527-page catalog of Italian foods, titled *A Gastronomic Guide to Italy,* for which journalist Paolo Monelli used to file reports from all over the peninsula in his effusively written *Il ghiottone errante* (the wandering glutton) that sang the praises of all he ate and drank. Of the aroma of the Ligurian coast, he wrote in 1934, "It is the odor of pesto. . . . The mere smell of it makes your ears ring with a dialect at once sharp and soft, full of sliding sounds, of whispered syllables, of dark vowels."[6]

But locals usually chose *not* to eat out, even if they could afford to, much preferring home-cooked meals (*casalinga*) with their families to the kind of food, however regionally based, served in restaurants that catered to wealthy patrons, luminaries from the arts, and American refugees from Prohibition who found sanctuary in Europe, a civilized oasis where they could drink beer, wine, and liquor freely. American novelists, from F. Scott Fitzgerald to Ernest Hemingway, reveled in the license to drink booze and wine on what had once been called the Grand Tour, whether it was in Paris, Biarritz, Pamplona, on the Riviera, or in Venice.

Americans were surprised, however, to find that Europe bars were not like the bars at home, where one could order a round of cocktails, stand with one foot on the rail, and not bother to order anything to eat. Europe's taverns and cafés were very different, so, in order to placate their new clientele, hotels began installing "American bars" of a kind that would be familiar to their guests. The staff had to learn to make American cocktails such as the martini, the daiquiri, the pink lady, and the sidecar, and how to use seltzer bottles and garnish drinks with maraschino cherries.

It was such a hotel bar, the Europa-Brittania Hotel in Venice, that a young American named Harry Pickering frequented over a two-month period in 1929, although his original intent was to go to Europe to dry out. He came from Boston money and was accompanied by his aunt and her lover. Pickering insulted them both, and they left him, penniless and alone.

Turning to the man he thought might be his one friend in the world—hotel bartender Giuseppe Cipriani, a Veronese raised in Germany—Pickering asked to borrow just enough money to pay his hotel bill and go home, an amount he figured to be about ten thousand lire. For some reason, Cipriani took pity on the young American and gave him the money, assuming he would never see it, or Pickering, again. For two years Cipriani heard not a word, not even a postcard of thanks. Yet true to his promise, Pickering eventually returned to Venice and handed Cipriani ten thousand lire, plus an additional forty thousand lire, with which the two of them could open a small watering hole to be called Harry's Bar. It debuted on May 13, 1931, just off the Grand Canal, and years later Cipriani would joke, "If all those who said they were at Harry's for the opening had really been there, this place would have to be the size of the Piazza San Marco."[7]

And a bar it was intended to be, with short, squat cocktail tables and chairs. It was not shadowy and secretive like other bars, because Cipriani believed that "darkness hides things and people talk in a low voice."[8] Food was merely an after-thought, but Cipriani had to serve something to his increasing number of foreign guests—which on a single day in 1934 included the crowned heads of Spain, Den-mark, Norway, and Greece.

There were some ham and cheese sandwiches available, even hamburgers, which the Americans loved; then, little by little, the menu grew: a little green *tagliarini alla gratinata,* Venetian risotto colored purple-gray with cuttlefish ink, and lavish meringue desserts. The wines were from somewhere in Veneto, served in small carafes and poured into small trattoria-style wineglasses. The prices were high and got progressively higher as the popularity of the place grew. The kitchen was noisy, so it was moved, but it was moved back again to retain the tenor of the place.

Throughout the 1930s, Harry's Bar acquired an international celebrity that had little to do with the food but everything to do with the clientele. Regular pa-trons visiting Venice included Somerset Maugham, Noël Coward, Charlie Chap-lin, and Sinclair Lewis. This clientele had adopted the bar as a place their kind of people could congregate and drink and eat simple Italian food that wasn't really like any they could have elsewhere. American food writer James Beard, once asked to describe the food at Harry's Bar, said, "Well, he doesn't serve Italian food; he serves Cipriani food."[9]

Meanwhile, Harry Pickering himself lost all interest in the venture and went back home. When the war came to Venice, Cipriani's clientele were prevented from going to their favorite place. Then, one day in 1943, a group of Fascists en-tered the bar and told Cipriani he had to put up a sign barring Jews from the es-tablishment. When the thugs returned a few days later and demanded to see the sign, Cipriani led them to the kitchen, where it was displayed on a back wall. The Fascists began tearing Harry's Bar up with their bayonets, and a few days later the German consul suggested to Cipriani that his bar was a hangout for "unaccept-able non-Aryans." Rather than accede to coercion, Cipriani closed the doors, sailed the Grand Canal, and went hunting on the isle of Torcello until the war ended. Harry's Bar was turned into a German soldiers' mess hall.

# Chapter 5

# The Good, the Bad, and the Delicious

The long war over, with Europe in miserable economic straits, America found itself soaring to world eminence. Americans' productivity, wealth, and population increased at unprecedented rates, the suburbs boomed, the new medium of television increased the availability of information, and the hunger and deprivations of the Depression and the war years were, for most people, things of the past.

As much as any other industry, food was quickly, radically changed by postwar technology, which also brought changes in the way Americans ate. In the 1950s, the evening meal might well be a frozen Swanson's TV dinner (first sold in 1953 for 98 cents, later lowered to 69 cents) served on folding snack tables in front of the TV screen. The low cost of food, not taste, drove marketing decisions, so that in 1957, per capita consumption of margarine in the United States exceeded that of butter for the first time. Innovations like canned and frozen food, powdered drinks, frost-free refrigerators, and hundreds of plastic products for the kitchen were advertised and sold as expressions of a wondrous new age, one in which it was possible to imagine that a family robot might someday do all the drudgery of housework and kitchen chores, including cooking.

Scores of new, modern cookbooks were published to tell Americans how to use new appliances from electric Crock-Pots to kitchen counter rotisseries. Electric beaters made instant pudding, electric blenders crushed ice, and electric hot trays kept food warm. Whatever was new was deemed necessary, and whatever was old-fashioned was deemed, well, old-fashioned. Why would a housewife trudge every day from store to store to buy her milk, vegetables, poultry, meat, bread, and seafood, if she could go to just one supermarket and buy it in convenient portion-sized packages or cans? Sauces need not be made but simply poured from jars onto meatloaf, chicken, or spaghetti, which were cooked in ovens or on stovetops with timers to indicate when the food was done.

Americans by then had become accustomed to spaghetti with tomato sauce, not least through the Chef Boy-Ar-Dee Spaghetti Dinner—"only about fifteen cents a serving," read the ads. It was a box of "tender, quick cooking spaghetti," canned meat or mushroom sauce, and grated Parmesan cheese, easily tossed together in minutes. The product was created by Italian immigrant Hector Boiardi, who came to New York in 1914, then moved to Cleveland, where he worked as a chef. Eventually, he opened his own restaurant, called the Italian Immigrant, which was a great success and became famous throughout the Midwest. He began canning his own sauces, then the cooked spaghetti itself, and started distributing them for sale. Not long before the United States entered World War II, Boiardi was sought out by the U.S. military to provide canned food for American GIs, many of whom had never tasted spaghetti with tomato sauce before. After the war, those same GIs sought out the product, and Boiardi capitalized on their appetite by putting his picture on the label and changing the name to a phonetic spelling to make it easier for the American consumer to pronounce—Chef Boy-*Ar*-Dee (though most people mispronounced it as Chef Boy-Ar-*Dee*).

Boiardi's products were among the first foods to be advertised on television. In a 60-second 1953 ad, Boiardi, dressed in chef's whites and hat, comes through the door of a modern, well-equipped kitchen, and says with a slight Italian accent, "Hello, may I come in? I'm Chef Boiardi," creating both a connection to and an intimacy with the viewer that was new for the medium. In another ad, two cartoon teenagers ask—in rhyme—if their mother wants to go out for pizza; she replies that Chef Boy-Ar-Dee's pizza—with crust, sauce, and grated Parmesan cheese (no mozzarella)—is just as good and "ready in minutes, with the Chef's touch in it."

Rice-a-Roni was created in 1959 by a San Francisco pasta maker named Vincent DeDomenico, who was inspired after watching his sister-in-law mix vermicelli and rice with Swanson's canned chicken broth. DeDomenico substituted dried soup for broth and began marketing the product in 1961, with sales of $100 million dollars its first year.

In 1965, aiming squarely at the children's market, Campbell Soup Company came up with SpaghettiOs, small pasta circles in a tomato sauce, advertised with the catchphrase, "Uh-Oh, SpaghettiOs!" Mothers loved the canned product because it alleviated the problem small children had trying to cope with long strands of spaghetti. To this day, Campbell's sells 150 million cans per year.

No matter that most Italian Americans would be horrified by the idea of pre-cooked pasta and sauce; such products sold exceedingly well to other Americans who, having grown up on the iconic macaroni and cheese packaged as the Kraft Macaroni and Cheese Dinner, introduced in 1937, had no prior knowledge of what true Italian food should taste like. For them, Chef Boy-Ar-Dee products and Rice-a-Roni *were* Italian food.

Nor was there very much interest in the subject. The American diet was largely based on meat, not vegetables or starches. When food rationing ended after the war, Americans took both greedy delight and pride in consuming 155 pounds of meat per person (which was the average in 1947). In America, the 1950s was a time when the food industry roared and created recipes for dishes no one could have imagined before technology allowed them to exist. Most appeared in newspaper and magazine ads from the food companies that supplied them directly to food editors for their columns. This connection between the editorial pages in women's magazines and adjacent advertising reinforced the dazzling novelty of the new, time-saving American gastronomy. Though less time-consuming than in the past, cooking was still cast as drudgery, a duty required of a housewife for her family, as satirized by Peg Bracken's bestselling, sharp-witted *The I Hate to Cook Book* (1960), with chapters like "Desserts, or People are Too Fat Anyway." Bracken's directions for "Skid Road Stroganoff" went, "Start cooking those noodles, first dropping a bouil-lon cube into the noodle water. Brown the garlic, onion and crumbled beef in the oil. Add the flour, salt, paprika and mushrooms, stir, and let it cook five minutes while you light a cigarette and stare sullenly at the sink."[1]

Recipes of the period were dazzling in their conception but depressing in their resolution. A bizarre but telling book entitled *Retro Food Fiascos* (2004) reclaims 1950s and 1960s recipes for onion soup with Coca-Cola, Ring-Around-the-Tuna Jell-O Mold, a bologna biscuit bake, a crown roast of frankfurters, and plenty of dishes made with SPAM. There are even pizza recipes: one is made with packaged biscuits for a crust, a topping of canned tuna, and a dressing made with Parme-san cheese and evaporated milk; another is called Yankee Doodle Pizza Pie—"a traditional Italian dish goes American" that will make you shout "Bravo!" and "your family will clamor for 'Encores.'" It is made from Ann Page spaghetti sauce on top of packaged biscuits with mozzarella cheese, Ann Page beans "any style," and green pepper. Ann Page, the motto for which was "Fine Foods Needn't Be Ex-pensive," was a store brand of the A&P supermarket chain.[2]

General Mills had a big hit with its Hamburger Helper packaged foods, designed to help families make five servings out of one pound of chopped beef by adding pasta, including a lasagna variation, all prepared in just one skillet.

A slightly more refined interpretation of Italian food was to be found in American cookbooks that had pretensions to international flare, meant for affluent housewives and party givers. Among the bestsellers of the wartime era was Marian Tracy's *Casserole Cookery* (1941), which became a requisite for new brides and housewives of the period. *Gourmet* magazine debuted that same year, with a French-born Austrian consulting chef named Louis B. De Gouy, who apparently had no use for commercial food products, but neither had he much use for Italian food in the magazine. In *The American Hostess* (1948), Mrs. Julia Cooley Altrocchi (apparently an Irish-American who married an Italian American) proposed a formal Italian dinner that began with frozen tomato salad and crackers, then *pollo alla cacciatora* with Burgundy wine, rounds of cranberry jelly on an orange slice, artichoke hearts fried in oil, wild rice with mushrooms, slices of French bread, zabaglione, cupcakes, coffee and candies—a meal that would at best puzzle and at worst nauseate an Italian hostess. For Italian Americans, it was a sin even to think of eating such things. Yet for most Americans, this *was* Italian food.

Surveying the field of cookbooks in the late 1940s before writing his own, Italian immigrant Angelo Pellegrini found that "the most offensive, and in some cases the most popular, are those inspired by an unassimilated foreign cuisine. These are phony, impractical, misleading, and decadent. All of them—excepting the honest few—give the impressions of being commercially inspired."[3]

One of the first Italian cookbooks to make its mark in the world's kitchens was the oddly named *Il talisimano della felicità* (*The Talisman of Happiness*) in 1927, by a well-to-do Roman woman named Ada Boni, who had originally compiled it for women like herself, with servant cooks. *Il Talismano* went through numerous editions, expanding from 882 recipes to 2,245 by 1976, and is said still to sell twenty thousand copies each year. When an English translation appeared in 1950, it introduced Americans to wholly unfamiliar regional dishes like "Fish brodetto Rimini style," "Green Lasagna Modena Style," mullet with "Piquant Sauce," and rabbit in egg sauce. Just as important to its inclusiveness was its conversion of European weights and measures to American kitchen usage. Of course, access to many of the fresh ingredients called for in Boni's book was a huge problem for American cooks, who could never find them on supermarket shelves. Nevertheless, the appetite was growing: starting in 1948, the sales of oregano in the United States would increase 5,200 percent over the next eight years.

Anglo-Irish writer Elizabeth David came out with a series of well-researched, bestselling cookbooks in England after the war, including *Mediterranean Food* (1950) and *Italian Food* (1954). These books introduced her readers to those cuisines, which unfortunately required ingredients unavailable in England. But the popularity of the books prompted interest in importing them. David's recipes were a welcome relief from the abstemious dishes promoted by the wartime cooking booklets, and in his review of *Italian Food,* Evelyn Waugh declared the book one of the two that gave him the most pleasure to read that year.

David declared that "English opinions of Italian cooking, being based mainly on certain dubious concoctions known as minestrone, spaghetti, risotto, ravioli, served in restaurants Italian in name only, are naturally inclined to be unbalanced," and went on to insist that "the term 'Italian' used in relation to food would in fact mean very little to most Italians. To them there is Florentine cooking, Venetian cooking, there are the dishes of Genoa, Piedmont, Bologna. . . . Not only have the provinces retained their own traditions of cookery, but many of their products remain localized."[4]

Far more accessible for Americans was a cookbook that featured an array of authentic Italian dishes: *The Italian Cookbook: 160 Masterpieces of Italian Cookery* (1954), published by the Culinary Arts Institute of Chicago and written by staff home economists—none Italian, though the publisher did enlist the consultancy of a woman named Marion Granato, owner of Granato's Pizzeria Restaurant in Chicago. Yet the book is remarkable for its comprehensive inclusion of everything from macaroni and lasagna to *stracciatella* soup and *zeppole* fritters. There are good recipes for pizza with a crust made from scratch (the alternative noted is to use English muffins), veal Marsala, *fritto misto,* lobster *fra diavolo,* polenta with sausage, even marinara sauce.

The book is illustrated with simple drawings, stereotypical images of Italian peasants such as two women in shawls with a pig on a leash, a mustachioed man with a donkey carrying kegs of wine, and women drawing water from a well, along with Swiss guards, Italian painters, Roman centurions, and St. Peter's Basilica. The preface to the book shows an admirable understanding of what Italian food truly was, not what was being served up by the magazines and newspapers. Acknowledging the influence of southern Italian cooking in America, the

unnamed author writes, "The bases of the most colorful Italian dishes are tomatoes, garlic, and olive oil. Yet, foods in Italy are as diversified as they are traditional. It is not at all unusual to find an Italian who likes neither tomato sauce nor
garlic—he probably has his spaghetti with a butter and cheese sauce and prefers
Melon and Prosciutto to an ordinary antipasto course."[5]

The section "Pasta, Polenta, and Rice" notes, "Lasagne, vermicelli, ditalini, ravioli and manicotti are only a small part of the Italian phenomenon known as
pasta"[6]—an early instance of an American cookbook using the word at a time
when most Italian Americans still called such dishes by their noodle names—
macaroni, vermicelli, spaghetti, and so on.

It was not the only Italian cookbook of its day, but it was one of the most popular: the 68-page paperback volume, sold mainly in groceries and supermarkets,
ran through at least four editions, all the way to 1965.

# Chapter 6

# Il Boom and La Dolce Vita

Upon agreeing to head the United Nations Relief and Rehabilitation Administration in 1946, former New York mayor Fiorello La Guardia shook his finger with missionary zeal and told the world, "People are hungry, and it is our responsibility to feed them." He implored Americans not to overeat or waste resources, noting, "In my own city we waste enough to feed a city of 350,000. . . . I know, I picked up that garbage for 12 years. . . . [We] learned through a period of depression that ticker tape ain't spaghetti."[1]

La Guardia, born in Greenwich Village to an Italian father from Puglia and a Jewish mother from Trieste, knew the deprivations Americans had endured for a generation, and as head of the Relief Administration sought to eradicate those deprivations in the rest of the postwar world, not least in Italy, which had lost its colonies, its industry, its manpower, and its means of food production—this in a country that had been overwhelmingly agricultural, with few mineral resources and no oil. In a bizarre turnabout, Italians were again resorting to polenta to keep body and soul together as the postwar Italian government struggled to stabilize itself.

In 1948, following the abdication of Victor Emmanuel III and the exile of his son Humbert II, a republican constitution went into effect; but the newly emergent political parties were often in disarray, falling in and out of power, foundering in deals and corruption, and making anything more than momentary stability impossible. Italian filmmakers such as Roberto Rossellini and Vittorio De Sica took to the streets to document the rigors of postwar living in neorealist films such as *Rome, Open City* (1945) and *Bicycle Thieves* (1948). These films, which were released in the United States in art house movie theaters, gave Americans their first sad, grisly, hungry look at the way Italians were coping.

Only with the tremendous help of the Marshall Plan in providing $12.5 billion worth of food (including 110,000 tons of pasta), oil, and industrial aid to Europe did Italy begin to dig itself, or rather, build itself, out of this postwar malaise. By 1948, the currency was stabilized, and the creation of the state-owned energy group ENI (Ente Nazionale Idrocarburi) in 1953 established much-needed resources to fuel the remarkable economic recovery that occurred in Italy between 1958 and 1963—a time that came to be known as Il Boom.

Most of the industrial growth came in the north. Cities such as Milan and Turin became capitals for textiles, plastics, and car and truck manufacturing. Fiats poured from assembly lines, while masterpieces of hand-tooled Italian automotive design such as Maserati, Lamborghini, and Alfa Romeo put *una bella figura* to Italy's industrial might. And when those cars were sold, they were driven on a great new *autostrada* system of superhighways.

In the south, land reform laws of the period allowed estates that had fallen into ruin to be sold off to the former peasants, although only 117,000 families actually acquired farms. The landlord system was finally defeated by regional governing boards, sometimes with European Economic Community subsidies. Roads were improved, schools were opened, and diseases such as malaria were eliminated. Yet as late as 1950, per capita income in the south was still only half that of northern Italy, and the problem persisted for decades. Between 1955 and 1970 more than three million people, mostly young men, left the south, seriously depleting the workforce. No one was starving, but there were beggars— *lazzarone*—on the streets of every city.

As it did in the rest of the western world, the new medium of television had a unifying effect on Italy. Although it had been introduced experimentally in 1939, Mussolini interrupted transmission during the war, so that it was really not until the mid-1950s that Italians had access to television, and then only through one station, RAI (Radiotelevisione Italiana). "Before television, Italy was little more than an assemblage of regions," said Dr. Lucio Caputo, who grew up in Palermo in the 1950s and later became a commissioner for Italian trade in the United States. "The families in Sicily and Rome and Genoa would watch TV and suddenly saw that something else existed outside their own region, in other parts of Italy and the rest of the world."[2]

TV brought Italians closer together as a twentieth-century postwar nation, and the population increased quickly. People had money and they wanted to go out and spend it, but most of it was spent on food to be made at home. The markets were teeming with fresh seafood, meat, vegetables, and fruit. By 1954, Italians were consuming 61 pounds of pasta per capita per annum (as they do today). By 1957, Italy was producing 370,000 refrigerators per year—up from a mere 18,500 in 1951.

Home cooking—*la cucina casalinga*—was still considered to be far superior to anything served in the burgeoning *ristoranti* of the 1950s, which were frequented more by businessmen and tourists than by locals. Then, too, the tradition of the siesta was still well entrenched at that time, so that banks and stores would close down from one until three or four o'clock. Most people had lunch at home, not at a restaurant, and then took a nap. When young people did go out, perhaps after dinner, they would head for a *tavola calda* (hot table) to pick up something small to eat, like a slice of pizza or a plate of anchovies, then stroll the piazzas, arm in arm. Perhaps they would get an espresso and a pastry or, as they did increasingly, a cold Italian beer. Many of their haunts had no name on the door and the only wines available were made by vintners who had not changed their growing and production methods or grape varieties in centuries. In Tuscany, they drank Chianti; in Rome, Castelli Romani; in Piedmont, Barbera; in Marche, Verdicchio—all of it plentiful and cheap, most of it never bottled but brought to the trattorias in bulk and served in carafes.

The trattorias in Italian cities remained rigorously devoted to regional form and tradition, so that in Rome, most offered more or less the same local favorites—*spaghetti alla carbonara,* with egg and guanciale; *bucatini all'amatriciana,* with tomato and onions; *abbacchio* (baby lamb); *coda alla vaccinara* (oxtail), and more. The cooks largely followed the old tradition of the *piatti canonici*—canonical dishes tied to the days of the week, so that on Monday, depending on the city, the special might be *bollito* (boiled broth with meat); Tuesday, *pasta e fagioli* (pasta and beans) and oxtail stew; Wednesday, a day free for the chef's creations; Thursday, *gnocchi di patate* (potato gnocchi); Friday, *pasta e ceci* (pasta with chickpeas) or *baccalà* (dried cod); Saturday, *trippa alla romana* (tripe with pecorino cheese); and Sunday, *fettuccine alla romana,* with tomato, and *abbacchio.* Novelty was not encouraged, and trattorias in each city would abide by their local tradition: Venetians were content with their *fegato alla veneziana,* calf's liver and onions, and their *risotto con seppie,* with cuttlefish; Milanese never tired of their *osso buco* (veal shank) or *cotolette alla Milanese* (breaded veal chop); Florentines were perfectly happy with their *bistecca alla fiorentina* (T-bone steak, see page 87 for recipe) and *pappa al pomodoro* (stewed tomatoes with garlic and oil); in Bologna, diners eagerly anticipated a plate of *lasagne verde* (green spinach lasagna), and a fat-speckled sausage called *zampone;* no Genoese would think of sitting down to lunch without ordering *trenette al pesto,* with basil and pine nuts, or fat-bellied *pansôti* ravioli; and in Naples, the appetite never flagged for *braciola* (stuffed beef roll), or a layered *timballo* of pasta.

Postwar Italy was not immune to the novelty and ease of new foods and technologies. Bottled pasta sauces and canned tomatoes were taken for granted by the 1960s. Milan had its first supermarket by 1972. Like their American cousins, by the 1970s Italians, now with a little more money in their pockets, were devoting less time to preparing food and more time eating it outside the home. The idea that stealing a bicycle could be of such vital importance to the characters of De Sica's *Bicycle Thieves* might well have been lost on the next generation of Italians, who were zipping around on Vespas, or driving the enormously successful, inexpensive, efficient Fiat 500 (*Cinquecento*). This new mobility allowed Italians to discover the foods and restaurants outside their own provinces, not least along the shore, where seafood was cheap and always fresh. Now Romans could enjoy the food of Naples and Neapolitans the food of Florence. And soon the regional dishes themselves were being adapted in other cities, so that an Abruzzo cook might open a restaurant serving his regional food in Perugia. And pizza was becoming almost as popular in northern Italy as it already was in the United States.

Indeed, when it came to food, there was a new, previously unimaginable exchange between Italians and Americans, albeit with certain limits, because of the ease of transportation. Americans could find spaghetti with tomato sauce easily enough anywhere in Italy but were puzzled when a request for dishes they loved back home—chicken Tetrazzini, Caesar salad, fettuccine Alfredo—was met with absolute bewilderment by waiters and cooks in Italy.

The curious story of fettuccine Alfredo tells a great deal about the gastro-gap between America and Italy in the 1950s and 1960s. *Fettuccine all'Alfredo* was created in 1914 by Roman restaurateur Alfredo Di Lelio to restore his wife's appetite after she gave birth to their son. Combining extra-rich triple butter and the core of the best Parmigiano cheese together with pasta ribbons made with plenty of eggs, he made a dish she responded to and thereafter added it to the menu at his restaurant Alfredo on the Via della Scrofa. Thirteen years would pass, however, before the dish became famous—at least in the United States. In

1927, Hollywood's two biggest movie stars, Mary Pickford and Douglas Fairbanks, married and took their honeymoon in Rome. They stopped to eat at Alfredo's, where they were served the fettuccine. Marveling at its flavor, they supposedly dined there every night of their vacation, at the end of which they presented Di Lelio with a golden fork and spoon engraved TO ALFREDO, THE KING OF NOODLES 1927.

Upon arriving back in the United States, the Fairbankses spread the word of this marvelous macaroni dish—without tomato sauce—they had encountered. It became an overnight rage among their colleagues and appeared in *The Rector Cook Book* the following year. However, American cooks and chefs were unable to obtain the same quality of ingredients for the dish and needed to bulk up the sauce with heavy cream, perhaps even adding a little flour as thickener, and that became the standard American recipe.

Like most restaurants, Alfredo's closed during the war. Di Lelio sold the original restaurant to his waiters, who reopened under the name Alfredo's when the war ended; Di Lelio opened his own restaurant under his name on the Piazza L'Imperatore, where it still stands. It was there, in the 1950s, that Di Lelio, ever the showman, with his big mustache and white jacket, cannily built on the reputation of his fettuccine recipe among visiting celebrities. He would have their photos taken as he held a huge bunch of the noodles above their tables or right up to their mouths. Those photos went straight onto his walls and include American actors Jimmy Stewart, Bob Hope (who draped the fettuccine over his head), Anthony Quinn, Bing Crosby, Gary Cooper, Jack Lemmon, Ava Gardner, and Tyrone Power, as well as Walt Disney and international film stars such as Sophia Loren, Cantinflas, and scores of others.[3]

It is safe to assume that there is no Italian dish, aside from spaghetti and meatballs and pizza, that ever achieved such an international reputation, not least because it was *not* a pasta dish with the traditional tomato sauce or garlic underpinnings. It even found its way into the frozen food sections of American supermarkets and as "Alfredo sauce" on any number of other foods.

Of course, no other Roman restaurateur would admit to serving the dish, even though many served their own version under the more traditional name *fettuccine al burro* (with butter). The word *fettuccine* (little ribbons) is itself a Roman term for what other Italians call *tagliatelle* or other names. Initially, and with no small degree of jealousy, Roman restaurateurs would shrug and contend there was no such dish, and it was decades before the recipe turned up in Italian cookbooks under the name *fettuccine all'Alfredo* (see page 88 for recipe).

The finer aspects of Italy's recovery after the war captured the attention of American and British magazines. The most notable stories appeared in *Life*, which covered postwar Europe in photos, as much for its culture and emerging style as for its politics. *Life* was always happy to put glamorous photos of Sophia Loren or Gina Lollabrigida on its covers. Then, in 1958, the company published a folio-sized *Picture Cook Book* (with no authors, only editors and photographers credited) taken from picture stories that had already appeared in the magazine from 1951 to 1958. Its purpose, as a "new kind of cook book," was to be a "showcase for delicious dishes of all kinds from many nations. It is designed in part for armchair gourmets who, far from the kitchen, may want to tempt themselves with culinary delights."[4]

Chapters treated everything from "Man's Job: Steak" to "The Chowder Controversy" to "French Lessons in Innards." "Perfect Pasta" included recipes for tomato meat sauce, chicken liver sauce, anchovy sauce, garlic sauce, manicotti, macaroni and cheese, chicken cacciatore and noodles, lasagna, and peas and pasta shells—all dishes Americans could easily find in Italian-American restaurants. The book then followed with photo essays on Europe's great restaurants, including La Tour d'Argent in Paris, Rules in London, and three in Italy—Passetto in Rome, Pappagallo in Bologna, and the Royal Danieli in Venice.

The large color photos dominated the pages, with a wide shot of Passetto's antipasti table ("a tremendous buffet") and a tight shot of a dining banquette at Pappagallo, showing its famous green *lasagne*, along with wine bottles and a wall of patrons' photos that included Hollywood stars Van Johnson and John Garfield, along with conductor Arturo Toscanini and assorted European opera singers. The Royal Danieli was shot from its al fresco aerie over the Grand Canal, showing a dark red tablecloth set with Venetian seafood dishes, polenta, and liver *alla veneziana*. The book provided recipes for all these local dishes, thereby allowing *Life*'s enormous readership to see Italian food as somewhat more exotic than the familiar Italian-American style—and in very elegant surroundings.

Ten years later, Time-Life published a series of single volumes on world cuisines, including *The Cooking of Italy*, by Waverly Root, whose vast reportorial experience and gourmand sensibility gave it an authority no other book on the subject had at the time. Even so, Root greatly expanded on *The Cooking of Italy* in 1971 in his exhaustive, 750-page book, *The Food of Italy*.[5]

Rome had emerged as the most prominent world capital of the 1950s, and in 1960 would host the Olympics. Along with Florence and Milan, Rome had become a trendsetter in clothes, textiles, leather goods, shoes, cars, and motor scooters—all shown off to Technicolor advantage in a series of Hollywood movies shot in Italy, where at the time it was inexpensive to rent studios, build sets, and even hire a brigade or two of the Italian army as extras.

Many of these films were made at Cinecittà studios, which was founded by Mussolini in 1937 to make propaganda films. It was later looted by the Germans, bombed by the Allies, and then used as a displaced persons' camp. Cinecittà offered filmmakers options they could not afford in the United States, starting with the extraordinary, huge sets of "spectaculars," based on stories of ancient Rome. There was *Quo Vadis* in 1951, the grandest of them, *Ben-Hur,* in 1959, and the disastrously overblown *Cleopatra* in 1963. Such films gave the world, not just Americans, a look at Italian—or at least Roman—splendor and decadence that had not been seen since Cecil B. DeMille's black-and-white epics of the silent era. Even stories from the Bible were riddled with debaucheries and extravagant Roman meals gluttonously gobbled down by fat noblemen on divans, served by half-naked slaves. The wine flowed into silver cups, the steaming roasted carcasses were brought through the rooms on spits, the bugles blared, and the girls danced to harp music.

Of course, nothing much resembling such antique shenanigans was going on at Roman dinner parties in the 1950s, but the titillation that such gastronomic excess provided was fascinating at a time when America was in the grip of a very conservative political and social climate. It showed all the forbidden fruit, in Cinemascope.

More important, however, in forming Americans' view of the postwar Italian lifestyle were those Hollywood movies about young Americans traveling to Italy and falling in love with a country that had become far more accessible to everyone than ever before. The first film to expose Americans to the postwar pleasures of Roman life was *Roman Holiday* (1953), made at Cinecittà. In it, a worldly newspaperman, played by Gregory Peck, pursues a European princess, played by Audrey Hepburn, showing her the joys of careering around the Seven Hills on a Vespa, licking gelato from a *cornetto* on the Spanish Steps, drinking champagne for lunch at a café, dancing in the moonlight beneath the Castel Sant'Angelo, and watching young lovers kiss in the shadows.

Audiences were in awe of handsome Italian actors such as Rossano Brazzi, who made a career out of playing the Italian lothario in *Three Coins in the Fountain* (1954), *Summertime* (1955), and twice in 1962, in *Roman Adventure* and *Light in the Piazza*. In all of these romantic reveries, the lira was weak, the food irresistible, and the wines heady.

At the same time, Italy's own filmmakers were creating their own fantasies of and commentaries on Italian life, including Eduardo Scarpetta's comedy *Miseria e Nobilta* (1954), which contrasts the lower and upper classes of Italy at the time, not least by showing the grossness with which the poor stuff spaghetti with tomato sauce into their mouths. That same year, *Un Americano in Roma* satirized Italians' infatuation with American culture through a character, played by Alberto Sordi, whose desire to eat American food—jam, mustard, yogurt, milk—brings him to yell in cowboy movie slang at a plate of spaghetti, "I'm gonna take you down!" After a few bites of a slice of bread spread with those American ingredients, he reverts to the plate of spaghetti, gorging on it while slugging wine from the bottle.

Federico Fellini's *La Dolce Vita* (1960), on the other hand, detailed a Roman decadence that was very unlike the Hollywood version. The story was about a world-weary tabloid journalist, played by Marcello Mastroianni, whose beat is on the extremes of Roman society—the rich, the fashionable, and the pseudo-religious visionaries. Scenes unreel in chic Roman restaurants, at provocative parties, in Roman nightclubs, and noblemen's castles, with the outrageous voluptuary Sylvia, played by the Swedish actress Anita Ekberg, romping in the Trevi Fountain. More Americans saw *Three Coins in the Fountain* than *La Dolce Vita*, but the title of Fellini's film became indelibly symbolic of its era, of Rome, of Italians themselves, and of the food, the wine, the trattorias, *caffés*, and restaurants inextricable from it.

All of these colors, contradictions, glamour, and emotions were caught by the paparazzi—a word culled from a photographer named Paparazzo in Fellini's *La Dolce Vita*—those voracious photographers who would do anything to get a photo of the celebrities sailing or flying into Rome in the 1950s and 1960s: a shot of Anna Magnani and Tennessee Williams drinking Campari at a café on the Via Veneto, Gina Lollabrigida leaning over a plate of spaghetti, Sophia Loren sipping espresso at Ciampini in the Piazza Trinità dei Monti. Asked how she kept her curvaceous figure, Sophia Loren was said to have told reporters, "I owe everything you see to spaghetti"—a story she later often and vehemently denied. No matter. All such effusions of Italian spirit exposed to the world the sweet life Italians supposedly lived.[6]

Maître d's in tuxedos or dark suits would swoon over their American and European guests, flattering the women with a kiss on the hand and a "*bellissima*" murmured sotto voce. Waiters in starched white jackets would show their dexterity carving fruit in ice water, folding napkins, spooning sauce, all with quick, light movements of the hands. Even the coat check girls and cashiers knew just how far to flirt. They all did so in restaurants with embossed, ironed linens, signature china, decanters half-filled with local wine. And they were the kind of restaurants that France's Michelin Guide, which first covered Italy in 1956, would grant their prestigious stars. The first Michelin star was awarded to an Italian restaurant in 1959, to a hotel restaurant in Rubiera, Emilia-Romagna, with the off-putting name Arnaldo Clinica Gastronomica.

The *ristoranti* tried to appeal to the international crowd. At Giannino in Milan, the menu in 1956 listed scores of dishes in a dozen categories, with two kinds of prosciutto, sardines in oil, half a dozen pastas (including *spaghetti alla marinara* "*Giannino*"), dishes in gelatin, a *gran fritto misto* of seafood, eight fish, and several desserts, including *zuppa inglese* and *crema caramella*—this, in addition to the daily specials, which might include osso buco, chicken *alla cacciatora*, even Hungarian goulash. Such a menu expressed a new pride in abundance, with an exuberance and gusto that was attractive to American tourists.

Many restaurants were known for their celebrities—Alfredo's, of course, and the rooftop restaurant at the Hassler Hotel, with its panoramic view of the Eternal City, made famous when President John F. Kennedy and his beautiful wife, Jackie, dined there in 1963. Al Moro, right near the Trevi Fountain, was favored by the Cinecittà crowd that included Anna Magnani, Michelangelo Antonioni, De Sica, and Fellini, who cast the proprietor, Mario Romagnoli, as Trimalchio, a vulgar nouveau riche known for the ostentation of his table, in the movie *Fellini Satyricon* (1969). Though Al Moro was once a simple trattoria, Romagnoli acquired a snobbery toward foreigners seeking to eat there, banishing them to a rear dining room called the *sala americana*.

No restaurants of the 1950s had a more glittering clientele than the reopened Harry's Bar in Venice, especially after American novelist Ernest Hemingway began visiting in 1949, when he stayed the winter at Giuseppe Cipriani's little hotel on the island of Torcello and went duck hunting with the restaurateur. Harry's Bar saw the return of the remaining prewar European aristocrats and wealthy American expatriates such as Peggy Guggenheim, who came with her lovers and small dogs, along with travelers on the grand tour of Europe. Baron Philippe de Rothschild brought his Labrador retriever and fed him a steak under the table. Aristotle Onassis arrived in the biggest yacht of all, though Cipriani considered the Greek shipping magnate something less than *"un grand signore."*[7]

Cipriani himself was the only real-life person ever to appear in a Hemingway novel, *Across the River and into the Trees* (1950), in which he wrote, "There he was pulling open the door of Harry's bar and was inside and he had made it again, and was at home."[8] Hemingway's presence gave the restaurant a literary cachet that drew the emerging writers of the day. Truman Capote wrote a travel piece saying the best part of his journey was eating shrimp sandwiches at Harry's Bar and that "Venice is like eating an entire box of chocolate liqueurs in one go."[9]

Cipriani said that Hemingway often paid the checks for the younger authors, filling "more pages of his bills than of his novels because of his generosity toward others."[10] On other nights, Hemingway could be less generous, as when he saw Sinclair Lewis in the restaurant and called him a snob whose complexion resembled the mountains of the moon. But when needled about Hemingway making Harry's Bar so famous, Cipriani quipped, "*I* was the one who made *him*. You notice he won the Nobel Prize after he came here, not before."[11] Hemingway was the first person Cipriani ever had a drink with in his bar.

The food improved year by year at Harry's Bar (it received a Michelin star in 1966 and a second in 1969), but the celebrity and flamboyance of its crowd gave the two-story restaurant a cachet that could never have come solely from its food. There was always something glamorous going on, something beautiful, something outrageous. Cipriani recalled how actor-director Orson Welles, whose laughter was heard "from halfway down the Calle Valleresso," would blow through the doors, immediately order a plate of chicken sandwiches and two bottles of Dom Pérignon Champagne, and dispatch them all within minutes. Once, late for his train, Welles rushed out of Harry's, tossed his host a handful of travelers' checks, and told him to "Sign my name, Cipriani!"

The date October 26, 1958, may well be said to be the real beginning of America's intense love affair with Italy, and by extension with its fashion, its art, and its food. That was the day a Pan American World Airways Boeing 707 took off from New York's Idlewild Airport and landed at Rome's Ciampino Airport. Earlier that month, British Overseas Airways had initiated a New York–London route, and two days before Pan Am first touched down in Paris. Coast-to-coast jet service across the United States did not even begin until January, so the fact that Rome was among those very first destinations for the new jetliners was of enormous importance and prestige for Italy; more important, it allowed overnight, easy access to Europe at a time when the alternative was a six-day sea passage. (Propeller-driven aircraft were smaller and more expensive.)

The term jet set had actually been coined earlier in the decade by *New York Journal-American* society columnist Cholly Knickerbocker to describe an international social set of wealthy people who used jets for travel within continents. But now, with transatlantic travel possible, the name took on a more worldly cachet. The term applied to wealthy society people, but there was another jet set emerging, one that had a far greater and enduring impact on European travel, opening up Italy to millions of young, well-educated, middle-class Americans who were as ready for a culinary adventure as they were for a romantic romp. The younger jet set alighted seemingly overnight, after the publication in 1957 of a 126-page paperback entitled *Europe on Five Dollars a Day,* which everybody who bought one called, simply, Frommer's.

Arthur Frommer was a Yale-educated lawyer drafted into the army during the Korean War and stationed in Germany, the cities and towns of which he loved to visit on his three-day passes. What baffled him was that, despite the tremendous buying power of the U.S. dollar then, his fellow servicemen stayed back in their barracks playing checkers. "They were frightened of the newness and the novelty of Europe," said Frommer in a radio interview years later. "People still regarded Europe as a war-torn continent just getting out from under the wreckage and ruins of World War II. The entire travel industry was telling you that unless you had a lot of money you should not travel to Europe, unless you could afford first class and deluxe hotels, and that it was not safe to go to Europe. You couldn't put yourself into a modest establishment or eat anything other than a top meal or you might be poisoned by it."[12] And, of course, you should *never* drink the water.

Inspired by that realization, Frommer decided to write and self-publish a little guidebook for his friends called *The GI's Guide to Traveling in Europe* "as an attempt to shake them up and introduce them to the wonders of Europe that I had experienced." The book was stocked at all the PXs in Europe and sold out fast. Frommer therefore returned to Europe for a month, "running around to all the major capitals of Europe,"[13] and printed up his guide anew as *Europe on Five Dollars a Day.*

"I realized that if I'd had any money I would not be at this sidewalk café," he recalled of those days. "I would have been in the bus, with those other Americans, their noses pressed against the glass looking out at the sights and the sounds of Europe, and I realized that the reason I was enjoying myself so much at this café, the reason I was enjoying the experience of Europe, was precisely because I didn't have any money, because I was forced to live off the economy and live with private families and live in the basements."[14]

He placed an ad in the book review section of the *New York Times* and drew 1,500 orders the first week. Only after Frommer reached 58 titles did he allow a major publisher, Simon and Schuster, to take over his immensely successful enterprise.

Frommer had hit on the desire of young Americans whose parents could not afford to send them to Europe and who had no tolerance for travel agency tours to cross the Atlantic and live out a dream previously unobtainable. In his research, Frommer "very quickly realized that the established tourist offices of the city were of no use to me whatsoever; that they all followed the course of least resistance; that they recommended to me the popular places to which everyone went. They were actually ashamed of their guesthouses, the bed and breakfast houses. They didn't want to recommend that type of facility. They wanted people to stay in standard hotels, in rooms with private baths, and to eat in famous restaurants. You didn't get complaints that way."[15]

He recalled that in his first forays into Italian cities, American tourists were few and far between: "In those days, when you walked in the Piazza della Signoria in Florence, it was empty! There were one or two tourists walking around. When you walked into the Piazza San Marco in Venice there were two or three tourists; you were there by yourself!" (Anyone doubting Frommer was exaggerating need only watch movies such as *Roman Holiday* and *Summertime* to see that tourists are barely evident anywhere in the streets of Rome and Venice.)

As difficult as it is to believe in the twenty-first century, in 1957 and years following, five dollars a day was actually sufficient for a traveler to find a clean room in a youth hostel or bed and breakfast (yes, breakfast included), two simple meals a day, and transportation on buses and subways while sightseeing. That luxury, combined with the airlines' offer of cheap student charter flights, made visiting Europe affordable, adventuresome, and just too tempting to turn down. Subsequent editions were changed to reflect inflation—*Europe on Ten Dollars a Day*—but costs did not change much through the 1960s and early 1970s.

Italy, vacant of tourists, was there for the asking. "Venice is a fantastic dream," wrote Frommer in his first edition. "Try to arrive at night when the wonders of the city can steal upon you piecemeal and slow. You'll step from the railway landing into a sea-going streetcar, and chug softly up the Grand Canal. Out of the dark, there appear little clusters of candy-striped mooring poles; a gondola approaches with a lighted lantern hung from its prow; the reflection of a slate-grey church, bathed in a blue spotlight, shimmers in the water as you pass by."[16]

The lure was irresistible and Americans flowed into Italy, Frommer's in hand, willing to try little off-the-beaten-track trattorias where the pastas—50 cents— were sublime, and filling; where one could linger over espresso for hours and watch the Romans and Florentines and Venetians and Neapolitans pass by, each in their own way; where a B&B family that spoke no English taught them a few dialect words of Sicilian or Genoese and had them taste a little glass of their wine; and where, if you were a pretty girl, you might find a handsome Roman boy to drive you up and down the Via Veneto till dawn.

This, too was a version of *la dolce vita* that gave Americans, and an increasing number of young Europeans, lovely lessons in Italian culture, food, and wine at the most impressionable times of their lives. Roughing it was part of the fun. Italy's intoxicating beauty took hold, and at a very low price.

## BISTECCA ALLA FIORENTINA

Simple, grilled foods are a hallmark of Tuscan cooking, and the Florentine beefsteak, traditionally made from a massive T-bone (*lombata*), was symbolic of Italy's post-war boom in good eating.

*T-bone steak, 1 $^1/_2$ inches thick*
*$^1/_2$ cup olive oil*
*salt and pepper*

Marinate the steak in the olive oil for about an hour. Prepare a charcoal fire. Season the steak with salt and pepper to taste. Grill for 6 to 8 minutes on each side, or until rare to medium rare. Serve with lemon wedges.
Serves 2.

## FETTUCCINE ALL'ALFREDO

*1 pound egg fettuccine (preferably fresh)*
*1 tablespoon salt*
*1 stick unsalted butter, cut into pieces*
*²/₃ cup freshly grated Parmigiano-Reggiano cheese*

1.  In a large pot bring 4 quarts water to a boil. Add the salt and the
    fettuccine, and cook until al dente. Drain, reserving a little of the pasta
    water.
2.  In a large saucepan, melt the butter over medium heat until it is just
    barely foamy. Add the fettuccine and toss with the butter. Add the
    Parmigiano-Reggiano and a little of the pasta water, and mix until well
    incorporated and creamy. Add salt and pepper to taste.

Serves 4.

# Chapter 7

# This Italian . . . Thing

The fond, romantic notions Americans developed from the movies about Italy, Italian actors and actresses, *la dolce vita,* and the country's food and wine, did not transfer to Italian-American food and restaurants, even after Italian restaurants in New York, Los Angeles, Chicago, and other cities made efforts to polish their image with fine cuisine, wines, and décor. Instead, Americans took a certain delight in believing that most Italian restaurants had a shady side to them. It became commonplace for patrons to make comments ranging from snide to completely bigoted. Non-Italians dining at an Italian restaurant, sometime during the evening would ask their Italian friends, "Hey, by the way, is this place, y'know, *connected?*"

It is the same question Italian Americans have been getting for decades, and people ask it with a mixture of coy naïveté and giggling titillation. Such people believe that every Italian would *know* if a restaurant is connected to the mob—some even assume all are—and hope actually to see large men in dark suits and sunglasses in the restaurant who look like they could be mobsters.

People are fascinated by mob killings at Italian restaurants—and the occasional barbershop—which occur, perhaps, once every 20 years. Yet the assumption that they may witness a shoot-out or rub-out of the kind that happened when Gambino crime boss Paul Castellano was gunned down in 1985 outside of New York's Spark's Steakhouse—owned by the Cetta brothers—makes people tingle.

Such fascinations, affections, stereotyping, and assumptions about Italians, their food, and their restaurants seem so ingrained in the global psyche that people see nothing offensive in asking Italian Americans if this or that restaurant is owned by the Mafia or even, "Is it *safe* to eat at that restaurant?"

It is obvious where such slurs and stereotypes come from, for Hollywood and the media have blatantly helped to create them. In many cases, once the stereotype of the Italian mobster was widely accepted, it was often softened and crafted like a commedia dell'arte character such as Brighella, the cowardly villain. The way he ate and the restaurants he frequented demonstrated his complete lack of refinement: he stuck his napkin into his collar, ordered too much food, gulped down red wine, and smoked cigars at the table.

The public had front-page familiarity with gangsters of various nationalities during Prohibition—Al Capone, from Naples; "Lucky" Luciano, from Sicily; Meyer Lansky, a Russian Jew; Dutch Schultz, a German Jew; and Dean O'Banion and Bugs Moran, both Irish-American, among others. But the association of Italian immigrants with criminal organizations has long been stoked by Hollywood, beginning as early as 1906 in a docu-melodrama titled *The Black Hand*. Two years after the notorious 1929 St. Valentine's Day Massacre in Chicago, when Al Capone had seven mobsters machine-gunned to death, the horror was depicted in the film *Bad Company,* starring Ricardo Cortez as "Goldie" Gorio. Edward G. Robinson's portrayal of Caesar Enrico in *Little Caesar* (1931)—with the very odd casting of fair-haired Douglas Fairbanks Jr. as Joe Massara—was based on Capone's life, as was *Scarface, Shame of a Nation* (1932), with Paul Muni as Tony Camonte, whose nickname refers to a deep scar like the one Capone got in a bar fight.

In both *Little Caesar* and *Scarface,* the Italians are shown running illicit bars and cafés. *Little Caesar* opens with scene at the sleazy Club Palermo—where the Italian mobsters show their boorishness by throwing food at each other— contrasted with the soigné, champagne-drinking swells at the swank, uptown Bronze Peacock. An Italian grocer provides a secret backroom for Robinson's character to hide out in. In *Scarface,* an Irish gangster (played by Boris Karloff) blasts away at Tony Camonte while eating at the Columbia Café, a scene intended to evoke how real-life Chicago mobster "Big Jim" Colosimo had been rubbed out in 1920 in the lavish Colosimo's Café, which he advertised as the "America's Finest Italian Restaurant."

A different image, equally as indelible, was epitomized, time and again, by Oklahoma-born actor Erik Rhodes, who played the fey Italian gigolo in two Fred Astaire–Ginger Rogers movies: In *The Gay Divorcee* (1934), he plays Rodolfo Tonetti, who declares, "Your wife is safe with Tonetti! He prefers spaghetti!"; in *Top Hat* (1935), he is dress designer Alberto Beddini. He continued the stereotype as Spaghetti Nadzio in *Music for Madame* (1937).

During World War II, the U.S. government branded more than six hundred thousand Italian-born immigrants and their families as "enemy aliens," requiring them to carry identification cards and seizing personal property. Thousands of Italian-American immigrants were arrested, and hundreds were interned in military camps. A new kind of depiction of Italian Americans appeared in movies—they were no longer associated with mobsters. Instead, when they were depicted at all, Italians were shown as good-natured, patriotic Americans. A few showed up in cinematic foxholes, on navy ships, or aboard Air Force planes, along with ethnic groups friendly to the Allies like the Poles, Czechs, Spanish, and Jews, promoting the idea that Italians could be counted upon in a war against Fascism.

Between 1950 and 1951, the U.S. Senate's Kefauver Committee was organized to expose the nationwide tentacles of organized crime in America. The hearings were broadcast on television so that Americans could see for themselves the swarthy, sunglass-wearing, thick-accented Italian mobsters who lived among them, with names like "Lucky" Luciano, Albert "Mad Hatter" Anastasia, Willie Moretti (after testifying, he was executed by the mob), Giuseppe Doto, known as Joe Adonis, "Don Vito" Genovese, and Frank Costello (born Francesco Castiglia), who refused to testify unless his face was hidden from the cameras, which focused solely on his hands.

Hollywood picked up on the public's fascination by bringing the Italian gangster back to the screen. In 1959, Rod Steiger starred in a violent biopic about Capone, and that same year a TV series debuted called *The Untouchables,* about federal agent Eliot Ness trying to put Capone and his gang in prison; it became an enormous hit, running for five seasons. In fact, the overwhelming number of Italian gangsters portrayed in the early series was protested by Italian-American groups as a perpetuation of the criminal stereotype.[1]

Hollywood Italian restaurants were not unaware of the commercial impact of this stereotype about Italian restaurants being mob hangouts. In 1953, Midwest mob boss Anthony "Big Tuna" Accardo, Los Angeles' Jack Dragna, and other gangsters met for a meal at Perino's restaurant in Hollywood, but after their bodyguards were harassed by the police, they moved to another venue. From then on, Perino's supposed association with mobsters never entirely faded, perhaps because owner Alexander Perino himself seemed to enjoy the aura, telling people about the time a customer pulled a gun on another guest and how Perino knocked it out of the man's hand and gave it to his waiter to hide, which the waiter dutifully did—in the soup pot. Perino also allowed mobster scenes for Hollywood movies to be shot in his restaurant.

The next wave of Italian gangster movies began with a masterpiece, Francis Ford Coppola's *The Godfather* (1972), based on Mario Puzo's 1969 potboiler novel. The Godfather began as a poor Sicilian named Vito Corleone, who emigrates to America only to be victimized by a local Mafioso, whom he murders. He rises to become one of the dons heading the New York Mafia families but fails to keep his son Michael out of the "family business."

I need not debate whether Puzo (who later said, "I never met a real honest-to-God gangster."[2]) and Coppola (who later became a respected California winemaker) sought to romanticize the brutal Corleones, but *The Godfather*'s more tender, familial moments are always connected to food, whether it is the enormous, joyous wedding banquet for Don Corleone's daughter or the sons' dinner-table planning sessions on how best to wreak vengeance on another mob family. Don Corleone himself dies of a heart attack while tending his vegetable garden in the backyard of his estate. At other times, Italians' respect for food is shown with ironic humor, as when two mobsters shoot a third, and one reminds the other, "Leave the gun. Take the cannoli!"

The most disturbing scene in *The Godfather* is when Don Corleone's young son meets with a rival don and a corrupt police captain at Louis's Restaurant in the Bronx. As the two eat spaghetti, their napkins tucked into their collars, the young Corleone comes out of the men's room and shoots both of them point blank. That chilling scene caused audiences to believe such a thing could happen in *any* Italian restaurant, the same way they wondered how safe the ocean was after watching the horrific shark attack in the movie *Jaws.*

Even before the Godfather movies, people seemed fascinated with restaurants frequented by Italian gangsters. In 1969, *New York* magazine restaurant critic Gael Greene fed people's fascination with mob hangouts in an article called "The Mafia Guide to Dining Out," sighing,

> I have waded through a roiling flood of tomato sauce to test the mys-
> tique of the Mafioso palate. . . . What is good for the Mafia is good
> for gourmet country. The Mafia is widely advanced as "the Miche-
> lin Guide for Italian restaurants," and a three-star police raid is a
> tribute to the excellence of the kitchen. . . . Characteristically, the
> menu is narrowly Southern—souvenir of Naples, Calabria and

Sicily; the bread is crusty and irresistible; the flowers are faded plastic; murals celebrate the Bay of Naples. You dine with judges, pols, fuzz in mufti, expatriate Italians from the suburbs, beehive-headed dolls in purple leather minis and stiletto heels . . . and maybe, seven solemn Dons along the same side of a banquet table, their backs against the wall.[3]

Greene then went on to note that the Carlo Gambino mob "has been eating up a storm at Villa Vivolo in Gravesend, Brooklyn"; how "Crazy" Joey Gallo got "pinched twice" at Luna's in Little Italy, where "rackets magnate Anthony Strollo, likewise known as Tony Bender, was an after-midnight regular until he mysteriously disappeared."[4]

Another Italian-American film director, New York–born Martin Scorsese, was drawn to those violent Italian street mobsters he saw around him while growing up on New York's Lower East Side. The biopic *Raging Bull* (1980) told the story of an Italian-American boxer Jake LaMotta, and his masterpiece, *Goodfellas* (1990) was about an Irish boy's infatuation with the Italian mob and his rise and fall under their protection and their spell.

Much of the appalling irony and grisly humor in *Goodfellas* comes from the way the Italian-American gangsters eat enormous meals, drink unlimited amounts of liquor and wine, and commit murder, all in the same scene. A busboy who idly interrupts their dinner has his foot shot off and is later murdered for complaining about it. After nearly beating to death a rival wise guy, the vicious, out-of-control character Tommy De Vito stops at his mother's house at two in the morning to borrow a carving knife so he can cut up the bloody body in the trunk of his car. But first he sits down with his mother to a full Italian spaghetti dinner.

Along the way, viewers also learned how Italian mobsters would take over and use a restaurant as a front in which to launder money, then, when it had outlived its usefulness, they would burn the place down for the insurance money. But the most astonishing revelation for viewers of *Goodfellas* was the scene in which several members of the gang are in prison together, where they have access to a fully equipped kitchen and get deliveries of fresh lobsters and steaks and where mob boss Paulie Cicero slices the garlic so thin with a razor blade as to be translucent, so it will melt into the olive oil. (In 2010, actor Paul Sorvino, who played Paulie, came out with his own line of pasta sauces—marinara and vodka—based on his Neapolitan mother's recipes.)

Audiences laughed nervously during such scenes, astonished at how the Italian-American love of food and drink was such an integral part of gangster behavior and how, no matter what the outcome, such men were still respected, powerful, and untouchable. Other Mafia movies followed, including comedies like *Married to the Mob* (1988), *Mickey Blue Eyes* (1999), and *Analyze This* (1999), all of them with plenty of scenes played out in restaurants with huge men eating huge meals, with huge bulges in their suit jackets.

A generation after *The Godfather* and *Goodfellas* came a foul-mouthed, bloody HBO cable series called *The Sopranos,* whose longevity—86 episodes—bolted Italian-American gangsters into the realm of myth, complete with a tragic hero, a fat mob boss named Tony Soprano—a dead ringer for Mussolini—whose twentieth-century angst and paranoia is fueled by his own family, including his own mother and uncle, who want him dead, and the burden of being a Mafioso—"This thing of ours."[5] Tony's cohorts include characters with nick-names like Paulie "Walnuts," Bobby "Bacala," Big Pussy, and Johnny Sack.

*The Sopranos* won every major media award and accolade possible during its six-year run, though it was also heartily condemned by Italian-American organizations as just more of the same stereotyping of socially disruptive, non-taxpaying murderers running drug and prostitution rings while enjoying themselves immensely eating spaghetti with red sauce and drinking booze and wine throughout the day. Yet as writer Bill Tonelli pointed out in his article "A 'Sopranos' Secret: Given the Choice, We'd All Be Mobsters" in the *New York Times,* Americans did not see the insult because they had were so fascinated by the lifestyle.[6]

The lifestyle of the Italian mob had become the American version of *la dolce vita,* and both non-Italians and Italian mobsters themselves picked up on the mannerisms. Their way of talking and the appetites of real-life wise guys were heavily reinforced by the media, who loved to characterize Mafia monsters like John Gotti, boss of the Gambino family, as "the Dapper Don" and "the Teflon Don." Gotti, who used to tip waiters by doubling the total on the restaurant bill, was the one who ordered the murder of boss Paul Castellano, shot down in cold blood outside Spark's Steakhouse in 1985. Media reports did not say whether anyone took the cannoli.

Given the prevalence of Italian stereotypes in the media, entrepreneurs began to use them as marketing ploys, no matter how egregious, not least in the food industry. Consider the major pizza chains in America—many of which opened units in many other countries: Little Caesar's Pizza was created by Mike and Marian Ilitch in 1959 in Garden City, Michigan, and is now the world's largest carry-out pizza chain. And even though their cartoon logo is of a toga-clad, cross-eyed, three-toed, hairy-chested Roman, the reference to "Little Caesar" clearly derives from the 1931 gangster movie of the same title. Even more blatant is Godfather's Pizza, founded in 1973 in Omaha, Nebraska, by Greg Johnson and Greg Banks. With obvious reference to the Godfather movies, the chain's ads have used paraphrases from the motion picture like "A pizza you can't refuse," and the slightly threatening "I know your neighborhood." Godfather's Pizza even has an actor dressed in the stereotypical white fedora and pin-striped suit who goes around and makes appearances at their stores; on the website, the character is quoted as saying, "As the boss, I feel it's my duty to make sure you get the goods. You may have noticed that I take my job very seriously. I demand that my crew serves you a pizza pie piled high with your favorite toppings every time you visit my joint or else they have to answer to me. Every so often, I like to watch 'em in action to make sure things are bein' done right."

There are also dozens of pizzerias around the United States that trade on the name "Goodfellas," including Goodfellas in West Fargo, North Dakota, the logo for which is a cartoon of a gangster in a pin-striped suit and fedora and wearing brass knuckles. Indeed, the fedora seems to be the most common icon of instant, winking recognition: Goodfellaz in Roanoke, Virginia, has a logo of a fedora-wearing man with his face blocked by the store's name. There is also a line of frozen Goodfella's Pizza products, including pizzas with Hawaiian and BBQ Chicken toppings. The name is trademarked by Green Isle Foods Limited in Dublin, Ireland.

In Nashville the owners must think it clever marketing to call their restaurant MAFIAoZA's—"a 1920s New York-style restaurant." Then there was a New York restaurant named Monzù, now defunct, whose ad used a black-and-white photo of a murdered man under a sheet on a barbershop floor, holding a loaf of Italian bread, with the line, "Sicilian dishes. French technique. Food to die for."

Perhaps worst of all are those Italian Americans trying to capitalize on the Mafia image in cookbooks, as if in some way suggesting that the criminals have any particular taste in food aside from the ability to gorge on enormous quantities. There is *The Mafia Cookbook,* written by Joseph "Joe Dogs" Iannuzzi, a former mobster with the Gambino crime family and FBI informant, who, according to its publisher's publicity materials, "took the quintessential Mob formula—murder, betrayal, food—and turned it into a bestseller, not surprisingly, since Joe

Dogs's mixture of authentic Italian recipes and colorful Mafia anecdotes is as much fun to read as it is to cook from."[7]

*The Mafia Cookbook* was reprinted and Iannuzzi followed up with *Cooking on the Lam*, which included an account of Dogs's recent years since he testified against the Mob in five major trials, all told in his tough-guy style. The publisher's description went, "Tested by Mob heavy hitters as well as FBI agents and U.S. marshals, these recipes are simple to follow, full of timesaving shortcuts, and liberally seasoned with Joe Dogs's stories of life inside—and outside—the Mob. This is the perfect cookbook for anyone who wants to make the kind of food that Tony Soprano only *dreams* about. . . . The 'can't fail' recipes for great Italian dishes whose ingredients can be bought in a small-town supermarket when you're a thousand miles from an Italian grocery store in Little Italy and couldn't go there anyway since there's a contract out for you. These are meals you can't refuse."[8]

There is another by the same title, *The Mafia Cookbook*, this one by Barbara La Rocca, subtitled, "Killer Recipes from Gangland Kitchens." Then there is *The Mafia Women's Cookbook: Quick Hit Recipes You Can't Refuse from America's Most Famous Italian Kitchens*, by Marnie Inskip and Penny Price; *The Mafia Just Moved in Next Door and They're Dropping by for Dinner Cookbook*, by Ziggy Zen; *The Sopranos Family Cookbook*, by Artie Bucco, Alan Rucker, and Michele Scicolone; and *The Wise Guy Cookbook: My Favorite Recipes From My Life as a Goodfella to Cooking on the Run*, by Henry Hill, the informant whose life was the basis for Scorsese's *Goodfellas*. Ironically, after getting out of the Witness Protection Program, the real-life Hill opened a restaurant named Wiseguys in West Haven, Connecticut. The restaurant was destroyed by fire, but police did not believe it was a mob job—it did not burn to the ground. In the movie, Hill's character helps burn down the Bamboo Lounge for the insurance money.

Italian Americans have for so long been stereotyped as lovable goombahs, wise guys, goodfellas, ginzos, guidos, garlic-eaters, macaroni benders, and greaseballs with names like Tony Soprano, Bobby Bacala, and Paulie Walnuts that Italian-American restaurants found it impossible to escape the taint. Many, seeing it was good for business, embraced it, as did Bronx restaurateur Anthony Paone, owner of Dominick's, when he treated delegates to the 1992 Democratic Convention to lunch and walked them around the Belmont neighborhood, telling the *New York Times*, "They thought the Bronx was just low-income and high-crime, so I obliged them, of course, by telling them to check their wallets, but they left knowing that Dominick's is not some Domino's."[9]

No wonder restaurant critic Hal Rubenstein of *New York* magazine thought it cute to write of Dominick's, "Arthur Avenue is not of this world. . . . What's the deal? Aren't the double-parked Cadillacs a big enough wink-wink? If you're still clueless, notice how everyone sitting family-style at Dominick's sounds . . . like family."[10]

# Chapter 8

# Stirrings

Despite the titanic changes in American society in the 1950s and 1960s—the Vietnam War, the Civil Rights Movement, the assassinations of John and Robert Kennedy and Martin Luther King Jr., as well as the cultural shifts in music, art, literature, and film—food and restaurants changed very little, except in design. The theme restaurant, which had been a part of American dining since the 1930s, when Hollywood had places like Pirate's Den, where mock pirate battles took place and females customers were "kidnapped" and thrown into the brig, flowered in the 1950s.

Fast food chains such as McDonald's, Kentucky Fried Chicken, White Castle, and Long John Silver's grew exponentially, using characters like clowns, kings, and pirates to tantalize children. In the big cities, French restaurants still dominated the fine dining market, while Italian restaurants held the middle ground. But there was a growing interest in international foods. During the 1964 New York World's Fair, American visitors developed an abiding taste for Belgian waffles, Spanish sangria, and French crêpes, but novelty, not good food, was the standard for new restaurants. (Italian food, however, was not available at the Fair, because Italy did not have a pavilion.)

At home, wives still did most of the food shopping and the cooking, and while supermarkets made fresh food more available, the aisles were overwhelmingly stocked with packaged, canned, and frozen foods—increasingly with more Italian, Chinese, and Mexican items, all produced in the United States.

Americans' annual consumption of pasta had actually dropped from 7.5 pounds per capita during the war (it was a cheap meal at a time of scarcity) to two pounds in the 1950s. Imported pasta was still a rarity, and products readily available to the housewife in Italy were not to her American counterpart. Obtaining good olive oil (there was no such thing as "extra virgin" then), true Parmigiano-Reggiano, Italian pork products such as prosciutto (which were effectively kept out of the United States by the FDA under pressure from American producers), and certain wines was difficult if not impossible in most of the United States. Only a handful of restaurateurs paid the extra money to have ingredients flown in from Italy, and even then, items such as true *scampi* came in frozen.

The same was true, it should be noted, for the finest French restaurants. Anything other than plain white mushrooms and canned truffles were impossible to find. Not that most Americans knew or cared: They still sought out the little Italian restaurant with the red-checkered tablecloths, the Chianti bottles with their dripping candles, and the fat proprietor who tweaked his cheek and promised everything he served was "*squisito!*" And what he served was what Americans knew—the red-sauced pastas, the veal cutlets with mozzarella, the minestrone soup, the cheesecake, and the drip-pot espresso. And it was cheap.

This entrenched style of Italian restaurant, which was by then thoroughly Italian-American, is what awaited the hundreds of chefs, cooks, and waiters who left their employ on the transatlantic liners—whose numbers dwindled in the new jet age—to take jobs in their field in the United States. Most in this new wave of restaurant workers came from Europe, where they had been schooled in the international style of cooking and service. Whatever they knew about Italian food derived largely from their own family background, but what they found upon landing in New York was a bewildering facsimile of Italian dishes with wholly unfamiliar names.

One of those Italians who sailed those seas and served that food was Tony May (born Antonio Magliulo), later to become one of the most important figures in Italian gastronomy. Born to a family with eight children in Torre del Greco outside of Naples, May sought his future abroad, washing dishes in Argentina at the age of 17, then becoming a maître d'hôtel in Australia by the time he was 20. To learn English he moved to England and worked at the Dorchester hotel, then, in 1960, he signed on to the *Italia* cruise ship, plying the seas from the Mediterranean to Singapore, New York to Nassau.

"In those days [after the war] fine dining meant 'international cuisine,'" he recalls. "It was hotel cooking, based on making everything with a demiglace and *sauce espagnole*. Everything was cooked with butter and cream. We had some Italian dishes on the cruise ships, but the menus were always more international, or what was later called 'Continental.'"[1]

One glance at the typical menus on the Italian liners reveals how pervasive the international style was. On the *Michelangelo,* which began service in 1965, menus were printed in Italian on one side and English on the other. They listed *risotto alla Milanese,* even a *pizza alla napoletana* at lunch, but most of the dishes might have been found on any ship or in any high-end dining room in Europe and America at the time: consommé, roast turkey with cranberry sauce, trout in court-bouillon with Hollandaise sauce, smoked ham with "California sauce," ox-tongue "Cinderella," rack of lamb with mint sauce, and "Wiener sausage with sauerkraut." The "chef's suggestion" for dinner might be orange juice, lobster bisque, pot roast with string beans, sultan cake Savarin, fresh fruit, and demi-tasse; a farewell dinner, served the night before disembarking, included prune juice, "Borscht Pirofjsky," capon "Côte d'Azur," and venison patty *en croûte,* along with *raviolini* in broth and lemon Italian sherbet.

Tony May left the *Italia* to settle in New York in 1963. "At that time, Italy still offered very few opportunities to young people," he says, "and I fell in love with New York—the excitement, the vitality, the modern outlook." Starting fresh in the New York restaurant world, he took a job at a society restaurant named the Colony, where the menu featured the usual international cuisine. When he visited Italian restaurants in the city, he remembers, "They spoke a language I didn't understand and served a food I'd never eaten. I'd open a menu and not recognize anything on it. The tomato sauces were cooked and cooked for hours, with too much garlic and oregano. The pastas were boiled for twenty minutes in advance. There were no good Italian wines."[2] Such had been the state of fine dining and Italian menus for decades, dating back before the war.

The Colony, which began as a clandestine bistro and gambling room during Prohibition, was eventually taken over by two Italian waiters, Gene Cavallero, formerly at London's Savoy Hotel, Boston's Copley-Plaza, and Philadelphia's Ritz, and Ernest Cerrutti, along with an Alsatian chef named Alfred Hartmann. They turned it into a club-like restaurant for New York society that appealed largely to women at lunch. *Vogue* magazine warned aspiring debutantes that it was harder to get a good table at the Colony than to join the Junior League. Within two years of taking over, the three owners had made $500,000.

The food at the Colony was resolutely Continental, with a few Italian-style of-ferings. The restaurant had an amazingly long and profitable run, finally closing in 1971. Cavallero and Cerruti were hardly the only Italian immigrants who es-chewed serving Italian food at their restaurants. John Perona ran a series of West Side speakeasies in Manhattan before opening the ultra-glamorous El Morocco nightclub (nicknamed Elmo's) on East 54th Street in 1931, with a clientele of show business stars and society lights from every capital in Europe. Those not in that firmament were shooed off to out-of-the-way tables, a section that became known as Siberia.

In a similar fashion, Sicilian immigrant Niccolò de Quattrociocchi, called "Coco," used his considerable charm with get Perona to help him open a New York French-Italian restaurant with a Spanish name, El Borracho (the drunk-ard), which he made to seem even more popular than it was by placing yellow cards on tables that read, "If you have enjoyed the dinner, the service, and the at-mosphere of El Borracho, PLEASE DO NOT tell your friends as our seating capacity is limited.—The Management." He also put mynah birds over the bar and had a "Kiss Room" with the autographed lip prints of contemporary glamour girls, an idea that caused *Life* magazine in 1947 to declare El Borracho the most popular restaurant in New York, attracting "a velvety following in theatrical and café so-ciety, together with its velveteen hangers-on."[3]

Then there was Toffenetti's, opened by Dario Toffenetti. It was a thousand-seat extravaganza, open 24 hours a day, in the middle of Times Square. Its pop-ularity owed as much to the modest prices and proletarian image as to Toffenetti's advertising expertise, acquired from Northwestern University's School of Com-merce. As William Grimes wrote in *Appetite City*, "In his psychology classes, Tof-fenetti studied the intricacies of stimulus response, and somewhere along the way developed a florid style of English that became the hallmark of his menus," with descriptions of "Rough Skinned But Tender-Hearted" baked potatoes. The restaurant décor and artwork was surrealistic, with food morphing into ma-chines. The menu offered something for everyone, even the occasional dish of spaghetti.[4]

New York's Theater District restaurant, Sardi's, opened by Italian immigrant Vincent Sardi in 1927, grew famous for the caricatures of show business stars drawn by a Russian refugee named Alex Gard (in exchange for one meal a day). After a while, it became a rite of passage that you had arrived in show biz if Sardi's put you on its walls, and the clientele was heavily peopled with press agents, producers, ac-tors, and radio personalities. Sardi's was where the cast of a new production would go on opening night to read the first reviews. The restaurant was also for many years where the nominations for the Tony Awards would be announced.

The food at Sardi's was secondary, never particularly Italian, but its fame was more than enough to ensure it would make its way into movie scenes, either pho-tographed on site or on a constructed set.

Though television seemed a natural medium for cooking shows, they could not draw enough viewers for network broadcasting, so they were shown on local stations and often as short segments on other shows. They were usually sponsored by the products used in the dishes shown. One of the few early cooking shows was hosted by an Englishwoman named Dione Lucas called *To the Queen's Taste,* which ran on CBS from 1948 to 1949.

No one could possibly have imagined the quirky success of a commercial-free 1963 PBS show out of Boston, hosted by a tall, gawky, odd-sounding California-born woman named Julia Child, who tried to convince Americans they really could cook classic French food. The show was called *The French Chef* and debuted two years after the release of the bestselling cookbook Child had co-authored, *Mastering the Art of French Cooking.* The local black-and-white half-hour show was an enormous hit that ran, in various forms, for decades, and Child provided a new impetus for Americans to take good food seriously.

Of course, none of it was Italian. Americans had to wait until 1973 for a PBS show, also out of Boston, called *The Romagnolis' Table,* hosted by Roman immigrant photographer Gian Franco Romagnoli and his American wife, Margaret, at a time when Boston's Italian restaurants all sold the same clichés of the Italian-American repertoire. Their show had modest success, and the Romagnolis subsequently wrote a cookbook and joined the new food media community then burgeoning in the United States.

Still, Italian food had not gained much traction. The best illustration of how difficult it was to get most Americans to accept any Italian food out of the ordinary is in the film "Big Night" (1996), a tender love story about two brothers who own a restaurant named Paradise in New Jersey in the mid-1950s. One brother, Secondo the front man (Stanley Tucci), insists that to stay in business they have to serve all the tired clichés of Italian-American food; the other brother, Primo the chef (Tony Shalhoub), rages with frustration at not being able to cook his own authentic Italian recipes, which he finally gets to show off at a make-or-break party planned for bandleader Louis Prima, who could bring much-needed publicity to Paradise. But the entertainer never shows up, and the dinner cost the brothers everything they had. The movie ends with the future of the restaurant in doubt but with the brothers committed to each other, whatever was to happen next.

The fact is that most Americans who went out for Italian food expected it and *wanted* it to be those entrenched clichés of Italian-Americana. Often diners would go for reasons beyond the food, instead enjoying the quaintness of a city's Little Italy. In each restaurant the menu offered no surprises: Guarino's, the oldest Italian restaurant in Cleveland's Little Italy (1918), expanded over the years to include a statue of St. Francis of Assisi in the garden, but the dishes never budged over the century—fried mozzarella, eggplant parmigiana, veal "francaise," and chicken piccata have never left the menu.

In St. Louis, Missouri, diners would drive to "The Hill" to eat at Ruggeri's, Charlie Gitto's, Cunetto House of Pasta, Gian-Pepe's, Giuseppe's, Mama Campisi's or Dominic's, all serving variations of the same dozen dishes; Providence had Federal Hill, where you would drop in at Angelo's Civita Farnese, opened in 1924, of which local food writers Deborah Moxham and John Schenck wrote, "If you're Italian-American, this is what you probably grew up on: pastine; escarole and bean soup; spaghetti aglio e olio; eggplant parmigiana; linguine with clams; braciole [*sic*]; tripe; pasta fagiole [*sic*], escarole and bean soup, linguine with clams; and, of course, fried calamari and fried smelts."[5] Which was actually something of a departure from the rest in town.

Chicago had scores of Italian restaurants, all serving more or less the same items—not least the local favorite chicken Vesuvio, supposedly created by a Neapolitan cook just after World War II, in which chicken is cooked in a casserole whose rim is topped with fried potatoes to look like Mount Vesuvius. You could have it, along with veal Marsala, shrimp fra diavolo, and baked clams at Bruna's in Little Italy; or at Club Lago, along with fettuccine Caruso, manicotti, and eggplant parmigiana; and at the Como Inn, along with fried calamari, cannelloni *della casa,* and veal in lemon butter. Bostonians and tourists went to Cantina Italiana, which claims to be the North End's first Italian restaurant (1931), not just for the chicken parmigiana and lasagna but to see the tall green-and-red neon sign outside the door—a Chianti bottle in a *fiasco* pouring drops of wine into a glass.

In Philadelphia, the locals have been going to Dante & Luigi's in the Italian Market district since 1899 for menu items like fried calamari, spaghetti "with Italian gravy," spaghetti Caruso, and chicken parmigiana. Baltimore had a dozen or more places crammed into the ten square blocks of its Little Italy neighborhood, where you could get a "bookmaker's salad" at Sabatino's or clams casino and fried ravioli at Chiapparelli's or gorge on the platters of heavy food at Trattoria Petrucci's, where, as the *Baltimore Sun* food writer Rob Kasper put it, "the key word in Little Italy is 'lotsa.' Lotsa pasta. Lotsa cheese. Lotsa sauce."[6]

Even such largess apparently wasn't enough: at most of these Italian-American restaurants the complimentary side dish was usually overcooked spaghetti in tomato sauce. None of it was expected to cost very much, so restaurateurs and chefs were unable to buy quality ingredients, even if any had been available.

Italian food varied little from New York to Los Angeles, although the appeal of restaurants in those cities would sometimes be the exclusivity of the place, meaning that it showed one had clout just to be able to get in or to get a good table. The food hardly mattered at all. The allure at Elaine's, an Italian restaurant on New York's Upper East Side since 1964, was its owner, Elaine Kaufman, who nurtured a long line of aspiring then immensely successful authors, whose book jackets and photos line the walls of the low-lighted restaurant.

Kaufman, a Jewish American from the Bronx, opened her first restaurant, Portofino, in Greenwich Village, where hungry writers and artists would come to eat cheap Italian food, and if they could not pay, Kaufman would feed them until they could, a generosity she would repeat uptown, where the rents on the Upper East Side were cheap enough for her to open up on a $10,000 investment. As many of those writers, such as Gay Talese, David Halberstam, and Tom Wolfe, became successful, along with established authors such as Norman Mailer and George Plimpton, they continued to go to Elaine's for the comfort and the camaraderie. A young writer named Winston Groom ran up a bill of several thousand dollars, but finally settled after he hit big with the novel *Forrest Gump*. Elaine's literary cabal inevitably drew other celebrities from the arts, including ballet star Mikhail Baryshnikov, who once danced a *pas de trois* with colleague Rudolf Nureyev and a chair in the dining room. On the night in 2000 when the New York Yankees won the World Series over the New York Mets, Yankees' owner George Steinbrenner was turned away from the door of Elaine's because the place was already packed with people celebrating the team's victory. Woody Allen, who said he ate at Elaine's every night for ten years at the same table, shot the opening dinner scene of his 1979 film *Manhattan* there.

This kind of clientele, of course, drew the unfamous but curious, who were invariably shunted off to another room—you did not dare ask for autographs, either—while there was always a table for her regulars and celebrities up front. Elaine's was the kind of restaurant that gave rise to the phrase, "We'll be eating out on this stuff all week," meaning the scene and gossip, not the food.

"You won't find your lips helplessly quivering with delight after the first bite of, say, some scallop with stupid top-secret caper-raisin-emulsion freckles," wrote a visitor from the New York *Observer.* "Who cares? And even those truffle-'n'-ink-stained professional masticators intent on pooh-poohing the place will undoubtedly turn up on Second Avenue in the upper 80s for some linguine with clam sauce and friendly conversation."[7]

Of course, many people went to Italian restaurants out of curiosity to see whether a place was "connected" or not. In the case of Rao's in New York's East Harlem, a neighborhood once home to Italian immigrants, the rumor of its being a mob hangout impossible to get into only gave the place a morbid cachet, especially after *Times* restaurant critic Mimi Sheraton gave a rave three-star review in 1977 about the food—meatballs, lemon chicken, sausage and peppers. At the time, Rao's had only eight tables, and Sheraton described the clientele as "mobsters, journalists, sports figures and assorted neighborhood types who hung around the bar in undershirts."[8] When the review appeared, Rao's had to take its phone off the hook because it never stopped ringing. Sheraton said she had been told by a New York police lieutenant that the restaurant had actually functioned as a sit-down place for mob discussions. "Such activities hardly drive the public away," she wrote, "as proven recently when a customer shooting at Rao's brought a renewed flood of requests for reservations. I even teased [owner] Frank Pellegrino about having staged it to renew luster to the restaurant's increasingly tame reputation."[9]

The fact was that Rao's eight tables had always been reserved by neighborhood regulars, ever since Charles Rao opened it as a saloon in 1896. His brother Joseph ran the place until 1930, when his sons, Louis and Vincent, took over. Louis died in 1958. Vincent, who was the chef, and his wife, Anna, ran Rao's with the help of her nephew Frank Pellegrino. Frank still runs the place, on the corner of 114th Street and Pleasant Avenue, with a partner, Ron Straci, Vincent's nephew. An arsonist burned Rao's down in 1995, but it was rebuilt just the way it had looked before, but with the addition of two tables, to make ten.

The regulars at Rao's have always been neighborhood people and might well include a local doctor, lawyer, or local priest. The only way to obtain a table, therefore, is to know a regular or someone who knows a regular who is not going to be using his table on a particular night. The priest might give up his table in exchange for a generous donation to the church.

No one ever picks up the phone at Rao's, and were one to drive up to Harlem and request a table in person, Frank Pellegrino will say they are entirely booked for the next year. This means that celebrities, too, are often turned away. No one just drops by hoping to get in.

Pellegrino and Straci still stroll their dining room, and a manager in a suit and tie will pull a chair up to your table, tell you what the chef is cooking that evening, and offer a couple of wine options. There are no menus, no wine list, and no change of silverware between family-style courses. Nicky "the Vest"—so-called because he owns 46 of them—is the bartender. Brightly lighted, with white tablecloths, varnished booths, little table lamps, and simple wineglasses, the place is cozy, familial, and not unlike a hundred other Italian-American restaurants. But none has Rao's clientele, one of whom, erroneously, took credit for its success: in his memoir *Eating* (2009), Random House editor and publisher Jason Epstein insisted that he published *Rao's Cookbook* not only so he could get the recipes but because he hoped Pellegrino would award him a table of his own—an offer that was never forthcoming.

Amid all this red sauce there were attempts, some quite successful, to show a broader face of Italian regional cooking in restaurants in New York. Urged by his bicoastal Los Angeles clientele to open a restaurant in New York, Romeo Salta made the leap in 1953 and opened a restaurant called Mercurio on West 53rd Street. The red-flocked wallpaper, Milanese display glassware, wooden coats of arms, and Chianti bottles on the table were not unusual, the food not much out of the ordinary. A 1960 guide to *The Best Restaurants of America,* called the cooking "predominantly *Piémontaise*,"[10] but then lists veal cutlet Milanese and *osso buco Cremolata* (Lombardian), and *fettuccine all'Alfredo* (Roman) among its best dishes, accompanied by Soave, Bardolino, and Valpolicella, all from Veneto.

Given its location, within blocks of the offices of fashion magazines, Mercurio became a hangout for publishers, editors, designers, and models, including a beautiful young starlet named Grace Kelly. At Mercurio it was considered good luck for a woman passing the nude male statue to tap its testicles.

Salta sold off his part of Mercurio and opened a newer, larger, grander restaurant under his own name on West 56th Street just off Fifth Avenue and near all the new television studios, theaters, publishing houses, and cosmetics companies. His name carried weight, immediately winning both his old regulars and new patrons who recognized that Romeo Salta was an Italian restaurant that aimed for "authenticity." Here adventurous diners with liberal expense accounts could feast on an array of dishes available nowhere else—artichokes stuffed with tuna; filet of sole in red wine sauce; squid in a spiced tomato broth; lasagna with pesto; brain croquettes; spaghetti with peas and truffles; even polenta *alla Milanese,* with fontina cheese; and for dessert, chestnut cake. Pastas were prepared tableside by captains. The restaurant stocked 40 different wines, the tablecloths were white linen.

Nine years after opening his restaurant, Salta wrote a cookbook, *Romeo Salta: The Pleasures of Italian Cooking* (1962), in which he explained, "Most of the food served in my restaurant is prepared in what might be called northern Italian-style, to differentiate it from the southern style, [which] has more garlic and herbs, makes a greater use of tomatoes, and in general, is a somewhat more highly spiced style of cuisine. Northern Italian food is lighter and more delicate, tending to use butter rather than making exclusive use of olive oil."[11]

As far as it went, Salta's assessment was reasonably sound and signaled a marketing difference between himself and the red-checkered-tablecloth, red sauce Italian-American restaurants elsewhere ubiquitous. Still, Salta hedged his bets: knowing his customers, however well traveled they were, wanted the southern tomato- and garlic-based dishes, he happily served them right along with his northern dishes, so that his menu listed all the traditional favorites—minestrone, spaghetti with white clam sauce, baked macaroni and cheese, *spaghetti alla marinara,* steak in tomato sauce, and so on—along with zabaglione, biscuit tortoni, and pastry fritters for dessert.

When Salta died, in 1998, the *Times* called him a "dining pioneer." His restaurant's menu was almost unique in the United States at the time. Salta would have imitators later on that tried to capitalize on the idea of so-called northern Italian cuisine. As in Italy, the term "Southern Italian" had a distinctly inferior connotation when it came to food.

Romeo Salta also inspired other Italian restaurateurs and chefs to upgrade their dining rooms and cooking to appeal to a postwar group of businessmen with generous expense accounts and the new Diners Club credit card, which appeared in 1950. There was a glamorous new industry in New York, where young advertising executives worked out of offices on the street that would become a metonym for their profession, Madison Avenue. These bright, creative, hard-drinking ad men (and they were almost entirely men) had an appetite for the good life in New York, and restaurateurs were only too happy to satisfy it; and if a guest did not have a credit card, it was easy enough to set up a house account to be paid at month's end, sent directly to the office.

This clientele afforded Italian restaurants the opportunity to charge higher prices for much the same food as before and in dining rooms with a bit more panache. Giambelli's Ristorante, opened in 1954 at Madison and 37th Street by Lombardian Francesco Giambelli, was one of the first to latch onto this new crowd, many of whom daily engaged in what came to be known as the three-martini lunch, which might also include a nice bottle of wine. Giambelli's dining room was not all that attractive—one article said its paintings "look suspiciously like those bought by the square foot"[12]—but its food was somewhat more refined than at the typical downtown Italian place of the time, and the restaurant drew U.S. Presidents, European royalty, and New York business executives daily. In October 1995, Giambelli served dinner to Pope John Paul II and 50 cardinals at the New York cardinal's residence.

San Marino, opened by Anthony Gugnoni on East 53rd Street off Madison Avenue, was condescendingly called by *Forbes* magazine "a spaghetti eater's '21,'" referring to the very exclusive Continental restaurant nearby, the '21 Club, which was once a speakeasy. The review went on, "The Hungry arrive looking important, acting important, and some actually are. Putting on the Suave is de rigueur here. . . . If you're dressed off the rack, you'll feel positively dowdy."[13] Still, the Italian food—shrimp Fra Diavolo, minestrone, veal scaloppini—was nothing unusual, even though *Great Restaurants of America* contended it was the best Italian restaurant in the country. Yet those same authors could not resist a nasty slur about an evening when the president of Italy and his wife sat at one table at San Marino and mobster Frank Costello with his bodyguard sat at another: "Despite the slight variance in their morals and methods of attaining eminence, they did share Italian parentage and devotion to good Italian food."[14]

Off Madison Avenue but going for the same kind of well-heeled clientele, there was the Italian Pavilion, on West 55th Street, done up in pinks and greens, with glass-enclosed garden. The menu included new dishes that came close to the Continental form, like *trota salsa Rafano* (smoked trout with horseradish sauce), along with newly named dishes such as "fettuccine Julian," and homemade pasta—something of a rarity then—with tomato and prosciutto strips.

One restaurant that had been around since 1953 but really flourished only in the 1960s was Orsini's on West 56th Street, designed, as *Forbes* wrote, "to foster an aura of romance, honeyed with sophistication."[15] Armando Orsini, an architect with wealthy jet-set friends, had first opened an elegant little coffeehouse, then expanded it into a restaurant in an old New York townhouse on two levels, where clients needed guidance on which was the preferred dining room. *Gourmet* magazine called the downstairs "a hideout for adulterous garment tycoons"; the *Times* called it "the place of banishment at night," while the upstairs drew "international film stars." Orsini's crowd was what became known as the beautiful people, especially after Michael Coady, then publisher of *Women's Wear Daily,* began frequenting the restaurant and wrote about it in his A page, creating an overnight wave of fashion media, designers, and models who wanted, *needed,* to be seen there.

In 1968, *New York* magazine's "Insatiable Critic," Gael Greene, wrote of the restaurant,

> It's not the greatest Italian food ever (nor the cheapest; $2.75 for an appetizer? $4.50 for osso buco risotto!). But at Orsini's, the tables are meant for people-watching. . . . Orsini's is theater. You could pay as much for an evening on Broadway with only half the dazzle. Lunch upstairs draws Gloria Vanderbilt and Arnold Scaasi; David Merrick with Candy Bergen in a mechanic's jumpsuit and Malibu tan; Social Moth Jerome Zipkin with Penelope Tree; Golda Meir, Sinatra, Princess Grace, Chagall, Roy Wilkins. One day Yul Brynner looks around and pokes his wife. "Over there," he hisses—"Mastroianni." And at that moment Mastroianni turns to his companion: "Look, it's Yul Brynner."[16]

The food at Orsini's was meant for its posh audience; it was a little lighter, with less tomato sauce and almost no garlic; its signature dish was a novelty called *paglia e fieno* (straw and hay)—really nothing more than white and green fettuccine mixed together with a cream sauce—along with old-fashioned dishes like *mozzarella in carrozza* (cheese sandwiched between thin bread and sautéed), baked clams, shrimp scampi, and veal parmigiana. Some of the food, as was the style at all finer restaurants of the era, came cooked in a chafing dish over a Sterno flame. Still, despite catering to the same clientele as New York's deluxe French restaurants, Orsini's did not dare charge the same prices; whereas a dinner for two at the Colony or Le Pavillon might cost $50 and up, Orsini's charged about $35, with a bottle of wine.

Italian restaurants like Romeo Salta and Orsini's—though not the food in par-ticular—were clearly gaining a certain cachet, at least in certain New York cir-cles. There was a sense that a modified form of *la dolce vita* could be found in Italian-American restaurants, but restaurants also needed to appeal to the com-mon man. A young crowd of creative minds working for Restaurant Associates, or RA, solved this problem. RA started in the early 1950s with coffee shops and expanded to an array of dazzling theme restaurants that included the Spanish- and South American–styled Fonda del Sol, the German sausage eatery Zum Zum, and the Forum of the Twelve Caesars. (The company eventually took over own-ership of Mamma Leone's.) The Forum was an elegantly appointed reverie of Roman extravagance, with flaming dishes, centurions' helmets used for wine buckets, and wholly invented dishes with silly names like "Tart Messalina," "Fid-dler Crab à la Nero," and "The Noblest Caesar Salad of Them All," none of them particularly Italian.

What *was* Italian was being served at the company's simply named Trattoria, which did not look like any casual, family-owned trattoria back in Italy. It was set on the ground floor of the new Pan Am Building, a 57-story skyscraper which opened in 1963. RA ran all the restaurants in the Pan Am Building, and Tratto-ria was its most successful. It displayed a highly colorful modern design, hung with candy-striped Venini glass globes, Italian travel art posters, a long mahogany counter in the shape of the Circus Maximus, windows overlooking the street, and a staff of young people who seemed to express a bit of that *la dolce vita* vi-vacity, however contrived. Trattoria was fun and open to everyone from business executives to secretaries, and its menu attempted to reproduce the true flavors of Italian food, which RA's top people had assiduously researched on well-budgeted trips for months on end to Italy. The place had the beguiling feel of a vast airport restaurant, indeed, Trattoria was similar to the restaurants run by RA at JFK In-ternational Airport.

At breakfast, commuters could rush into Trattoria—which acquired the snappy American nickname "the Trat"—for espresso and Italian pastries. For lunch and dinner, there was an excellent *lasagne alla bolognese,* eggplant salad with capers and stuffed sardines, and *granita* (frozen ices). And the prices were just right for plenty of people—with main courses at night $1.35 to $5.75. The restaurant had a 27-year-run before being changed into an equally handsome pizzeria/restaurant named Naples 45.

RA did give a big-city boost to Italian food and design in the mid-1960s. Trattoria was not a cramped little Italian eatery or Little Italy tourist trap. Neither was it fashionably exclusive nor expensive. It had its own youthful, sexy cachet that made people happy to be there and gave a little sense of Italian brio. Trattoria was unique in its day, but it was but a ripple in an ocean of dated Italian restaurants in America.

Celebrity was also the draw at Hollywood hangouts like Dan Tana's, which opened in 1964 and is still thriving, serving the same standard-issue ravioli with meat sauce, eggplant parmigiana, and "steak & peppers Sinatra" over the years. For years, Perino's reigned in competition with Chasen's as the number one place to spot movie actors. In Beverly Hills, the restaurant La Scala (run by a Spaniard named Jean León) was easily more famous for the Hollywood stars who came than for a menu that rarely changed or the straw-covered *fiaschi* of Chianti bottles hanging above Italian urns.

London, where rationing did not end until the mid-1950s, was the only city in Europe outside of Italy to see new Italian restaurants appear—these restaurants shared in the mediocrity of their contemporaries in the United States. So ignorant were the British about Italian food that a 1957 BBC broadcast of an April Fools' Day program showing spaghetti growing on trees in Switzerland was widely accepted as fact.

Owing to London's social class system, London restaurants were even more snobbish about their clientele than those in New York; they catered to aristocracy and celebrities in club-like restaurants that were usually French or Continental. Italians worked in such restaurants but ran few of their own—these were cheap and forgettable, restricted to whatever ingredients were available, and there was far less available in London than in the United States. In 1955, Britain's *Good Food Guide* listed only seven Italian restaurants in London, most predating the war.

A significant departure came in 1959 with the opening of La Terrazza by two waiters, Mario Cassandro and Franco Lagattolla, formerly at the Savoy Hotel, with a dream of offering London true *cucina italiana*. The story of La Terrazza and several other successful restaurants opened by the two men has been told exhaustively in *The Spaghetti Tree* (2009), by Alasdair Scott Sutherland, who credits the two Italians with starting the "trat" (for trattoria) revolution in London.

La Terrazza did not have the heavy décor of other London restaurants—at first the restaurant had a mural of an erupting Mount Vesuvius and a string of plastic grapes—and its food was somewhat lighter. The menu was extensive, with both Italian and Continental dishes, ranging from seafood cocktail ("Cocktail Positano") and steak tartare to *Scampi alla Provinciale* and baked lasagna with meatballs. There were many dishes Londoners had never tasted before, such as *vitello tonnato, penne alla matriciana,* and *salsiccie fresche con spinaci,* and a good number of Italian wines on the list. La Terrazza caught on quickly among people from many facets of London society, not least new musicians, the producer of the James Bond movies Cubby Broccoli, and the international movie crowd that filmed at Shepperton Studios, such as Gregory Peck and David Niven, along with American entertainers Jerry Lewis and Frank Sinatra.

The London fashion and society magazines like *Queen* and *Vogue* caught on to all the excitement and created much of it among themselves, so that Mario and Franco's next restaurant, Alvaro, on King's Road, became the most popular, toughest table to get in London, which led inevitably to a backlash about the exclusivity of the place. *The Good Food Guide* reported that it was "crowded with noisy second-rate talents, the photographers and the photographed. All the nobodies who are supposed to be somebodies go there all the time, and it is fun watching them projecting." The food was said to be good but overpriced.

By 1970, Quentin Crewe, restaurant critic for *The Evening Standard,* would write that Mario and Franco had a major impact on dining out in London, with "headwaiters, waiters and even kitchen boys from La Terrazza splitting off to found their own places, faithfully modeled on the original design by the indefatigable Enzo Apicella."

The first pizzerias in London date back to the 1930s, but a true infatuation developed with the opening in 1966 of the first Pizza Express eateries. The owner, Peter Boizot, at first gave away free slices to people passing by the shop who had no clue what the item was. To the extent that Italian food had entered the world's consciousness at all, it was pizza that had the most widespread recognition, and such a humble pie was not much on which to build a world-class gastronomy.

# Chapter 9

## Simmerings

In the autumn of 1977, my wife and I set off on our honeymoon, driving back and forth across the United States, a blissful, idyllic tour that required us to eat out for breakfast, lunch, and dinner every day for 14 weeks. We had looked forward to wonderful meals in every state we would visit and planned to visit famous restaurants in Charleston, Atlanta, New Orleans, Dallas, San Antonio, Phoenix, Los Angeles, and San Francisco, then back east through Las Vegas, Colorado Springs, Kansas City, St. Louis, Cleveland, and Pittsburgh. We would be home to New York for New Year's.

What we found was a depressing and dismal array of restaurants of every stripe—French, American, Mexican, Chinese, and Italian—that disabused us of any idea that America had come of age as a gastronomic power. Frankly, not even in New York was there more than a handful of good restaurants at that time, but the relentless and numbing number of truly awful restaurants all around the country was astonishing—frozen fish cooked in margarine, salads with canned olives and vegetables, watery gumbos, grits and mashed potatoes from a box, pies made with canned fruit in syrup, cakes topped with fake whipped cream.

Even in New Orleans, long regarded as America's premier food city, we found restaurants with stained walls, out-of-date wine lists, inedible turtle soup, gummy rice dishes, and overcooked shrimp, all dropped on the tables by geriatric waiters in tuxedoes shiny with age who seem not to give a damn what we ordered.

After a wretched steak dinner served by a waitress in velveteen shorts at a well-recommended restaurant in Birmingham, Alabama, my wife burst into tears and said, "We can't go on eating like this all the way to California."

I knew she was right, for the amount of bad food, spooned from cans, de-frosted, and poured from bottles was an appalling testament to just how little food and restaurants in America had progressed in the past century. Among the worst of all were the Italian restaurants, including one in Wichita, Kansas, called the Godfather, where the mustachioed owner with slicked-down hair wore a gangster's striped suit, tie pin, and spats, and the kitchen served slop it called lasagna in aluminum foil unwrapped at the table so that it flowed like lava onto the plate.

My notes from that trip describe horror after culinary horror. In Charlotte, North Carolina, a restaurant called Little Italy served tasteless bread dusted with garlic salt, sweet, overcooked tomato sauce covered every dish, and stale Parme-san cheese was shaken from a bottle. "This cook should be drowned in his own rotten tomato sauce," I wrote. At Gene and Gabe's in Atlanta, the waiter told us the kitchen was unable to cook spaghetti al dente; when I complained to the owner, he sniffed that since he had been in business 12 years, he must be cook-ing great food.

Mario's in Nashville made three attempts to make fettuccine Alfredo edible; the owner of Giovanni's in Memphis told us candidly that, if we were from New York, we would not like his gnocchi. He was right. At Bella Napoli in El Paso, the pizza tasted as if it had just been thawed, the cheese was like rubber, the sauce was full of sweeteners; in Colorado Springs, Marretta and Dalpiaz claimed on its menu to be Colorado's "only genuine Italian restaurant," which it definitely was not. And at every restaurant the choice of Italian wines was *always* Valpolicella, Chianti, or Soave. There was little else imported at the time.

By the time we left Birmingham, we had actually learned to keep away from fine dining restaurants of any kind and to eat at the casual eateries serving re-gional American fare—crab shacks, chili parlors, gumbo shops, taco stands, bar-becues, diners, cafeterias, and fish camps. We had brought with us Jane and Michael Stern's *Roadfood* (1977), the first eating guide to the true repositories of *culinaria Americana,* places they treated with great affection, real appetite, and true respect. But *Roadfood* was of little help in finding decent Italian restaurants around the country, nor were any of the other travel or restaurant guides of the 1970s, not even the *Mobil Travel Guides,* which awarded thousands of restaurants one to five stars; the inspectors had never eaten at most of them. The best Mobil-rated restaurants were of the kind that writer Calvin Trillin described as "some purple palace that serves 'Continental cuisine' and has as its chief creative em-ployee a menuwriter rather than a chef." Trillin also suggested that, given the amount of frozen food such restaurants used, the continent referred to in the word "continental" was Antarctica.[1]

There were no Michelin Guides to the United States in the 1970s, although that series, bankrolled by the French tire manufacturer, did cover Italy beginning in 1956. Being French, the editors and inspectors were reluctant to award stars to restaurants in Italy because most of those establishments lacked the traditional elegance and classic cuisine that were the hallmarks of French gastronomy. If a restaurant was fortunate enough to receive one or two stars, it was invariably very formal, very expensive, and probably located within a hotel where the food was not very Italian at all.

At that time no restaurant in Italy rated three stars, which meant "worth a special journey." Given that descriptor, perhaps there *were* no such restaurants of that caliber anywhere in Italy. But what Michelin ignored, as did all the other guides except Frommer's, were the good, honest regional trattorias and osterias that served wonderful food in modest surroundings and at a cheap price. One restaurant that had earned two Michelin stars—"worth a detour"—was Harry's Bar in Venice, which just happened to be the most expensive restaurant in Italy.

In the 1970s, any traveler to Rome willing to seek out the small, local restaurants would be rewarded with wonderful food based on the freshest ingredients the cooks could procure—excellent veal and beef, tasty poultry, remarkable eggs and cheese, vegetables plucked from farms hours before serving, and fish bought that morning at the market just as the boats or trucks arrived with their supply. There was more meat than ever, with Italians consuming an average of six ounces per capita per day—three times what they ate in 1960 and five times what they ate in 1861.

It was the kind of food that caused well-traveled Americans, who by the end of the 1970s were by far the most numerous among tourists in Italy, to return home asking, "Why can't we get food that tastes like that here?" There were legitimate reasons: the ingredients did not exist in America; the supermarkets would not stock them, and restaurant cooks complained that they could not sell that kind of food, which would be too expensive to provide. Indeed, it was easier to go to a "gourmet" supermarket in those days and find exotica like salmon roe, kiwi fruit, even chocolate-covered ants, than it was to find a head of arugula, *mozzarella di bufala,* made from buffalo's milk, or fresh prawns.

There had, however, been some improvement in Italian restaurants in the big U.S. cities by the 1970s. In San Francisco, Tuscan-born Bruno Orsini and Lorenzo Patrone opened North Beach Restaurant, where they prided themselves on serving the best seafood in the market, curing their own hams, and making their own pastas. In the wake of Perino's and La Scala in Beverly Hills, Venetian chef/owner Gianni Paoletti opened Peppone in 1974 in Brentwood. Typical of the trajectory of culinary immigrants, Paoletti learned French and Spanish at restaurants in Italy, then English in London, where he trained at L'Ecu de France as *entremetier* and graduated to saucier. Then, in 1963, he went to the United States. At Peppone he introduced a few items of his native cuisine to his affluent clientele— calf's liver *alla veneziana, lasagne venete,* and *spaghetti col tonno* (tuna), along with the usual chicken parmigiana, veal Marsala, and cannoli for dessert.

In New York, the food got better as the owners and chefs attempted to persuade customers that Italian food was not all spaghetti with red sauce and fettuccine with cream sauce. Patsy's, opened by Pasquale "Patsy" Scognamillo and his family in 1944 in the Theater District, attracted a huge and enduring show biz clientele whose photos they hung on the walls, including all the Italians who made it big in the 1950s, from Sinatra (who once cooked up his own spaghetti back in the kitchen) and Tony Bennett to Perry Como and Dean Martin. The food was honest, cooked by Patsy's son Frank, served in big portions— pastas costs $1.25—and proudly Neapolitan, like stewed tripe with onions, peas, and tomatoes, mussels *alla marinara,* chicken cacciatore, and baked ziti à la Patsy.

One of the best restaurants, largely because of its owner's commitment to buying top quality ingredients, was Amerigo's in the Bronx. Amerigo Coppolla began selling pizzas in 1932 from a Tremont Avenue stand to people coming back from sailing and fishing on the Long Island Sound. Soon he was able to open a restaurant across the street, called Amerigo's, with a full kitchen, good Italian-American food, and a fine wine cellar. Eventually he stopped selling the pizzas—not because customers did not want it, but because *ristoranti* did not serve pizza. Hedging his bets, though, he retained the pizza oven in his kitchen, lighting it only for special friends who begged him to make the pizza they missed so much.

What was to distinguish Amerigo's from most other Italian restaurants in the 1970s was Coppolla's insistence on purchasing the very best meats, fish, and provender available. With these ingredients, Coppolla's wife, Millie, would turn out freshly made potato gnocchi, superb osso buco, thick pork chops with broiled vinegar peppers, and the kind of dry-aged steaks that distinguished Italian steak-houses from all others.

Coppolla eventually sold Amerigo's to his head waiter, a Neapolitan named Tony Cortese and his wife Anna, who not only maintained the restaurant's quality but improved upon it year by year. The Corteses also built one of the most comprehensive Italian wine lists in the country. Amerigo's distinction, then, was not that it was doing anything revolutionary but that it was doing everything as well as possible, within the Italian-American canon. The restaurant drew its share of celebrities, sports figures, doctors, judges, and clerics.

But despite the strides made in Italian restaurants in America, they were still not very much like those in Italy. Most Americans did not know enough to care, and those who had eaten in both countries were puzzled but content with the status quo, which was about to change.

One of the principal reasons there had been so few advances in Italian food and wine by the 1960s and 1970s was that there were so few experts or authorities in Italian cuisine to depend on. Not since Ada Boni's *Il Talismano,* published in Italy in 1929, had there been a book on Italian cookery that covered all the changes and improvements in Italian kitchens that caused regional cooking to move forward. Despite Italians' traveling, moving from region to region, to Europe, and to the United States, no one was documenting how that affected the gastronomy of a country that had entered the global market.

Indeed, few books after Pellegrino Artusi's *La Scienza in Cucina e l'Arte di Mangiare Bene* even addressed the diversity of a country composed of 20 distinctive regions, each with its own culinary traditions. One that did was written by a Roman named Luigi Carnacina, born in 1888, who left Italy during the Fascist era. He worked as a waiter at the hotel restaurants in Monaco and London that were overseen by the great French master chef Escoffier and eventually became restaurant director in grand hotels in Europe and the United States. In 1966, Carnacina and his younger colleague Luigi Veronelli published a four-volume series in Italian called *La Cucina Rustica Regionale* (Rustic Regional Cooking) that treated of everything from tripe *alla Milanese* and crabs *alla veneziana* to pizza from Catania and *malloreddus* pasta from Sardinia. Though never published in English, the series was praised highly and sold well in Italy among readers who might well have had occasion to travel inter-regionally or even sample some Sicilian dishes at a trattoria in Rome or Milan.

Carnacina's training in the international style was the basis of his next work, published two years later, into which he poured out all he knew of the culinary arts. It was a massive volume, titled *La Grande Cucina Internazionale* (1968), and was notable for its inclusion of scores of Italian dishes along with English kedgeree, Russian coulibiac, Waldorf salad, and peaches *flambé Brillat Savarin.*

Carnacina annotated many of the Italian recipes by region, providing occasional anecdotes like this on the elaborate dish of boiled meats and vegetables with garnishes, *bolliti misti:* "Although popular throughout Italy, *bolliti misti* is a specialty of Piedmont. An annual scene in Bergamo, an hour's ride from Milan, is the hundreds of summer visitors sitting outside under the trees making a difficult choice from a large cart of *bolliti misti.*"[2]

The pasta section runs to 40 recipes made with egg pasta—including a less-than-abstemious "Lenten ravioli" stuffed with fish and topped with a sauce of lobster, clams, anchovies, and tomatoes—and another 33 with dried pasta, including macaroni with meatballs. There are even seven recipes for pizza and one for calzone.

Curiously enough, the English translation, weighing in at 851 pages, took the title *Great Italian Cooking.* Carnacina offered only a brief introduction on general matters of cookery, but editor Michael Sonino positioned the book as presenting "as wide a range as possible of recipes falling within the limitations defined by 'Italian' and 'international.'"[3] Sonino noted distinctions between northern and southern Italians, then excoriated Italian-American cooking as being in no way representative of true *cucina italiana,* describing examples of the former as "gastronomic horrors"—"tomato sauces overflavored with oregano and garlic, that soggy pasta swimming in watery tomatoes and studded with over-cooked, anonymous meatballs, . . . and 'Veal Parmigian' fried to leathery toughness, bathed in the omnipresent tomato sauce, and overcooked until the sauce and meat achieve the same texture."[4]

Sonino noted that while the book's recipes were adapted to "present-day American cooking ingredients, in no way has it been transformed into an 'Italo-American' cookbook." Ingredient substitutions were made—songbirds were omitted because they were illegal to hunt in the United States. He also wrote that "it would be impossible to list *all* the Italian regional specialties in a book of less than five volumes."[5]

Carnacina's associate, Luigi Veronelli (1926–2004), went on to become Italy's leading wine and food critic in the 1970s and 1980s, when he began to publish his own guide, *I Ristoranti di Veronelli,* which concentrated not on grand dining rooms but on the trattorias and osterias popular with his readers. Unlike the Michelin Guides, which gave out only graphic symbols for ratings, Veronelli actually discussed the character of the restaurants he covered, what products and wines they sold, and what dishes to order.

That he was also a dedicated fomenter of controversy is obvious from the title the Communist newspaper *Liberazione* gave him: "anarcho-oenologue and theorist of peasant-hood." Ever the Milanese socialist, his harangues on TV in the 1970s caused authorities to try to jail him for six months (sentence suspended) for instigating rebellion; he had exhorted Piedmontese winemakers to rebel against the government's regulations regarding what to plant and how their wines must be made. Veronelli's jeremiad encouraged winemakers of the region to begin experimenting with new blends and grape varieties to improve the quality of their wines.

Good cookbooks on Italian food were rarities outside of Italy in the 1960s and 1970s. When France's gastronomic bible, *Larousse Gastronomique,* was translated into English in 1961, Italian food barely made a dent in its 1,100 pages. There is a single paragraph for "Italian Pastes (Pasta Products)," followed by this entry: "ITALIENNE (À L')—A name given to various dishes made of meat, poultry, fish and vegetables. In all these dishes finely-diced or chopped mushrooms are used. The name *à l'Italienne* is also given to a method of preparing macaroni or other pastes. See MACARONI."[6] Turning to that entry, the reader finds that macaroni should be boiled 15 to 20 minutes then topped with any of variety of sauces, including *à l'anglaise, à la créole, à la mirepoix,* and a few Italian-sounding sauces such as *à la napolitaine* (with tomato sauce), *à la piemontese* (with butter, cheese, and truffles), and *à la milanaise* (with tomato, shredded ham, pickled tongue, mushroom, and truffles). *Macaroni à l'Italienne* is dressed with nutmeg, Gruyère and Parmesan cheese, and butter. Noodles (*nouilles*) get the same treatments. And that was that for Italian food.

In the United States, the more general cookbooks invariably included a few of the more familiar and easy-to-make Italian recipes. *Gourmet* magazine's *Gourmet's Menu Cookbook* (1963)—"A Collection of Epicurean Menus and Recipes"—had a slew of dishes in its "Pasta and Grains" chapter, only a few Italian, including "Sicilian spaghetti," with tomatoes and anchovies; manicotti with ricotta and ham; potato gnocchi; and risotto Milanese with saffron. There is pesto, two tomato sauces for pasta, and Bolognese sauce. Still, in their section of recommended "formal dinners," every single dish is French, from *faisans aux Champagne* to *Pommes de Terre Nanette*.

The well-respected food editor of the *New York Times* Craig Claiborne published several cookbooks during his tenure in the 1960s and 1970s, including *The New York Times International Cook Book* (1971). It included a section on Italy, among 42 other countries—but not on France. The Italian recipes focused mostly on Italian-American favorites like stuffed clams, minestrone, shrimp marinara, tomato sauce with meat balls and sausages, and even a ghastly thing called "Veal Roast with Frankfurters."[7]

Anyone looking for a comprehensive, well-researched Italian cookbook written in English would find very little in bookstores during those decades. In the early 1970s, the bestselling cookbooks included *Diet for a Small Planet, The Cuisine of Hungary, James Beard's American Cookery, The Chinese Cook Book; and Couscous and Other Good Food from Morocco*. By the end of the decade, books such as *When French Women Cook,* and *The Flavor of the South* all sold well. Italian cookbooks did not sell at all.

Except one. In 1969, Marcella Pollini, born in Emilia-Romagna and married to Italian American Victor Hazan, came to the United States. Even though she did not have a background in cooking—in fact, she was professionally trained in biology and the natural sciences—Hazan began teaching Italian cooking classes in her home, using Italian cookbooks—including Ada Boni's *Il Talismano*—and the memories of food she grew up eating. She named her little business the School of Classic Italian Cooking, which soon came to the notice of the *New York Times'* Craig Claiborne, who asked to publish some of her recipes. This quickly brought her to the attention of editor Peter Mollman at Harper's Magazine Press, and the result, in 1973, was *The Classic Italian Cook Book*. It was followed five years later by *More Classic Italian Cooking* and several more books over the next three decades. Hazan could be doctrinaire about instructions, but they were always based on the traditional principles of true Italian cooking. She insisted on using good olive oil—not readily available then—buying fresh ingredients in season, making homemade broth, and using the best Parmigiano-Reggiano, though, oddly, she uses the French/English term Parmesan throughout the book. In her introduction to *The Classic Italian Cook Book,* Hazan explained, "What is important is to be aware that these [regional] differences exist and that behind the screen of the too-familiar term 'Italian cooking' lies concealed, waiting to be discovered, a multitude of riches."[8] She also reminds readers that Italians always enjoy two courses at a meal, but neither need be large in proportion, the way Italian-American dishes so often were.

She was not dogmatic, accepting that "of course, no one expects that the Italian way of eating can be wholly absorbed into everyday American life. Even in Italy it is succumbing to the onrushing uniformity of an industrial society."[9] By the same token, as Hazan would soon see, Americans were trying to be more like Italians.

For most Americans, however, the stereotypical Italian family sat down to a big plate of spaghetti and meatballs, as parodied in a hilarious 1970 TV commercial, titled "Magdalini's Meatballs," for the indigestion remedy Alka-Seltzer. The viewer is watching the making of a commercial for a spaghetti and meatball product in which a fat, mustachioed actor named Jack sits at his kitchen table with his fat, smiling wife hanging over him, awaiting approval for the meal she has prepared him. The husband is supposed to say, with a thick Italian accent, "Mamma mia! That's-a-spicy meat-a-ball!" but something goes wrong with take after take until we see Jack becoming sick at the thought of putting another meatball in his mouth. A voiceover is heard saying, "Alka-Seltzer to the rescue," followed by a shot of the restored actor doing a perfect take, only to have the oven door crash to the floor.

Italian Americans loved the commercial as much as anyone, even if the stereotype of the fat, overeating husband and wife was becoming tired by then. They watched it, laughed, then went back to cooking their mother's or grandmother's or great-grandmother's recipes. They took enormous pride in their cooking, happily inviting their non-Italian friends and their children's non-Italian friends over to the house for dinner.

# Chapter 10

# From Dago Red to Super Tuscan

The history of Italian wine may be ancient, but until the mid-twentieth century, the wines in question were not of very high quality. For while vine growing probably dates back to the Etruscans in the ninth century BC, and despite the Greeks' calling Italy *Enotria Tellus* (land of vines), the vast majority of wines were made on small plots by peasants who had little knowledge of how to get the best from whatever grapes grew on their land.

Wealthy Romans prized certain regional wines for their quality and positioned vineyards for optimum results. The opening of trade to Gaul and Spain gave Roman winemakers new markets, so vineyards were often planted near seaports for easy shipping. Roman wines were aged two or three years and stored in ceramic amphoras lined with pitch and set in rooms with smoke-pipes to flavor the wines.

Emperors created the fashion for their favorite wines, so that those made in Rome's province of Lazio and nearby Campania were accorded the most serious attention. It was Pliny the Elder who pronounced, "*In vino veritas*" (in wine there is truth), and Latin poets reveled in verses about the quality of wine, as when Horace apologized to a friend for serving him "cheap Sabine" wine:

> *At your house you enjoy the best—*
> *Caecuban or the grape that's pressed*
> *At Cales. But whoever hopes*
> *My cups will taste of Formian slopes*
> *Or of the true Falernian*
> *Must leave a disappointed man.*[1]

The barbarian invasions did not exactly wipe out vineyards in Italy, but they destroyed the market and appreciation for finer wines. Throughout the Dark Ages, European viticulture languished, kept alive only in monastery vineyards, where each monk was allowed a quarter of a liter per meal under the Rule of St. Benedict, who explained that it was "better to take a little wine of necessity than a great deal of water with greed."[2] The ancient Roman varietals mostly disappeared, but new ones were planted that have survived to the present day, including Aglianico, Albana, Aleatico, Vernaccia, and Trebbiano.

The improvement of the Italian economy in the late Middle Ages spurred both wine production and trade, which the Florentine banking family of Antinori found highly profitable, allowing them both to grow grapes and sell wines while expanding their own vineyards in Tuscany, which to this day are huge holdings. Grape selection, plantings, and trellising of vines improved somewhat during the Renaissance, though wines were by then no longer sealed in ceramic amphoras but instead stored in large oak casks prone to oxidation and contamination. Even when wine bottles (used since the first century BC) with cork stoppers came into widespread use in the rest of Europe, Italian winemakers shrugged at the idea.

By the end of the eighteenth century, French, Portuguese, and Spanish wines were being shipped to European and even American markets, principally by the British, while the Italian *sfuso* (bulk) wine trade suffered as a result. Toward the end of the nineteenth century, all European vineyards were devastated by the plague of phylloxera, an aphid that destroyed *Vitis vinifera*. It was decades before graftings from resistant American root stocks allowed for replanting. But Italian vintners did not respond as quickly or with the resources necessary to salvage much from the phylloxera disaster, and for most of the next century, there was little done to improve the health of vineyards or the quality of Italian wines.

Even after it was abolished in the 1950s, the old landlord system in Italy still retained its grip, surviving as a sharecropping system by which a farmer gave over most of what he grew to the land's owner, retaining only a small parcel for his family to live off of. This meant that minimal acreage was left for grape growing, and whatever grapes did grow were whatever had already been there and were self-propagating—a situation called *la coltura promiscua* (promiscuous cultivation). Those vines had to compete for nutrients with many other crops on meager land, so the end product was bound to be wine with little character, lean in body, and, after being stored in a wooden barrel, it would likely be oxidized.

The wines most Italians drank were those produced locally, and those were the same wines sold in the marketplace. Tuscany's Chiantis became popular in the

mid-twentieth century merely because they were sold in straw-covered *fiaschi*
that managed to look quaintly rustic and could be easily turned into candle-
holders after the contents were finished off. A white wine from the Marches called
Verdicchio de Castelli di Jesi gained a similar following because it came in a green
bottle shaped like a fish, scales and all, a cheap objet d'art. Even the most lavish
*ristoranti* carried only familiar labels: Giannino in Milan offered a total of seven
wines: two Soaves, one Chianti "*fiaschetto*," a Bardolino, a Valpolicella, and a Re-
cioto. Most were bottlings by Bertani.[3]

There simply was very little demand for fine wine in Italy for most of the twentieth century, and the destruction of land wrought by two world wars only made
prospects dimmer.[4] Even if twentieth-century Italian winemakers wanted to improve their wines, there was scant information on how to go about it. The technical advances in viticulture and vinicultures were being made in France,
Germany, and even the United States. Indeed, the first serious Italian work on
the subject since Andrea Bacci's seven-volume *De naturali vinorum historia* of
1595 did not appear until the 1950s, when Luigi Veronelli began writing about
modern winemaking. As an admirer of France's viticultural advances, Veronelli
insisted that Italy would never become a great winemaking country until it
adapted a classification system like France's *appellation contrôlée*, established in
the 1930s. After visiting California in the 1980s, he crusaded to get Italian vintners to switch from using huge *botti* barrels, which held 264 gallons, to smaller,
59-gallon *barriques*.

Oxidation was considered normal, even essential to the flavor of the wines.
So until the mid-1960s there was very little anyone could say about the thousands of wines made from region to region in Italy, often from grapes that had
cross-pollinated years or decades or centuries before. Few growers knew anything
about their grape varieties, the best way to tend them, or which ones made good
wine. There were simply no rules to follow except stultified tradition.

Then, in 1963, the whole Italian wine industry was radically altered by the installation of government regulations, under the Ministry of Agriculture, as to
just what constitutes a particular wine from a particular region. Created along the
lines of France's *appellation contrôlée* laws, Italy's DOC (*denominazione d'origine
controllata*) and DOCG (*denominazione d'origine controllata e garantita*) designations were a bureaucratic attempt to make sense of the maverick way Italians
grew grapes and made wine.

Only a few Italian wines had been legally protected since the 1930s, but the
DOC and DOCG laws passed in 1963 were amazingly comprehensive. Hundreds

of zones—today, there are more than three hundred—were given appellations based on tradition and history, the predominant grapes grown in a region, and the blends of grapes typically used in a wine of a particular name. Thus, varietals were delimited in those areas, ceilings were placed on yields, acidity, and alcohol, and winemaking practices were regulated in conformity with existing practices so as not to change the nature of the wine. There were also subzones allowed to be called "*classico*" and "*superiore.*"

Quality, however, was *not* guaranteed by the DOC laws; this was the purpose of the appended DOCG, which would not simply control regional winemaking but would guarantee that certain wines were of real quality. By 1980, five wines—Barolo, Barbaresco, Chianti Classico, Brunello di Montalcino, and Vino Nobile di Montepulciano, all made in the north—were awarded DOCG status; soon the reputations and fortunes of wineries making those wines soared. The credibility of the system seemed admirably proven by such a narrow listing of "quality" wines, which, under the rules, could not be labeled with those names unless the wines met standards of taste as measured by government analysts. Such requirements surpassed even the strictures of the French wine laws, which never designate quality, so that in a bad vintage, French winemakers still label their wines with the same château name and appellation as in a good or great year. In Italy, a poor year can prevent an individual winery or an entire region from putting its own label on the bottle or using the term DOCG.

Yet DOCG did little to stifle objections to the basic DOC rules, which many traditional winemakers found restrictive, if not wholly dubious, when so many wines of no particular value suddenly acquired appellation status.[5] In fact, the actual average production of DOC wines is still today only a third of the two thousand wines that might be so labeled, and production of some DOC appellations is too small for commercial sale. The issues came to a head in 1986, when a DOCG was awarded to Albana di Romagna, a wine few connoisseurs would rank anywhere near the level of quality of the first five awarded DOCG. (Currently there are 24.) Veronelli, an early advocate for a classification system, now led the opposition to DOC and DOCG, accusing government bureaucrats of being controlled by large commercial producers that made Albana di Romagna and other wines such as Sagrantino, Vernaccia di San Gimignano, and Soave.

Nevertheless, at the beginning of DOC's installation, centuries of confusion had been replaced by codification and control, allowing Italian wines—good and bad—to get a toehold in the global market. Thus, within two years of DOC's being introduced, the Italian ocean liners were suggesting regional labels on their menus, such as Cirò di Calabria, Chianti Melini Classico, Frecciarossa Vigne Blanche, and Martini & Rossi Riserva Montelera.

The DOC and DOCG gave wineries and importers an opportunity to say something specific about Italian wines at a time when Americans and the British had only the faintest idea what a wine such as Chianti was or where it came from.[5] Progress was slow. In 1960, only about 73,000 hectoliters of Italian wine were exported to the United States. By 1965, the figure had risen only to 89,000; by 1970, to 142,000, with a value of only $13.9 million, representing a mere 18.4 percent of the U.S. import market.

There were a few notable successes by the end of the 1960s. Among them was Lambrusco, a sweet, *frizzante* (fizzy) wine made from a grape of the same name in Emilia-Romagna, where in 1950 nine producers formed the Cantine Cooperative Riunite, which enabled them to improve the technology of their wineries. Lambrusco, at 9 percent alcohol, was well positioned at the time to appeal to Americans' preference for sweeter, low-alcohol wines that tasted like soda pop, like Cold Duck, a blend of American sparkling wines created by a Detroit, Michigan, restaurateur, and sold nationally under various labels. Along the same lines were two very successful Portuguese sweet rosé sparkling wines, Mateus and Lancer's, both sold in distinctive bottles.

Riunite capitalized on that market in the United States by linking up with New York–based Banfi Vintners, America's oldest family-run wine importer. The founder, John Mariani (no relation to this writer), was born in Connecticut, studied for ten years in Italy, served in World War I, then founded Banfi in 1919. During Prohibition, Banfi marketed to Italian immigrants, bringing in foodstuffs and alcoholic medicinal bitters called *amaros,* labeled as a "mild laxative." Following Repeal and after World War II, Mariani and his sons John Jr. and Harry focused on imported wines as well as shipping California wines.

Working with the Riunite cooperative, John Jr. crafted Lambrusco to be enjoyed by Americans who could drink it at any time, mixed with spirits or with soda; he also convinced the Italian winemakers to use chilled stainless steel fermentation tanks of the kind that were growing popular in California wineries, which kept the wines fresh and free from oxidation.

Riunite hit the U.S. market in 1967 with the TV jingle "Riunite on Ice, That's Nice." They even used the French cancan melody "Ta-Ra-Ra-Boom-de-ay!" that in the 1950s had been the theme song of TV's immensely popular children's series "The Howdy Doody Show," whose viewers reached drinking age in the late 1960s, when a bottle of Riunite sold for $2.

By 1976 the wine became America's number one imported wine, selling a million cases a year, holding that position for 26 years and setting sales records that have never been broached by any other import. Banfi never stopped pushing for higher and higher sales, aiming for increases of 200 and 300 percent each year. By 1981, 11.5 million cases were being sold; if they could have produced more, that figure would have been even higher.

Fontana Candida, a cooperative founded in 1958, became synonymous with the white wine Frascati. Ads for Frascati promoted it as "the wine of popes and of the people" and recalled the legend that during the papal elections of Innocent X in 1644 and of Clement X in 1670, Frascati "spouted from the fountains, the marble nostrils of Marcus Aurelius's horse and the lions of the Capitol to the delight and amusement of the people. Citizens rushed out with bottles and cups to capture the wine and enjoy it fully." Here was a pleasant but undistinguished wine, the sales of which Fontana Candida was able to build up to eight million bottles per year, exporting 6.5 million of them. One significant difference, however, between Frascati and other popular Italian wines was that it was dry, with only a faint suggestion of sweetness.

The Fratelli Bolla winery of Veneto was founded by an innkeeper named Abele Bolla, who in 1883 began serving guests his own vineyard's Soave, then branched out into wider distribution of Bardolino and Valpolicella. By 1935, Bolla was putting its wines into 750-milliliter bottles rather than jugs, thereby creating a better image for the brand. Bolla began shipping to the United States in 1947 with only two hundred cases, but Bolla sensed that if Soave could be positioned the right way, there was a fortune to be made selling it to Americans with no familiarity with any Italian wines besides Chianti.

In 1968, the Italian government permitted a tripling of the area of Soave production in Veneto, and Brown-Forman of Louisville, Kentucky, took over the marketing of Bolla (buying a minority share in the company four years later). The brand was among the first to advertise on American television. It was portrayed as a prelude to and part of falling in love, featuring a series of extremely romantic ads that always ended with the handsome Franco Bolla, in a white linen suit, surrounded by beautiful young Italians, toasting the viewer. Viewers thought that the name of the wine was not Soave but, inextricably, Soave Bolla, which accordingly is how they would ask for it in wine stores and at restaurants. In 1984, Bolla declared itself "the Official Wine of Pizza"—a title that had unofficially belonged to Chianti.

While none of these Italian wines were DOCGs, they were higher in quality than what was available in the past and a far cry from what Americans had been drinking as "dago red," a term derived from a contemptuous slur used for Italians since the middle of the nineteenth century. With reference to a cheap red wine, the term dates in print to 1906, about the same time immigrant Italians started being called "guineas" and "wops." As time passed, "dago red" became closer to a slang word than an intentional slur.

Much of the time, the red wine in question was Zinfandel, produced in the United States. During Prohibition, it was made in cellars and at home from grapes shipped from California. Zinfandel had Croatian origins, with cuttings from a Vienna nursery entering the United States around 1829 through George Gibbs, a Long Island nursery owner. He then introduced it to New England, where it went by various names, and by 1859, the vine was growing in California's Napa and Sonoma valleys, where it became a favorite among growers because it produced large quantities of grapes and was adaptable to various styles of wine.

Italian Americans in both the west and east loved Zinfandel for its heartiness, its yield of strong, consistent wine, and, for some at least, its reminiscent flavor of the wines they drank back in Italy. Only in the past decade has DNA profiling shown that, in fact, the grape is identical to what Italians call Primitivo, which had crossed over from Dalmatia (where it was called Crljenak Kaštelanski) in the eighteenth century. In Italy, Primitivo was and still is propagated mostly in Puglia and commonly used as a blending varietal, but now, given its popularity in the American market, it is used as a single varietal, sometimes even appearing under the name Zinfandel on Italian labels.

The California Zinfandel's versatility beyond making "dago red" gave it renewed interest in the 1970s as sweet, salmon-colored white Zinfandel, while other vintners made "zin" in darker, heavier, higher-alcohol versions. In the 1990s, a group called the Zinfandel Advocates and Producers, representing three hundred Zinfandel bottlers, tried to get the wine designated the official state wine of California, but the effort failed because of opposition from makers of other varietals considered better representative of the state's viniculture.

Not unlike Italy, California had for centuries lacked a reputation for fine wines, having gone through fits and starts ever since the Spanish missionaries brought European grape vines to California in the eighteenth century, planting the so-called Mission or Criolla varietal. After the Gold Rush of 1849 in California, many ex-miners switched to grape planting; there were more than 12 million vines in the ground by 1863. In 1857, Agoston Haraszthy, a Hungarian who would later to be called "the Father of California Wine," opened a winery in Buena Vista, California and brought technical expertise to the enterprise of making wine, along with one hundred thousand vine cuttings from Europe, thereby firmly establishing those varietals in the state.

But winemaking remained a boom-or-bust business, the latter usually the result of overproduction, which led to significant depressions in the 1880s at a time when California, like Europe, was already infested by the phylloxera blight that ultimately destroyed 250,000 acres of the state's vineyards. This last disaster finally led the legislature to establish a State Board of Viticultural Commissioners and to fund a department of viticulture at the University of California, which would become the leading research and teaching facility in the world.

Even after the San Francisco earthquake and fire of 1906 destroyed huge stocks of wines stored there, the industry kept restoring itself, or at least tried to stay alive. But then, starting in 1919, Prohibition effectively put American wineries out of business; those that survived grew and shipped grapes or made sacramental wine for religious services.

The repeal of Prohibition began as a boom but again resulted in overproduction of grapes and oversupply, while market forces and contemporary taste prevented California from developing beyond its bulk wine business for the next 30 years. Ernest and Julio Gallo, sons of Italian immigrants in the grape-growing business, founded their winery in Modesto at the end of Prohibition, believing that the true market for California wines was the European ethnic groups that already drank wine on a daily basis. The Gallos therefore set out to make better wine for that market and over the next few decades became the world's largest winery, selling everything from table wines to "Hearty Burgundy" and wine coolers.

Jug wines were sold cheaply and sold well, and dessert wines sold far better than dry wines. Although no one in the industry would ever admit to pandering, there was a considerable market for cheap, fortified high-alcohol wines among alcoholics in inner-city skid rows, where Gallo's heavily advertised Thunderbird label was the most popular. The brand's jingle went, "What's the word? / Thunderbird. / How's it sold? / Good and cold. / What's the jive? / Bird's alive. / What's the price? / Thirty twice." Others had suggestive names like Ripple, Night Train Express, and Sly Fox.

By the 1960s, with better technology, producers were finally able to make respectable if bland wines from grapes like Thompson Seedless and Flame Tokay, even sweet sparkling wines that could be sold at very low prices. By 1971, "pop" wines, made from blends of Thompson Seedless and fruit flavorings, were all the rage with young Americans who previously showed no interest in wines, but by attracting millions of new customers to the pop wines, the industry was laying the groundwork for converting drinkers to drier wines. Once Americans accepted drier wines, the Unites States would become a wine-drinking nation. But at the end of the 1960s, per capita wine consumption was still only less than a gallon, which included sparkling, dessert, and fruit-based wines and vermouth.

Then the boom hit. As wine historian Leon D. Adams wrote, "When the consumption of table wines first outstripped dessert wines in 1968 and set off the wine revolution, it caught both the California grape growers and the vintners by surprise. In 1849 the cry was 'gold,' now the cry was 'wine grapes.'"[6] Prices for wine grapes and vineyard land soared, new varietals were planted, and some producers even began vintage dating their bottles, a practice they had previously thought expensive and of no interest to consumers. By 1975, there were more than 18 times more acres of Chardonnay in the state than in 1960, 50 times more of white Riesling and Pinot Noir, 90 times more of Cabernet Sauvignon, and 200 times more of Barbera.[7]

Poised to take advantage of this new order of winemaking were a significant number of Italians, many of whom had entered the industry in the early part of the century. Italian Swiss Colony, which after Prohibition was the third-largest wine company in the world, was founded in 1880 as a philanthropic venture. A grocer-turned-banker named Andrea Sbarboro settled indigent Italian and Swiss farmers in Sonoma Valley at Asti, and in 1887, he opened a winery there with San Francisco pharmacist Pietro C. Rossi managing the business. They constructed the world's largest wine storage cellar—it held three hundred thousand gallons—and a church in the shape of a wine barrel. The two men grew rich and soon began making red wines they called Chianti. After objections from the Italian government, it was renamed Tipo, but for decades California wineries blithely appropriated the name Chianti for the labels of their jug wines.

Louis M. Martini came from Genoa to San Francisco in 1899 to work at his father's fish market and to make wine at home. His fervor for the latter led him to return to Italy to study enology, then go back to California to sell wine. During Prohibition, he was able to buy a winery in Kingsbury to make dessert wines, then another in Napa Valley to make table wines under his own name; his son joined the business, and the winery increased their vineyards from ten to a thousand acres. The winery was one of the first to plant merlot, to use cold fermentation, and to install wind machines to combat frost in the vineyards. In 1943, the Martinis helped establish the Napa Valley Vintners Association.

Italian names abound throughout the California wine industry—Simi (founded in 1876), Foppiano (1896), Martinelli (1896), Bargetto (1910), Delicato (1924), Pedroncelli (1927), Parducci (1933), Pellegrini (1933), Tedeschi (1946), and others. Of these, none was more important than Robert Mondavi, who is widely acknowledged to have been the single greatest influence on the way the California industry developed in the 1970s.

Though he was hardly alone in his belief, Mondavi insisted that the Napa Valley could produce wines that were far superior to those that were being made after Prohibition. With his father, Cesare, and brother Peter, the Mondavi family bought the old Charles Krug Winery in St. Helena in 1943 and set out to improve its production year by year. They made quality red table wines, which, as of 1946, included their proudly named Vintage Selection Cabernet. Robert wanted to go much further with the new technologies and to make wines that could rival the best from France. His ideas, delivered with his usual confrontational zeal, distanced him from his father and brother, who felt that the investment was not worthwhile. Cesare and Peter ultimately drove him from the winery, whereupon he started his own venture, the Robert Mondavi Winery, which he opened in Oakville in 1966.

Over the next decade, with his sons Michael and Tim in the business, Mondavi succeeded in proving his theories about the quality to be derived by careful use of clones, planting, trellising, harvesting, making, and aging his wines, which included not only superb Cabernet Sauvignons but Pinot Noirs and Chardonnays. By the mid-1970s, Robert Mondavi wines were not just being touted as fine California wines but were thought to be among the finest wines in the world.

So triumphant was Mondavi in attaining the wine world's attention and admiration that in 1978 he entered into business with Baron Philippe de Rothschild, owner of the Premier Cru Bordeaux estate Château Mouton-Rothschild, to make a Napa Valley Cabernet Sauvignon to be called Opus One that would marry the expertise of both the French and American style. It was as much a brash marketing ploy as it was a serious undertaking, for failure would have made both men a laughing stock. But it did not fail; instead, it achieved recognition among the finest California Cabernets, thereby prompting other foreign investments in American wineries, including Christian Moueix, owner of one of the most illustrious estates in Bordeaux, Château Pétrus, who came to believe he could make a great wine in Napa Valley. The result was Dominus, which was established in 1983 and is now regarded as one of the state's best.

By the late 1960s, then, Mondavi had provided the impetus for others like himself seeking to radically shift the image of California wineries away from the bland jug wines that had for so long determined their reputation—the same reputation that characterized the majority of wines in Italy, though for the most part the Italians were perfectly content with the status quo.

The man who played the greatest role in improving the quality and worldwide reputation of Italian wines was the formidable Dr. Lucio Caputo, a strong-willed Sicilian, ex-Italian Air Force, doctor of law, journalist, economist, and Italian Trade Commissioner in New York. Caputo was tall, slender, and impeccably dressed, with the manners and wit of a courtier and a canny understanding of the market—knowing just when to strike. He had been appointed to the New York outpost in 1971 with the assignment to promote Italian products, from tiles to textiles, from fashion to leather goods, all of which he sought to tie together as an expression of a dynamic Italian style. Into this mix he wished to add Italian wines, a product never before seriously promoted by the government officials in Rome.

Caputo sensed the time was ripe for an expansion of the wine industry. He insisted that what was needed was an "organic program" that required an expensive commitment to public relations and advertising, not just in New York but across America. "I knew that interest in wine—all wine—would grow," says Caputo, whose efforts on behalf of fashion had been impressive. "But when I proposed pushing Italian wines in the U.S., Rome and the other trade commissioners were opposed. They did not want to spend the money. So, I had to fight to get any credibility for wines, and every time I went back for more money, Rome got angrier with me."[8]

Nevertheless, Caputo was set on the idea and began to assemble information and consult Italian enologists on what was going on in Italian vineyards. "The

DOC helped, of course, but there were so few people to turn to for up-to-date information," says Caputo. He helped distribute a new Italian wine magazine begun by Pino Khail in 1974 called *Civiltà del Bere;* Caputo made sure the English-language edition, *Italian Wine & Spirits,* was sent out to key people in the industry and to the small but growing wine media that Caputo both courted and helped educate.

At that time the title of wine writer was almost unknown anywhere outside the trade. A wine writer would be an inhouse expert on Bordeaux or German wines or Champagnes, compiling notes and background on wine regions and wines imported and exported. One of the first comprehensive works written for both the trade and consumer was by Bordeaux winery owner Alexis Lichine, whose 1967 *New Encyclopedia of Wines & Spirits* was a massive and authoritative volume; still, out of 716 pages, Italian wines were accorded just four and a half. (Israel's wines received two and a half.) *The New York Times Book of Wine,* by Terry Robards, (1977) spent less than two pages on Italy.

Few magazines and newspapers had wine columns, which were usually written either by bon vivants or regular news reporters with an interest in the subject. Erudition was not required and sweeping generalizations were encouraged, not least about Italian wines, which was to be expected, since there was so little to write about. Caputo began sending young food, travel, and wine writers to Italy's vineyards to learn about the old traditions and the modern innovations in regions like Piedmont and Tuscany. He brought them to the international wine fair in Verona called Vinitaly, put them up in good hotels, and showed them what was happening in Italian restaurants.

His strategy worked. Many of these writers became well-versed, serious, scholarly advocates of Italian wine, and they reported back with enormous enthusiasm about old wines like Barolo and Barbaresco, the wide range of Chianti Classicos, and some remarkable new wines from innovators in Tuscany who had begun experimenting with blends of the traditional Sangiovese with French varietals such as Cabernet Sauvignon. Caputo also took *New York Times* wine columnist Frank J. Prial to lunch to try wines from Piedmont; Prial wrote glowingly about them and became a true advocate of the new wines coming out of Italy.

Wine articles began appearing everywhere—in the food and travel magazines, city magazines, airline magazines, men's magazines, and fashion magazines such as *Vogue, Queen, Elle, Tattler,* and *Marie Claire.* Wine was, in fact, becoming inseparable from fashion and style, and good taste had as much to do with one as with the other.

Easily as important as connecting the American media to Italian wines was Caputo's reverse strategy of bringing Italian winemakers to California to observe wineries such as Robert Mondavi's and others in the forefront of American viticulture. There they saw the latest technologies and received information on ampelography, cloning, trellising, and terroir. For many, these innovations were a revelation; for others, they seemed to threaten a way of making wine, even a way of life, going back hundreds of years.

In one particularly telling incident Caputo invited a dozen Sicilian winemakers to New York's Rainbow Room in order to show their wines to an increasingly knowledgeable New York wine media. I attended that tasting and met the winemakers—most of whom were smoking cigarettes—and I recall that all of the American writers sniffed, swirled, and sipped the wines and found most of them musty, oxidized, even rank. When Caputo later spoke with the Sicilians—forcefully, and in their own dialect—about the Americans' responses, the winemakers were outraged, insisting, with centuries of tradition to back them up, that this was the way they had *always* made their wines and that they were *supposed* to taste that way.

Caputo shook his head and said, "Maybe so, but if you ever want to sell your wines in America or the rest of the world, you've got to clean them up and get rid of the oxidation, which you get because your wines are flawed." He then suggested that they go out and buy a bottle of a great French Bordeaux or a California Cabernet if they wanted to see what wine could and *should* taste like in the twentieth century. Some went away furious, but others learned a great lesson that they brought back to their wineries. Sicilian wines improved at an astounding rate over the next two decades.

"Everyone was waiting for me to fail," recalls Caputo, who created an ad campaign with the line "Some of my best friends are Italian." He also managed to get money to open a lavish Enoteca at the new trade commission on Park Avenue that stocked more than two thousand Italian wines, including vintages dating back to 1864, for media and trade tastings and dinners. (He also founded the Italian Fashion Center, the Italian Jewelry Center, and the Italian Shoe Center at around the same time.) Designed by Roman architect Piero Sartogo and furnished with elegantly modern Italian furniture, the Enoteca was a complete showcase of Italian design and good taste. Pino Khail had even gotten producers to donate money to buy a Giorgio de Chirico painting for the Enoteca entitled "*Le Musa Inquietanti*," which was the first thing visitors saw upon entering the room. "It was the first time Italian winemakers ever donated anything to a government body," says Caputo. "Before that, all they did was ask for money."

Caputo's master plan was to tie Italian style into Italian wine, aligning up-and-coming designers such as Giorgio Armani, Roberta di Camerino, Valentino, Missoni, and Ferragamo with an Italian lifestyle—*la dolce vita,* if you like—that absolutely required a bottle of good wine in the mix. "I remember Dustin Hoffman in the movie *The Graduate* in 1967 driving a red Alfa-Romeo sports car," says Caputo, "not an American Corvette or Mustang, and I thought that this was a change in the way Americans looked at Italian style."

Back in Rome, his bureaucrat bosses kept trying to restrain Caputo's exuberance and budgets, but they simply could not argue with his results: In 1970, when Caputo became commissioner, Italian wine exports to the United States were 142,000 hectoliters; by 1975, they were 449,000; by 1979, more than a million and a half; and by 1980, more than two million—11 times more than they had been a decade earlier. By then, Italian wines constituted 55 percent of *all* wines imported into the United States, even though about 50 percent of that was still Lambrusco. In Great Britain, Italian wine sales soared more than tenfold in the same period.

"Every month the increase was incredible," he says, "four hundred percent in one year! So whenever Rome refused to go along with my plans, I threatened to quit, and they gave me what I needed."

Eventually, he did quit, in 1982, to open the Italian Wine & Food Institute, a nonprofit corporation established to promote and further improve the image of Italian wines and foods in the United States. As part of his promotions, he ran the "Gala Italia" in New York, bringing hundreds of Italian winemakers and chefs together with importers and media, always with a guest of honor from the entertainment, sports, or corporate world, including Lee Iacocca, Mario Andretti, and Gina Lollabrigida, along with fashion designers La Perla, Missoni, Biagiotti, Fendi, Krizia, and others. Food was prepared by chefs from leading Italian restaurants such as Gualtiero Marchesi, Don Alfonso 1890, San Domenico, and Il Bersagliere. The marriage of Italian food, wine, and fashion was crucial to the image of each independently and together, especially at a time when French food, wine, and fashion were regarded as increasingly predictable and less than exciting.

In recognition of his work in favor of Italy in all his activities, the President of the Italian Republic awarded Dr. Caputo the title Commendatore in 1981 and Grande Ufficiale in 1996.

With the kind of access Caputo and American importers provided for Italian wineries in the mid-1970s, the industry responded quickly. As in California, Italy needed forward-looking, even radical ideas to shake its wine industry out of its complacency. The DOCG laws gave the nod to certain wines of proven quality, and more vintners accepted the improvements wrought by clonal selection, cold fermentation, shorter maceration times, and use of *barriques*. Italian wine authority Burton Anderson wrote in 1980 that since 1963, "Italy has made greater progress in defining and improving its premium wines than has any other nation, with a subsequent impact on the entire scope of wine production that has been truly revolutionary."[9] By 1980, there were eight hundred *cantines* producing 40 percent of the country's wines, and although large-scale wineries rarely turned out the highest quality, the wines were well made, clean, and consistent, thanks to ever-present, on-premises technicians and trained vintners.

Ironically, the outrageous abundance of grape-growing territory in Italy that had for a century overwhelmed the industry became a boon in the 1970s. Italy began to produce good wines at very modest prices for the new global market, even if occasional price cutting and flooding of the market created antagonism among other European vintners.

Italian wineries could thus provide the production, but what Italy needed was an image of both the highest quality and the most persuasive style. Young winemakers such as Piedmont's Angelo Gaja were going very much against the grain of their ancestors by tearing out vineyards and rebuilding wineries, replanting with better grapes that included varieties that had rarely, if ever, been grown in the region.

Gaja's family had opened a tavern in Barbaresco in 1856, where they served their own wines and became successful by supplying the Italian Army in the 1930s. After the war, their plantings, in the best vineyards of the Barbaresco zone, were developed to produce fine wines that brought the Gaja name further prestige. Angelo Gaja labeled his Barbarescos by their single estate names, like Sorì San Lorenzo and Sorì Tildin, a significant departure from other producers in Piedmont, as was his use of *barriques* as early as 1975. But his planting of Bordeaux varietals such as Cabernet Sauvignon, Chardonnay, and Sauvignon Blanc in the family vineyards to produced highly unconventional Piedmont wines was a radical step that caused enormous controversy in the tradition-bound wine region; Gaja even called the wine Darmagi, meaning "what a pity!"—the phrase his father used when he passed the new Cabernet vineyards that had once been planted with traditional Nebbiolo grapes.

Nevertheless, Gaja won raves from the new wine media. Speaking English with a fierce, staccato zeal, he won over media, importers, and wine store owners to his radical innovations; the proof, however, was clearly in the bottles of his wines.

In Tuscany, a number of wine families were also creating new styles from traditional wines such as Chianti, Vino Nobile de Montepulciano, and Brunello di Montalcino, all with DOCGs. Fame came slowly for the Brunello, a big, tannic wine created in 1888 by Ferruccio Biondi-Santi from the Sangiovese Grosso clone at his Il Greppo estate. Known among only a few cognoscenti in Tuscany, Biondi-Santi's wines were drunk locally, after decades of aging. When they could be found outside of Tuscany, they sold for the then-astounding price of $15 a bottle. A consortium of brunello producers was formed in 1967, but not until the mid-1980s did the wines acquire DOCG status.

Then, when Caputo introduced the wine media to Brunello, the handful of Brunello makers in Montalcino awoke to find themselves the new darlings of the wine world. Within a few years there were scores of brand new Brunello wineries, most with brand new plantings that the old-timers such as Biondi-Santi and the Colombinis insisted could not possibly produce good wine, or at least not the kind of wine that had made the Brunello famous. In 1960, there were only 11 Brunello producers; by 1980, there were 53, and by 2005, there were 220. At a meeting of Brunello producers in the late 1970s, Ferruccio Bondi-Santi's grandson Franco looked around the room, turned to the owner of Barbi-Colombini, and said, "Who *are* all these people?"[10] One of the newcomers was in fact the American company Villa Banfi (which would be renamed Castello Banfi). As early as 1970, Banfi had imported Poggio alle Mura to the United States, but in 1978, it began to buy and develop vineyards around Montalcino to produce its own Brunello. Careful not to antagonize the local traditionalists, Banfi hired a respected Tuscan enologist, Ezio Rivella, and worked rigorously to be environmentally diligent; the company financed ampelographic research to choose the 15 best, healthiest clones out of 650, then freely shared the results with all their competitors in the region. As Castello Banfi's wines entered the market, the company would achieve great prestige; the International Enological Concourse has named Banfi International Winery of the Year four times and Italian Winery of the Year nine times.

In the Chianti Classico zone, there was a wide-ranging focus on upgrading the wine's image, first by ridding it of the *fiasco* bottle, then by blending Sangiovese with better grapes and dropping some, such as the white Trebbiano, which many felt compromised the potential for Chianti, even though DOCG

rules stipulated Trebbiano and other grapes had to be in the blend. That re-
quirement was later dropped.

Thus, winemakers such as Marchese Piero Antinori, whose aristocratic banking family dated back to the Renaissance as winemakers, broke not just with tradition but with government rules when they began shifting the blends even to
include Cabernet Sauvignon to bolster the Sangiovese. Antinori's experiment
produced a powerful, tannic wine of surprising complexity, called Tignanello.
Antinori tried other blends, like Solaia, and promoted the wine of his relative
Marchese Mario Incisa della Rocchetta, who made Sassicaia.

Though just as revolutionary as the intense showman Angelo Gaja, Piero
Antinori represented a contrast in personal style: Every inch the *marchese*, Antinori seduced the global market with both patrician grace and Tuscan charm.
With the media and buyers he would always stress his respect for a tradition of
high quality that dated back to the Renaissance within his family, while at the
same time manifesting the image of a modern Renaissance man for whom innovation was as crucial to Italian wines as it was to Italian art. If Gaja's Piedmontese style might be compared to the mannerism of Parmigianino, Antinori's
Tuscan style was more like the muscularity of Michelangelo.

The appearance of these new wines in the world market in the 1980s was
greeted with praise that would have been previously unimaginable for Italian
wines. Indeed, they were ranked with the greatest red wines of France and the best
out of California. They won high ratings of 90 to 100 points from the American
wine media, and Antinori's wines acquired the unofficial moniker "Super Tuscans" in the British wine trade. With that kind of heroic title being bandied about,
Tuscan wineries scrambled to come up with their own Super Tuscans—
Flaccianello by Fontodi, Le Pergole Torte by Montevertine, Ornellaia by Tenuta
dell'Ornellaia, Sammarco by Castello dei Rampolla, Il Pareto by Tenuta di Noz-
zole, and many more. Their prices soared to levels that until then only the finest
French wines could charge.

But of course, the DOC and DOCG rules had no allowance for such a name as
Super Tuscan, so these much-applauded new wines had to carry the ignominious
label tag of *vino da tavola*, mere table wine; in 1992 the authorities came up with
a compromise: IGT, *indicazione geografica tipica*, meaning a wine typical of a particular geographic region. This allowed the bureaucrats to save face more than it

benefited the Super Tuscan winemakers, who had achieved international renown despite their lacking a DOCG or any other government sanction. According to the Italian Trade Commission's website pronouncement, "The IGT opened up new paths for winemakers who wanted to venture outside the relatively strict confines of the DOC and DOCG categories without, however, making concessions on the level of quality."[11]

The lesson of marketing an Italian wine as a Super Tuscan was not lost on other Italian vintners, who saw that making higher-quality, limited-production wines on small estates was a way to both get a foot in the global market and take a huge step up in prestige. Of course, cheap Italian wines continued to outsell all the experimental ones of the 1970s and 1980s, and far too many producers from every region believed they could get $100 a bottle for wines that had no track record whatsoever. Clearly, however, the improvement of Italian wines went hand in hand with the recognition that they were every bit as good as the wines of any other country, including once-dominant France.

By the mid-1980s, the wine media had grown exponentially, right along with the popular interest in wine. Journals such as *Wine Spectator, Wine Enthusiast, Wine Advocate* (all American), and Britain's *Decanter* happily promoted Italian viniculture, eventually appointing columnists who wrote only about Italian wines; beginning in 1986, Italy's *Gambero Rosso* began covering restaurants and wine with both typical Italian exuberance and scholarly rigor. Ratings, rankings, and awards always showed Italian wines among the best of any year. In just a single decade, Italian wines had achieved legitimacy and fashionable clout beyond what anyone might have imagined a decade before. By the 1980s, Italian wines were sought out not for their bottles but for their beauty, refinement, and taste.

Only then did the term "dago red" pass out of existence—and that was a hugely satisfying triumph for Italian wine.

*Macaroni sellers eating pasta in Naples, Italy, 1890s (Library of Congress)*

*Pasta makers drying their pasta out in the dirty streets of Naples, Italy, circa 1897 (Library of Congress)*

*Italian bread peddlers, Mulberry Street, New York, circa 1900 (Library of Congress)*

*A "street macaroni restaurant" in Naples, circa 1903, shows how pasta was eaten from a plate with one's fingers as street food. (Library of Congress)*

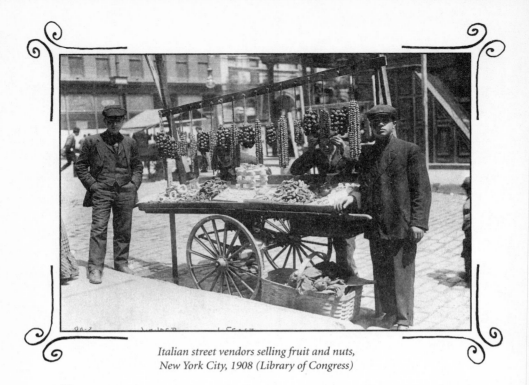

*Italian street vendors selling fruit and nuts,*
*New York City, 1908 (Library of Congress)*

*The Palm opened during Prohibition as a speakeasy but soon set the standard*
*as the quintessential New York Italian steakhouse, serving spaghetti,*
*Prime steaks, and cottage fried potatoes to regulars who had their*
*cartoon caricatures painted on the walls. (Library of Congress)*

Harry's Bar was opened in Venice in 1931 by bartender Giuseppe Cipriani to appeal to wealthy American travelers who wanted to drink at an "American-style" bar, then a rarity in Europe. The bar developed into a restaurant that after the war drew most every potentate and celebrated figure from Europe and the States, and was famous for its signature cocktail, the bellini, and its raw beef dish, carpaccio. (Arrigo Cipriani)

Patsy's, opened by the Scognamillo family in 1944, is one of the last remaining Neapolitan restaurants still operating in New York's Theater District, where it has drawn hundreds of show business figures whose photos line the walls and where Frank Sinatra once made his own spaghetti dish in the kitchen. (Library of Congress)

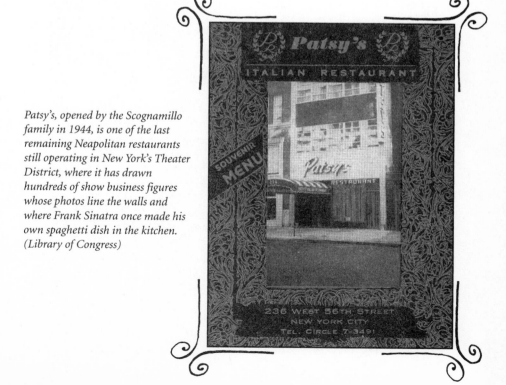

American author Ernest Hemingway (right) made Harry's Bar restaurant
in Venice famous in his 1950 novel Across the River and into the Trees,
along with the restaurant's owner, Giuseppe Cipriani (left).
They are seen here carousing at Cipriani's trattoria on
the island of Torcello. (Arrigo Cipriani)

# Dinner's all here, with sauce all ready

Chef Boy-Ar-Dee puts in one box *everything* for your spaghetti dinner. You don't add a thing. Just heat authentic Italian mushroom sauce to release flavor that's been slow-simmered in. Cook spaghetti to taste, top with lots of zippy cheese.

Serve onion bread. Cut French loaf almost through. Mix ¼ cup softened butter with 1 pkg. onion soup mix. Spread. Foil wrap, bake in moderate oven (375°) 15 min. Try Chef Boy-Ar-Dee Spaghetti Dinner with Meat Sauce or Dinner with Meat Balls.

## A meal in a minute with the Chef's touch in it

# CHEF BOY-AR-DEE®

Immigrant Hector Boiardi sold canned spaghetti to the U.S. military during World War II, and later made Chef Boy-Ar-Dee Spaghetti Dinner one of the most successful postwar food products, introducing many Americans to Italian food. He was also one of the first food producers to use the new medium of television as a venue for advertising. (Con Agra Foods)

## Luncheon

| | |
|---|---|
| **COCKTAILS** . . . | Juices:      Grapefruit      Pineapple |
| **HORS D'OEUVRE** . | Emilian cooked ham      Varzi salami |
| | Tunny-fish with onion      Mixed olives |
| | Smoked eel with capers      Gherkins in vinegar |
| | Mixed Italian olives      Stuffed eggs, Angel |
| **SOUPS** . . . . | Hot or cold double consommé in cup |
| | Consommé Mimosa      Cream Judic |
| | Manhattan Chowder |
| **FARINACEOUS** . . | Spaghetti in butter; Bolognese, mushroom sauce |
| | "Ravioli,, Genoese style |
| **EGGS** . . . . . | Scrambled with cheese      Omelet Parmentier |
| **FISH** . . . . . | Fried squids with lemon |
| **ENTRÉES** . . . | Veal scaloppine, Forestale |
| | Lamb curry, Madras |
| **FROM THE GRILL** . | Pork cutlets with sauerkraut |
| (15-20 minutes) | Mixed grill, Italian style |
| **VEGETABLES** . . | Buttered green peas      Artichokes Bordolese |
| **POTATOES** . . . | Boiled    Chips    Mashed    Lyonnaise |
| **COLD BUFFET** . . | Roast beef, horseradish sauce |
| | Smoked ox-tongue with mixed pickles |
| | Rack of pork, apple sauce |
| | Game patty in jelly |
| **SALADS** . . . . | Beet-root      Escarole |
| | *Dressings:*   Thousand Island   French   Vinaigrette |
| **SAUCES** . . . . | Carmen      Cranberry      Mayonnaise |
| **CHEESE** . . . . | Fior d'Alpe   Gorgonzola   Hollanl   Emmenthal |
| **SWEETS** . . . . | Lemon Pie      Hazelnut eclairs |
| **ICES** . . . . . | Grape sherbet      Vanilla cream |
| **FRESH FRUIT** . . | Oranges    Pears    Apples    Grapes |
| **BEVERAGES** . . | Italian or American coffee    Sanka    Ceylon Tea |
| | Linden   Hag   Camomile   Mint   Fresh milk |

*Passengers on a Diet or needing special Baby Food are requested
to apply to the Maître d'Hôtel*

*Well into the 1960s Italy Line cruise ships appealed mainly to American travelers, and while the menus featured many Italian dishes, they also served a wide variety of international dishes and American favorites, as shown on this 1966 menu from the oceanliner* Michelangelo. *(Author's collection)*

*In a former Greenwich Village carriage house once owned by John Wanamamker, Italian-American Chef Mario Batali opened Babbo in 1998, where he diverged from the entrenched Italian menus of the time and offered a heartier, more authentic trattoria-style food that became increasingly popular in the twenty-first century. (Colleen Lawrie)*

## Chapter 11

# Breaking Away

Culinary historians rightly credit a New Jersey–born former Montessori teacher who fell in love with France's Provence with creating a revolution in American cuisine. I need only refer briefly to what Alice Waters innocently, naïvely wrought at a time when the kitchen was still the domain of the American housewife and the word "gourmet" connoted a rarefied, even effete world of affluent gastro-dilettantes.

When Waters opened her restaurant Chez Panisse, in Berkeley, California, in 1971, in effect, she was asking the same brash yet simple question many travelers did: Why does the food in America not taste the way it does in Europe?

Her solution now seems so ridiculously simplistic: begin with good ingredients, the guiding principle of all good cooking. Yet in America, good ingredients, not necessarily exceptional ingredients, were still impossible to find. At that time there were *no* mushrooms in the market except white Paris mushrooms. So, when Waters began ferreting out the best tomatoes, potatoes, cheeses, meats, and seafood she could find from California's vast cornucopia, she was going against long-entrenched tradition in American restaurants, where most chefs bought whatever was readily available and rarely bothered to buy the best ingredients or even to find out where they might be obtained.

This was then as true of America's French restaurants as it was of its Italian, Chinese, or Mexican restaurants, all of whose cooks wanted the same ingredients, in or out of season, every day of the year, even if they were packaged, frozen, or canned. Tomatoes were shipped year round and genetically modified to have a longer shelf life but at the expense of flavor; brown spots, which indicate sweetness, were eliminated from fruit, which were sold in plastic-wrapped packages;

fish were sold pre-cut into fillets; chickens were raised by the tens of thousands in farm pens; steers were bulked up on steroids. Cookbooks of the time recommended freshness and quality but at the same time listed alternative canned and frozen ingredients in the recipes.

Many of those who cooked with Waters in Berkeley had come from careers that had nothing to do with food; they were, however, college educated and, like her, graduates of the 1960s counterculture, which had railed against the previous generation's infatuation with booze, sirloin steaks, fried potatoes, and mile-high layer cakes. Instead, the counterculture embraced the diets of peoples from the developing world: whole grains, beans, nuts, and cheeses, which poor people had subsisted on for centuries.

The intensity of interest in such ethnic foods gave rise to new kinds of cookbooks and magazines that explored the food cultures of indigenous Peruvian, Cambodian, and Biafran tribes, as well as Italian mountain villagers. Restaurants aligned with these trends followed either those ethnic models or the one set by Chez Panisse, which was resolutely Provençal French.

This post-1960s American interest in better, healthier food and ingredients came as a jolly surprise to Italians who, since Il Boom, had had easy access to the freshest and the best-quality ingredients on a daily basis. Tourists were fascinated by street markets in Italy crammed with wonderful artichokes, lemons, broccoli, and wild mushrooms; butchers whose windows were hung with grass-fed beef, baby lamb, and goat; and seafood markets where the fish were still alive and twitching in the stalls, having been pulled in from the Mediterranean that very morning. Nothing in those markets was packaged; nothing was wrapped in cellophane.

These same tourists had also come to realize that the best cooking in Italy was *not* in the grand hotels or posh *ristoranti,* where elaboration of the Continental style was still stringently followed, but in the trattorias, or, even better, at Italians' homes, where simplicity had always been the rule. Even the *vini della casa* (house wines), once to be avoided, were now of good quality. The distinctions between Sardinian and Tuscan and Umbrian and Ligurian food were coming into focus, and what was rustic was preferable to what was pretentiously elegant.

Classic French haute cuisine, which underpinned the Continental style, had in fact been languishing for years, with unvarying menus that slavishly copied each other and quite literally opposed innovation—this, despite what the French gastronome Jean Anthelme Brillat-Savarin famously said in the nineteenth century: "There is more joy in the discovery of a new dish than in the discovery of a new star."[1] Whether it was a restaurant in Paris, London, or New York, dishes such as *canard à l'orange, pâté maison,* Dover sole *à la meunière,* and *soufflé au Grand Marnier* were omnipresent and never left the menus.

Then, in the late 1960s, a generation of younger chefs such as Paul Bocuse, Alain Chapel, Roger Vergé, and others brought about what came to be known as *la nouvelle cuisine,* a movement never intended to destroy classic cuisine but only to allow young chefs to modify, expand on, and invigorate it with new ideas. The unofficial guidelines of *la nouvelle cuisine* were outlined by French food writers Henri Gault and Christian Millau in the October 1973 issue of their *Gault Millau* magazine. They encouraged innovation but, more important, asked cooks to consider the health and nutrition of their patrons, shorten cooking times, avoid unnecessary complication, learn new techniques, use the finest and freshest ingredients, and return to regional cooking. Taken together, those guidelines were already in force in kitchens throughout Italy.

Waters' ideas found fertile ground in Northern California, but progress was slow everywhere else in America. Italian restaurants were instead promoting the idea of so-called Northern Italian cuisine. This was actually more of a style than a regional cuisine, and while restaurateurs insisted their food was lighter, fresher, and more refined, most of the menu still featured penne with vodka sauce, ravioli filled with lobster, fettuccine Alfredo, cannelloni, and steak *pizzaiola.* The more refined word "pasta" had by then replaced "macaroni," with all its red-sauce connotations. Freshly made pasta was deemed far superior to dry spaghetti from a box. Garlic was reduced to a minimum—dishes were said to have "just a touch of garlic!"—and basil nudged out oregano. The running joke by the captains was always to tell a woman who asked about a rich pasta dish, "No problem, Signora, we take out all the calories!"

Carpaccio, a dish of paper-thin slices of raw beef dressed with a little mayonnaise, created at Harry's Bar in the 1950s, became the epitome of the new, light Northern *cucina italiana.* Smoked salmon, caviar, and vodka were tossed with fettuccine—the pasta shape then preferred to the outdated spaghetti—not because they were part of northern Italian cooking but because they denoted luxury, even if they tasted terrible. The vodka, of course, had no flavor at all, so it was usually marinated with chile peppers and blended with tomato and cream. And the veal chop, once the basis for a breaded cutlet *alla Milanese,* was now served as a massive cut, 12 ounces or more, slit open and stuffed with a mixture of prosciutto and fontina cheese, roasted, then doused with a brown mushroom sauce. It was christened *alla valdostana,* suggesting it was a classic recipe from Val d'Aosta in Piedmont, where it would be difficult to find a cook to make such a dish.

The rich, often heavy, Italian cheesecake was still being offered in these restaurants, but it was now joined by chocolate desserts, and a rich, achingly sweet confection of sponge cake, chocolate, espresso, and cream cheese called tiramisù, created at El Toulà restaurant in Treviso in the 1960s. For some reason, this dessert became a phenomenon to be found on every upscale Italian menu in the United States by the 1980s, while in Italy it was almost unknown. Later the tiramisù craze caught on even in Italy, where by the 1990s it was became a staple on the menu.

New York had always had a handful of expensive Northern Italian restaurants such as Romeo Salta, but in the late 1970s they proliferated, with names like Il Menestrello, Il Monello, and Il Nido, where the captains wore tuxedoes and the waiters white jackets, and both were adept at preparing pastas tableside. The checkered tablecloths were exchanged for white linens, the Chianti bottles replaced by fresh flowers in Venetian glass, and the décor was invariably white stucco walls and dark wood wainscoting.

Prices at these new Northern Italian restaurants were still well below their French competitors', but the clientele, who paid with expense accounts and favored the Italians, happily ordered whatever they were told was the best, including outrageously overpriced *tartufi bianchi*—white truffles—from Piedmont. Barbetta had been serving them for years, but they became requisite on fall menus after having been sanctioned in 1976 by Craig Claiborne in the *Times* as uniquely Italian and decadently expensive. Claiborne, who had first tasted white truffles at Passetto in Rome, wrote, "We may have remarked a few hundred times that there is almost no food known to man that, given a purse of sufficient size, cannot be purchased in America in or out of season, be it Australian kangaroo tail, scotch grouse or reindeer from Finland. One rare and notable exception is a delicacy, peculiarly Italian . . . fresh white truffles, one of the most extraordinary luxuries ever to touch a person's palate."[2] Claiborne noted that they would be selling that fall for $400 a pound and listed Mercurio and Parioli Romanissimo among the handful of New York restaurants that would be serving them, usually shaved over renderings of *fettuccine all'Alfredo.* From then on, the arrival of white truffles was announced each autumn in the media, and New York Italian restaurants had to offer them, with an astonishing price per plate of $50 and up.

The wine lists at these new restaurants were much improved, now with access to the best of Italian viticulture; in fact, the best Italian wines were more likely to be found on a restaurant wine list in New York, Los Angeles, or London at that time than in most restaurants in Italy, where placing a few antique, dusty bottles on a dining room shelf constituted a new dedication to regional wines. Many New York restaurants shared exactly the same list, thanks to a local distributor who crafted leather-bound wine lists, written in his own calligraphic script, and gave them to restaurateurs.

Il Nido and Il Monello were both run by Tuscan-born Adi Giovanetti, who prided himself on serving authentic Italian cuisine such as *ravioli malfatti* (badly made ravioli), the filling of which (ricotta and spinach) was not enclosed in ravioli dough but cooked on its own. *Farfalle* pasta came with a duck *ragù*, and risotto was scented with saffron and laced with radicchio. He even served *crostini di polenta*, little rounds of crisply fried polenta that were, to those unfamiliar with that cornmeal of poverty, quaintly delicious.

All of this cost customers more than they would usually spend in Italian restaurants, which raised the hackles of those who believed Italian food should never be priced at the level of the French cuisine. Dining out, as opposed to eating out, was still the world of French cuisine, a world of privilege and expense, fueled by liquor, not wine. French haute cuisine was synonymous with extravagance, and the "haute" meant haughty. Social position counted more than wealth, and knowing the rules was more important than gustatory taste. Aside from the occasional forays to Orsini's or Romeo Salta, New York society women congregated at the French restaurants each day over salads, poached salmon, and Perrier. These "ladies who lunch" (a phrase from Stephen Sondheim's lyrics for the 1970 musical *Company*) had already been fodder for Truman Capote in his *Esquire* story "La Côte Basque 1965," about the women who came solely to gossip, plan benefits, flirt with the staff, and reassure themselves that there would be a table for them tomorrow.

The pompous owner of New York's Lafayette, Jean Fayet, once ordered a guest to remove her sunglasses because they caused a reflection on the ceiling; refused a table to the beauty editor of *McCall's* magazine because her Pucci dress was too short; and banished the Italian designer Valentino for wearing a turtleneck; Fayet even refused to accept credit cards because he "didn't want to be another name on a list."[3] Robert Meyzen, owner of La Caravelle, once told the *Times*, "I don't care if you call three weeks ahead. When I can have someone like Mrs. Lytle Hull and Mrs. Burden [two New York socialites], why should I take Mrs. Somebody from Kalamazoo? Even if I have ten tables empty, if I don't feel like taking someone, that's *my* privilege. We don't sell tables here. You couldn't get a table here for $200. If you belong here, you get a table."[4]

No Italian restaurant of that era would dare trying to get away with such arrant snobbism, even if the restaurant was wildly popular. Armando Orsini told the *Times* in 1973 that restaurants "are not to be taken so seriously, like a temple. [Our customers] can even have a Coca-Cola with spaghetti. My headwaiter and I, we don't judge people. But if we see a woman in her fifties in jeans, with a big fanny, we don't accept her. Now a bare-backed halter dress, on a woman like a model—we love that. We parade her around the room."[5]

Tuscan-born Sirio Maccioni had been a maître d' at the Colony and was well aware of the snob factor that came with celebrities—on his first day at work, Frank Sinatra, Cary Grant, and the Duke and Duchess of Windsor all came to lunch within minutes of each other (and all wanted the same table). Maccioni also knew that serving French, really Continental, cuisine was the way to attract such a clientele, so that when opened his own restaurant on East 65th Street in 1973, he did not have the audacity to make it Italian. At the Colony he had seen plenty of celebrities—but he regarded the French restaurants of the day as places "for masochists willing to submit to the French culinary act."[6] He knew that much of the food in French kitchens, prepped long in advance, was left sitting in a bain-marie, which he said was "disgusting."[7] Still, he named his new restaurant Le Cirque—the circus—with a French chef named Jean Vergnes as partner, and a $100,000 loan undersigned by real estate titan William Zeckendorf Jr.

In his autobiography, Maccioni tells how he could never have attracted a clientele if he served the kind of food Italians ate and which he preferred.

> Let's be very clear. To me the way Italian food works, in the kitchen, on the plate is the best. Salt, olive oil, pepper, that's it. A grilled piece of fish or meat, a little thyme or rosemary. Wild garlic roasted until it is sweet. Even when we opened Le Cirque, there was no way to present that kind of food in a restaurant. I mean you could not do it. Who needs a chef? I could go back into the kitchen, put a little olive oil in

a pan, sauté a fish, bring it out on a plate, and lay it in front of Mrs. Colgate. She would have had a heart attack. Right or wrong, the way of restaurants in America was French. I love the trattorias of Italy, but America was not ready for this kind of cooking.[8]

Maccioni had himself come from poverty, born in the Tuscan town of Montecatini. "Americans don't understand how terrible Italy was then," he recalled. "I mean, yes, as a child, I had a home and a bed and a father who had a bicycle, but it was terrible to be my mother and father and my grandfather and my uncles."[9] His mother passed away in 1938, his father went off to the war; at one point German soldiers ransacked his house, attempting even to steal the family's one cow, but were turned away by his grandmother brandishing a wooden board. In 1944, his father was killed by a bomb set at the Montecatini train station. When the Germans finally left, the Allies moved into the town, and Maccioni recalled of them, "The Americans? Well, they looked like a circus coming to town."[10] Maccioni's father had worked at the local hotel before the war, and that seemed a natural route for the young man to make his way in a world where he had always admired the elegance and the beautiful women who filled those old hotels. The slender, handsome Tuscan rose through the ranks of hotel service, eventually working on the Home Lines cruise ship *Atlantic,* which brought him to ports such as Nassau, Port-au-Prince, Havana, and New York, where in 1956 he disembarked to pursue his career in America.

Still without money, Maccioni had acquired a great deal of worldliness, which he put to good use in his first New York waiter jobs. He joined the union, got a job at Delmonico's, and waited on some of the wealthiest people in the world. Still, he realized, "There is no one more stupid than the waiter who thinks that just because a rich person smiles at you, you are set for life. Usually, it's the opposite. They use you when they need you and then don't remember you when you have a problem."[11] It was a lesson he bore in mind after becoming maître d' at the Colony, then after opening Le Cirque.

It was Maccioni's name and reputation that brought immediate attention and a glamorous clientele to Le Cirque from the start. From any seat, guests could see who was coming through the revolving door: former president Richard Nixon, fashion designer Bill Blass, Paloma Picasso, Sophia Loren, Woody Allen, Luciano Pavarotti, and all the world's social elite. Everyone seemed to bask in Maccioni's radiance as much as they brought their own. Soon paparazzi were parked outside Le Cirque's entrance and the restaurant appeared frequently in magazines such

as *Town & Country, Vogue, New York,* and *W,* whose editors Maccioni courted. Inside, the impeccably tailored host greeted his guests, kissed hands, designated
who was to be seated where, and by his sheer charisma—a mix of savoir faire
and a sad-eyed, operatic soulfulness—gave the place a distinct air of amusement.
In contrast to the staid, formal, cookie-cutter décor of French restaurants of the
era, Le Cirque was brightly lit, with walls depicting monkeys cavorting on vines.
As food editor Michael Batterberry explained in Maccioni's memoir, "He dares
to have fun. He is the quintessential dashing Italian. But behind all the bravura,
he's in a perpetual state of high hysteria. And all of his best customers are a part
of it. He involves you in some kind of ancient Italian agony that is far beyond
the dashing maître d.'"[12]

Maccioni's customers, knowing his Tuscan background, would often ask him
for a good pasta dish, but Vergnes fought the idea because he considered it completely antithetical to his cuisine. He even refused to serve pasta to conductor
Zubin Mehta and French chefs Paul Bocuse and Roger Vergé. As co-owner, Maccioni finally insisted there *had* to be at least one pasta on the menu each day, so
Vergnes reluctantly complied, but, Maccioni moaned, "I got what I wished for.
Each one was more awful than the next. It was like beating a dead horse."[13]

How ironic, then, that Le Cirque's most famous dish became something called
pasta primavera. The story of how this dish came to be has at least two versions,
though Maccioni's has the most support. He says that his wife, Egidiana, merely
tossed it together from whatever was in the refrigerator to feed Vergnes and guests
Craig Claiborne and Pierre Franey of the *Times* while on a trip to Canada. The
dish, which means "springtime pasta," was made with pine nuts, tomatoes,
chopped string beans, frozen peas, and broccoli, with heavy cream (see page 153
for recipe).

Whatever pasta primavera origins were, Vergnes never listed the dish on Le
Cirque's menu and refused to make it, saying it would "contaminate" the
kitchen.[14] If requested—which it was, dozens of times a day—the dish was
cooked up in a pan of hot water in the kitchen corridor and finished at the table
by Maccioni or a captain. Then, after Claiborne published a recipe in the *Times*
for the dish he called "inspired," pasta primavera became all the rage among Le
Cirque's clientele. It even supplanted *fettuccine all'Alfredo* as the most famous
non-red-sauce pasta dish in New York. Of course, in Italy, chefs had no idea what
the dish was when Americans asked them to make it.

The food at Le Cirque in the 1970s was very good—FFF was the slang back
then for "fine French food"—but it was the presence and savoir faire of Maccioni

himself that made his restaurant something fresh and important. By then, the Colony and several of the old-line French restaurants such as Lafayette, Le Pavillon, Le Voisin, and others had closed, though Lutèce, La Côte Basque, La Caravelle, and La Grenouille still thrived. What Maccioni brought to Le Cirque was a divertissement at which he was both the ringleader and central player, that of the exquisitely refined Tuscan gentleman who could teach the rich and famous a thing or two about food, wine, and good taste.

And as time went on, Le Cirque's French cuisine, under successive French chefs, was widely considered to rank among the finest in America. In the kitchen each night, 18 sauces were readied for the *mise-en-place.* There was always caviar and smoked salmon, consommé and soups, salads, pâtés and terrines, cold seafood, hot seafood, roasts, grilled items, poultry, filet mignon and lamb, game in season, an array of desserts and soufflés, chocolates, and cookies. Yet as much as Maccioni would have liked to serve Italian food, the times demanded that a restaurant of Le Cirque's caliber be French and charge accordingly.

This was a lesson not lost upon another restaurateur, in Houston, Texas, whose own affluent clientele believed the only fine restaurant was a French- or Continental-style restaurant. Tony Vallone was born and grew up in Texas to a family in the restaurant and catering business. His father had been a gambler who ran eateries of questionable purpose where the young Vallone learned the rudiments of the business. More important, when he was a child, his grandmother had fed him the traditional food of her native Sicily. Her kitchen, said Vallone, was "a kind of church and marketplace and workshop all in one room. Simmering an honest Italian sauce or soup all day long, with the aromas perfuming our house, was not work for her but pleasure."[15]

The simple fact that he was an Italian in Houston required him to work harder to win over the city's dining crowd. This was during the 1960s, when Houston was a dry city, and only "private clubs" could serve liquor by the glass. (Restaurants got around this law by making patrons "members" for the evening.) "I knew that Houston was going to boom and people with money would want to eat somewhere with class," Vallone recalled. "They didn't just want to eat and drink at their country clubs anymore. They'd eaten in New York and Paris and Rome and would spend the money to get the same quality here in Houston."[16]

Vallone opened his first namesake restaurant, Tony's, in 1965, with six tables, dancing, and a little Italian food along with the mostly Continental menu. But things really took off after Houston changed its laws about on-premises drinking (in 1969). Tony's developed a small crowd that followed him in 1972 to much larger, glitzier quarters in the posh Galleria area, where Vallone honed his skills as master restaurateur, catering to a clientele that was increasingly upscale, well-heeled—albeit it in hand-tooled cowboy boots—and as well-traveled as any in America.

As an admirer of Sirio Maccioni, Vallone said, "Everybody knows Le Cirque as the most famous restaurant in the world because of who goes there, but Sirio gets all due credit for also having some of the best food and wine in the world."[17] Vallone's mission was to emulate Maccioni—that and to get away from the Continental cuisine and the clichéd Italian dishes his guests still craved. Vallone gave them whatever they wanted, whether it was Chateaubriand with béarnaise sauce, fish mousse with rose petals, oysters Bienville, veal chops Parisienne, or even Texas chili.

Through the 1970s, Vallone's culinary ambitions were shackled by the poor availability of good Italian ingredients. "We couldn't get fresh clams," he remembers, "so we had to use canned clams with the linguine. I started doing it with oysters, which were abundant in the Gulf. Nobody sold calamari, so I had to go down to the fishing docks and buy it out of the guys' bait bags."[18]

Over the next three decades, Tony's was the principal arena for Houston society, duly reported on in the newspaper gossip columns on a daily basis. Vallone had a lock on visiting presidents of the United States, Nobel Prize–winning surgeons, Hollywood actors, and every sports figure who came through town. Luciano Pavarotti once got up and sang two impromptu arias in the dining room. Tony's prepared takeout for Frank Sinatra, and Vallone personally brought espresso to Sophia Loren's hotel room. And no one was more discreet than Vallone about keeping a local tycoon and his new mistress out of sight—especially when the same tycoon's wife was in his dining room.

Little by little, Vallone came in sight of his goal of serving Italian cuisine, regularly putting osso buco and *fettuccine alla carbonara* on the menu along with a few of his own childhood favorites, which he named after his family, like "breast of chicken Nonna," "oysters Zia Maria," and "filet Nino." He was also busy building a huge wine cellar that held the best wines coming out of Italy along with those from Bordeaux, Burgundy, and Champagne. If Tony Vallone could succeed at that level in Houston, fine Italian food was ripe to succeed at the fine dining level anywhere in America.

## PASTA PRIMAVERA

Pasta primavera became one of the most fashionable dishes of the 1980s. After the *New York Times* published a recipe for the dish, it became not only Le Cirque's most popular dish but one people expected to see on Italian menus in the United States and Italy.

*1 cup sliced zucchini*
*1 cup sliced broccoli*
*1 ¹/₂ cups snow peas*
*1 cup baby peas*
*6 asparagus spears, sliced*
*10 white mushrooms, sliced*
*1 heaping tablespoon salt*
*1 pound fettuccine*
*2 tablespoons olive oil*
*¹/₃ cup pine nuts*
*2 teaspoons minced garlic*
*¹/₂ cup chopped flat-leaf parsley*
*Freshly ground black pepper*
*¹/₂ cup freshly grated Parmigiano-Reggiano cheese*
*5 ¹/₂ tablespoons unsalted butter*
*1 cup heavy cream*
*¹/₃ cup chopped fresh basil*
*2 tomatoes, coarsely chopped*

1.  Place a steamer basket into a large pot, add a small amount of water and bring to a boil. Place the zucchini, broccoli, snow peas, baby peas, asparagus, and mushrooms in the basket, cover, and steam until tender, about 3 minutes. Rinse vegetables under cold water and drain.
2.  Bring a large pot of water to a boil. Add the salt and the fettuccine. Cook until al dente and drain.
3.  In a sauté pan, heat 1 tablespoon of the olive oil over medium heat. Add the pine nuts and garlic and cook until they begin to turn golden, about 2 to 3 minutes. Add the remaining olive oil, and the steamed vegetables,

then the parsley. Salt and pepper to taste. Cook until all the ingredients are heated through, 2 to 3 minutes.

4.  Add spaghetti to the sauté pan, then the Parmigiano-Reggiano, butter, cream, and basil, and heat thoroughly. Toss, then scatter the tomatoes on top. Serve immediately.

Serves 4.

# Chapter 12

# Coming to a Boil

The fatuous word "foodie," like hippie and yuppie, was hardly meant as a compliment when it first appeared. It was used in an essay called "Cuisine Poseur" in the British magazine *Harpers & Queen* (August 1982), and by 1984, there was *The Official Foodie Handbook,* by Paul Levy and Ann Barr, who wrote, "A Foodie is a person who is very, very interested in food. Foodies are the ones talking about food in any gathering—salivating over restaurants, recipes, radicchio. They don't think they are being trivial—Foodies consider food to be an art, on a level with painting or drama."[1]

By the beginning of the 1980s, there was a growing tribe of omnivores who played games of one-upmanship by being the first to eat at the new Michelin stars each spring, the first to know about a hidden dim sum place in Chinatown, the first to obtain the unlisted phone number at a red hot new bistro in Beverly Hills.

A good deal of this new frenzy about food was driven by Northern California chefs, farmers, cheesemakers, vintners, and grocers who saw fortunes to be made from the trend Alice Waters started. At the same time, in the early 1970s, there was the expensive glamour of France's *la nouvelle cuisine,* in which eccentricity and presentation played a far bigger part than its originators intended. Suddenly fine dining everywhere had come to mean being served on oversized Villeroy & Boch china plates, with Christofle silverware, on Porthault linens. *Beurre blanc* replaced Béarnaise and Hollandaise, kiwi fruit became all the rage, even with fish and meat, and sauces were dripped or scattered or streaked over plates in Op Art patterns. Huge white umbrellas imprinted with the Perrier logo were hoisted on restaurant patios over rattan bistro chairs. The combination of these forces electrified the media: The marriage of the casual California style with the posh of French cuisine was simply irresistible. In Los Angeles, the most highly regarded and tough-to-get-into restaurants had names like L'Ermitage, Le Dôme, and L'Orangerie, each, depending on its location, appealing to a segment of the entertainment business. One of the most important restaurants of the era was Michael's, opened in 1979 by a brash ex–New Yorker named Michael McCarty, who combined a French *nouvelle* menu—he insisted it was American because *he* was American—with paintings by contemporary, cutting-edge artists such as Jim Dine and David Hockney.

Books on the subjects of *la nouvelle* and California cuisine poured out of the publishers, and new magazines in both Europe and the United States fed the frenzy with beautifully stylized food photography of dishes that looked too precious to eat, cooked by young chefs too handsome to ignore. The acknowledged French masters of *la nouvelle,* Paul Bocuse, Roger Vergé, and Gaston Lenôtre, were even asked to open a French restaurant at the futuristic Epcot Center at Disneyworld in Orlando, Florida.

Most Italians chefs felt *la nouvelle cuisine* was ridiculous, over-hyped, constructed to dazzle rather than satisfy, and in the end, mere decoration rather than honest cooking. Nevertheless, a handful of Northern Italian chefs, all trained in France, took up the *nouvelle* banner in the early 1980s and emblazoned it with the name *la nuova cucina.* With backing from industrialists and bankers in Milan, Turin, Bologna, and Florence, these chefs opened extravagant restaurants, often as inns outside the major cities, where their backers could spend a reclusive weekend with wife or mistress. They might seat no more than 20 guests each day but had ten cooks in the kitchen. The china might well be Villeroy & Boch, or it could be the new Italian designs by Vietri, the linens by Frette, the silverware by Buccellati. The wine lists brimmed with the best vintages of the new Italian wines such as Tignanello, Sassicaia, and Gaja. And prices rose as portion sizes fell; *il menu degustazione*—a multi-course tasting menu—copied the French *le menu dégustation,* and lavish French-style desserts were accompanied by an array of jellies, candies, and chocolates. There was no doubt in anyone's mind: these chefs saw stars—in the Michelin Guide.

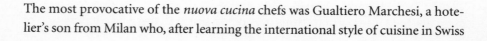

The most provocative of the *nuova cucina* chefs was Gualtiero Marchesi, a hotelier's son from Milan who, after learning the international style of cuisine in Swiss hotels, worked in the early 1970s at Michelin-star restaurants in Paris, Dijon, and Roanne, where early forms of *la nouvelle cuisine* were evolving. Marchesi returned home in a fever to create his own dishes. In 1977, he opened a restaurant under his name in Milan, which, within one year, garnered a rare Michelin star, a second the following year, and finally, in the mid-1980s, the illustrious third star. It was one of only three restaurants in Italy to have ever done so.

True to form and fashion, Marchesi had outfitted his restaurant expensively, in a stylishly modern décor, and charged accordingly. The first time my wife and I tried to dine there, in 1980, I opened the menu to find I could not afford dinner—$15 to $20 for a main course!—so I made up a story about forgetting my wallet and exited quickly without ordering anything. A few years later, when I had the money, I dined at the restaurant and ate splendidly, although the food was not what I expected to find in Italy. Marchesi never *said* his food was Italian; he called it "global cuisine."[2] Indeed, although he was forced to serve it, Gualtiero, like Marinetti before him, railed against pasta, saying Italians filled up on it and then had no appetite for a main course; thus, he served a small pasta *after* the main course.

In an interview I had with Marchesi in 1982, he spoke of "the ecology of food" and the "reaffirmation of naturalness," sounding much like the California New Age counterculturists, and insisted that the youth rebellions of 1968 helped change perceptions about everything, including cuisine. He was critical of contemporaries who still "repeated the cooking of yesterday."[3]

Marchesi's menus could be deliberate fantasies, with French names, like his 1979 "*Le Diner de l'Apocaypse*," at which he served *Les Fleurs du Mal sautées et arrosées de néguentropie, L'Implosionde Turbot Sémilogique à la façon de Umberto Eco,* and *Les Symmulacres des Viandes Stochastiques au feu de touché-bois.*[4] Such Marinetti-like effusions were intended to spark debate, of course, for Marchesi actually demanded simplicity in its purest form, like placing a sheet of gold foil on saffron risotto; he would scramble eggs then place them back into their shell garnished with tiny pieces of chub, preserved tomato, and chervil; he would take old ideas like pressed duck and *tournedos Rossini* and prepare them in entirely new, lighter ways. He mimicked the French passion for foie gras in many dishes, sprinkled then-fashionable pink peppercorns on many dishes, made a *savarin* of fish with caviar and crispy onions, combined salmon with rhubarb, sprinkled *amaretti* cookies into a cream of zucchini soup, and used kiwi in his desserts.

His plate presentations were not ostentatious, but his tables were set with small silver sculptures and his dining room was a showcase for the contemporary

Milanese interior design. Marchesi was interested in technology, methodology, and spa cuisine, and he got attention along with criticism from more traditional colleagues. He ate it all up and shrugged. He might have called his cooking "global," but his 1980 cookbook was titled *La Mia Nuova Grande Cucina Italiana*.

Other restaurants in Italy took up *la nuova cucina* in the 1980s with less fanfare, but still caught the media's attention, which was both positive and negative. One of the most respected was San Domenico, in Imola, under chef Valentino Marcattilii. With the support of the owner, banker Gianluigi Morini, the young chef was eager to prove he could cook in his own style while preserving Italian tastes and traditions. His most famous dish was *uovo ai tartufi*, a single large *raviolo* stuffed with ricotta and an egg yolk that cooked along with the pasta, then oozed out when the pasta was cut, with shavings of white truffles (see page 164 for recipe). He was clearly indebted to French training and *la nouvelle cuisine*, as evidenced by his duck foie gras with brioche toast, and his raw marinated salmon with three peppers. But in dishes such as his *branzino* ravioli with shellfish, risotto with meat glaze, butter, and Parmigiano, and monkfish with tomato, he showed persuasively how Italian food could move beyond its regional underpinnings and win worldwide attention as being on a par with French haute cuisine.

There were other chefs of the same merit, some more conservative, others more adventurous. At Antica Osteria del Ponte, outside of Milan, Ezio Santin served ravioli with carrots, asparagus, and fava beans, and stuffed zucchini flowers with potato puree, but most of the dishes were closer to France than Lombardy— poached salmon with *fines herbes*, a sauté of fresh foie gras, and white chocolate mousse. Antica Osteria del Teatro, in Piacenza, began as resolutely French, with the menu listing *salade de champignons sauvage en cerfeuil, la petite folie de langouste amoreuse*, and *aiguillette de canard aux artichauts à la menthe*. As a balm to Italian guests, the restaurant also offered ricotta-spinach *tortelli*, gnocchi with tomato and butter, and zabaglione of strawberries.

Since 1926, four generations of the Santini family have helped keep Dal Pescatore, in the middle of a farm in Canneto sull'Oglio outside of Milan, on a middle track. The refined rustic design of the restaurant and exquisite food by Nadia Santini (who married into the family) earned it three Michelin stars. Enoteca Pinchiorri, outside of Florence, opened in 1972 and is run by Giorgio Pinchiorri and Annie Féolde, who garnered three stars for a cuisine the couple described as "an always-evolving voyage into the memory of taste; it is a simple and careful exercise in style which refers to, at the same time, the application of the French techniques and an interpretation of the Tuscan cuisine tradition."[5] A *menu degustazione* there might begin with three kinds of *burrata* cheese (one deep-fried); move on to a poached egg with Jamaican pepper, Parmigiano fondue, zucchini cream, and sliced pancetta; then to *agnolotti* filled with polenta and tossed with scampi, candied tomatoes, black olives, and oregano.

Such restaurants catered to wealthy clients—at the time, a parade of Japanese, who later bankrolled a branch of Enoteca Pinchiorri in Tokyo—who were prepared to pay high prices for such food and for the best Italian and international wines, from cellars that stocked deep holdings in large formats and old vintages. The American media caught on, and more rich foodies followed.

The direct effect *la nouvelle cuisine* had on Italian food is not easy to judge, for many expensive new restaurants copied the trappings of décor and plate presentation. Some lightened their cuisine; most adopted the lengthy *menu dégustation* format. With a steady flow of tourists and business travelers into the principal Italian cities, the restaurateurs could afford to set an elegant table, stock a fine wine cellar, and hire a well-trained staff, but they were not ready to abandon the long traditions of their beloved regional cooking. New planes, trains, and roads brought food in from everywhere, so that there was no longer any real reason that a Sicilian restaurant could not open in Florence or a Florentine restaurant in Palermo.

Nevertheless, Italians overwhelmingly kept to their local cooking, so that while they would venture out on vacation to Taormina to sample Sicilian food or to Vasto to enjoy Abruzzese food, they were always happy to get back home to their own. Indeed, nothing is sadder than an Italian in a foreign country deprived of a good plate of spaghetti, and in most European countries in the 1980s, the fare was likely to be a weak facsimile of Italian-*American* food—the same meatballs and spaghetti, the same chicken parmigiana—that people in London, Dublin, Madrid, Brussels, Oslo, and even Paris found on their menus.

The same modes of transport that brought the best of ingredients from all over France into Paris's old Les Halles food market now brought the best ingredients from all over Italy to the markets in Rome, Genoa, Milan, and Turin. Palermo's Vucciria and Venice's Rialto seafood markets teemed with freshly caught fish. *Aceto balsamico,* albeit in a much diluted form, could be found everywhere. This made the odds of having a good meal anywhere in Italy higher than anywhere in Europe. It was quite common for people to express amazement at the good food served at an AGIP gas station on the Autostrada—my own notes from a drive from Rome to Pisa recall an AGIP lunch of risotto with prosciutto, *tortellini alla bolognese,* roast veal, and rabbit stew.

I filled scores of index cards with notes on *ristoranti* and *trattorie* throughout Italy in the 1980s that show, in retrospect, that while the menus differed little within regions, the high quality of the oil, butter, cream, mushrooms, tomatoes, greens, fish, and meat made the prospect of getting a poor meal nearly impossible. These were simple dishes, such as lasagna with artichokes at Trattoria all'Amelia in Verona; pumpkin ravioli at Il Cicogno in Mantua; risotto with cuttlefish in All'Ancora in Padua; baby lamb with roast potatoes at Il Matriciana in Rome; *pappardelle* with hare *ragù* at Mariotti e Mugulone in Siena; veal stew in tomato sauce at Camillo in Florence. Dish after dish, antipasti, pastas, meat, and fish—but never desserts, which Italians still had little talent for—we always ate well and, in the 1980s, still inexpensively. Then we would come home to the United States and wonder all over again why the Italian food did not taste as good as in Italy, just as Alice Waters had wondered about the food in California. The answer was the same: American chefs lacked the same quality of ingredients they had everywhere in Italy.

In the early 1980s, that was about to change, but American chefs were by then in the throes of what they called New American Cuisine, broken out into New California Cuisine, New New England Cuisine, New Southwestern Cuisine, New Texas Cuisine, and so on. Each region had its own passel of young chefs from many backgrounds—Larry Forgione of An American Place in New York, Michael Roberts of Trumps in Los Angeles, Jimmy Schmidt of the London Chop House in Detroit, Jasper White of Restaurant Jasper in Boston, Barbara Tropp of China Moon in San Francisco, Stephan Pyles of Routh Street Café in Dallas, and many others—all of them media savvy, all of them promoting the quality of local ingredients, from littleneck clams and fiddlehead ferns to heirloom tomatoes and sand dabs and blue crabs. Symposiums were held among food writers and chefs to determine just what constituted American cuisine, which had evolved from so many immigrant roots.

These New American chefs had respect for but showed no fealty to the strictures of French classicism, international cuisine, or even regional cooking—unless it was American. By the 1980s, Italy's young chefs in the United States realized this but lacked the persuasive power of Julia Child or Alice Waters or Craig Claiborne to demonstrate what strides had been made in Italian cuisine.

The Italian Americans needed a spokesman, a Savonarola, really, someone who could both fire up the faithful and expose the corruptors. He needed to be on good terms with the media, speak excellent English, and have the experience to put things into perspective. The man who took on the job, more or less singlehandedly, was Tony May, who, when we last heard of him, was working as a waiter at the Colony in New York.

May left that moribund restaurant to go off on his own—to great success, first opening more or less conventional Italian restaurants, then taking over the spectacular art deco masterpiece the Rainbow Room atop Rockefeller Center in 1974. The restaurant had opened in 1934 as the swankiest of New York dinner and dance clubs, an aerie above the city, with a 360-degree panorama. It endured through the next four decades as a Continental restaurant and banquet facility, a style May maintained upon taking ownership, but he also introduced a series of "Italian Fortnights," for which he brought some of the best chefs working in Italy at the time to show off how Italian cuisine had gone far beyond the clichés of Italian-American food.

A fierce crusader for authentic Italian food, May became a founder and president of a nonprofit association called the Gruppo Ristoratori Italiani (GRI) in 1979 to foster "authentic Italian cuisine and enhancing its image through education" and to provide "a constant flow of information about Italian cuisine to member restaurants, US press, culinary schools, importers, distributors and general consumers with the intent to achieve a better understanding of Italian food and wine in North America."[6] As Lucio Caputo had done with the wine media, May invited the food and wine media to join Italian restaurateurs from the United States on trips to a different region of Italy each year, visiting both the *nuova cucina ristoranti* and the *trattorie* and touring prosciutto makers, dairies, and fisheries, where everyone could be exposed to the true flavors and culinary concepts of modern Italy.

May also brought together an array of Italian and American food writers to a three-day 1983 GRI convention in New York titled "The Presence of Italian Cuisine in the World Today, Particularly in the United States." He knew very well that the subject would be controversial on all sides; it would force issues that had rarely been touched on and lay the basis for discussions of the issues for years to come.

May cordially welcomed everyone then said, "We want to divert our attention from pizza to white truffles, from spaghetti and meatballs to *pappardelle alla lepre,* from inexpensive table wines to Brunello di Montalcino." He also said, "It has taken a long time for Italians to learn how to live together, let alone eat together. We still can't get together on who should govern us; we have changed forty different prime ministers since World War II!" He went on to say that a similar convention in Milan the year before yielded little agreement and nothing of substance. "But believe me," he said, "did you ever see thirty people argue!"[7] The battle was quickly joined in New York.

Food and wine writer Anthony Dias Blue drew first blood, maintaining that "in this country, Italian food does not have cachet. In this country, French food is glorified, it's spoken of with awe. And most of the awe that people who eat French food can muster comes when the bill is presented at the end of the French meals. . . . It's very hard to cook a national cuisine, a cuisine with as much character as Italian cuisine, if you have not grown up in a home where that cuisine is served."

Los Angeles restaurateur Mauro Vincenti moaned about how difficult it was to open a great, authentic Italian restaurant in America, insisting that "most Italian *ristoratori* lose sleep trying to import the best possible items from Italy[.] To talk to us about truffles when we pay $400 a pound and when they arrive, fifty percent must be thrown away because no reliable freight service can guarantee delivery from Italy in two days? We buy French fish or black truffles because they arrive on time."

Gianluigi Morini, of San Domenico, explained that he had committed himself to creating a restaurant that was every bit as refined as a French restaurant, as in the days when Italian noblemen had a score of cooks in the kitchen, saying that his restaurant had 20 tables, 15 cooks, and 6 pastry makers. Sicilian-born Piero Selvaggio, whose restaurant Valentino in Santa Monica, California, was trying to refine Italian cuisine in the same way, sighed and said, "Mr. Morini is a great inspiration, but his type of restaurant could not survive in America, because the economics and the labor laws are very hard [and] would not allow us to staff twenty people in the kitchen of a fifty- or sixty-seat restaurant."

The next day, the highly respected Italian food authority Vincenzo Buonassisi spoke of the postwar "gross consumer morality" that stifled creativity in Italian food through the 1950s. "For some time following World War II, Italians confused noble cuisine with French cuisine. This was the mentality of a nation defeated in war." In the late 1950s, he said, Italians "began to rediscover the cuisine of their grandmothers, of the peasant women, the cuisine of our past heritage," New creativity followed in the 1960s, on all fronts—fashion, cars, moviemaking. He also insisted that "we are witnessing the birth, or a rebirth, of a healthier, more 'natural' cuisine that makes ample use of the foods commonly available in the Mediterranean area, the grains, the vegetables, the natural vegetable oils"—all ideas that would later be developed into what was called the Mediterranean diet.

Shaking his head, Buonassisi smiled and said, "In Italy there is no longer such a thing as truly autonomous regional cuisines. This is a romantic American notion, not a modern reality. In the modern Italy that actually exists, regional cooking is traveling from region to region."

On the third day, Piero Antolini, food and travel journalist and director of *Il Cuoco,* the official magazine of the Italian Federation of Cooks, acknowledged that Italian-American food was better known abroad than Italian food, but he offered a balm to those Italian-American restaurateurs who had created their own cuisine, saying, "This Italian cuisine for export may have done damage to our culinary image; on the other hand, this probably could not have been avoided. The early Italian immigrants were in no position to behave differently."

Next came the restaurant critic for *Gourmet* magazine, Jay Jacobs, who blasted away, saying, "I find, generally speaking, I don't even have to look at a menu when I go out to most Italian restaurants; I know what's going to be on every single one of them. . . . The typical Italian restaurateur is overly concerned with his own conception of what will and what will not appeal to American tastes and what will and won't sell."

Although the seminars were not widely reported on, they had set a tone, if not an agenda, for what needed to be done by the restaurateurs and media. May closed by saying that the Italian character was given to obeisance and eagerness to please, a posture that had allowed them to survive millennia of invasion and occupation. But there was a new post-war self-respect among Italians and a worldwide respect for what Italians could achieve, and with the increasing availability of better ingredients and well-trained cooks, they were ready to fight for their reputation, not loudly but with *sprezzatura*—the Italian art of concealed effort.

## EGG-FILLED RAVIOLI WITH TRUFFLES

As an example of both the *alta cucina* and *nuova cucina* movements of the 1980s, this sumptuous dish showered with white truffles in which a raviolo contains an uncooked egg whose yolk flows onto the plate was the creation of San Domenico restaurant in Imola, Italy, made even more fashionable at a branch of the restaurant in New York City.

*Fresh pasta dough, purchased at a good Italian pasta store*
*1/2 cup cooked spinach*
*1/2 cup ricotta cheese*
*2/3 cup freshly grated Parmigiano-Reggiano cheese*
*5 large eggs*
*Pinch of freshly grated nutmeg*
*7 tablespoons unsalted butter*
*2 ounces white truffles*

1. Cut eight 5- to 6-inch circles from the pasta dough, using a cookie cutter or a knife.
2. Chop the spinach finely; combine the spinach with the ricotta, half the Parmigiano-Reggiano, and 1 of the eggs. Season with the nutmeg and salt and white pepper to taste.
3. Place 4 rounds of the pasta dough on 4 sheets of wax paper. Divide the ricotta-spinach mixture among the rounds.
4. One at a time, separate the yolks from the whites of the remaining 4 eggs. Make a slight indentation in each mound of the spinach mixture, and carefully place 1 egg yolk and 1/2 of its white in the indentation. Season with salt and pepper.
5. Brush the edges of the pasta rounds with a little cold water, cover with the remaining 4 pasta rounds, and press together to seal.
6. Bring a large pot of water to a boil. Add 2 heaping teaspoons salt, and carefully ease the ravioli into the water. Cook for 2 minutes. While the ravioli are cooking, melt the butter in a saucepan over high heat and cook just until the butter takes on a light brown color.
7. Drain the ravioli and place them on 4 individual heated plates. Sprinkle with the shaved white truffles, if using, and the remaining Parmigiano-Reggiano. Then pour the browned butter over the ravioli, and serve.

Serves 4.

# Chapter 13

# A New Respect

In 1980, when *Playboy* magazine, then with a circulation of five million readers, did a poll of food critics and restaurateurs to rank the "25 Best Restaurants in America," it came as no surprise that 15 of them were French and most of the rest French-Continental. The top vote-getter was New York's Lutèce, as classically French as a restaurant could possibly be, with a menu that changed little. This description also fit the other award-winning French restaurants around America, from Le Bec Fin in Philadelphia and Le Perroquet in Chicago to Le Lion d'Or in D.C. and Maisonette in Cincinnati. Only one Italian restaurant—Trattoria da Alfredo in New York's Greenwich Village—made *Playboy*'s list, at number 17.

Four years later, *Playboy* asked me to conduct the same survey, but I insisted that this time only food writers be asked to vote; in the previous survey, a passel of French restaurateurs, simply voted for their friends, who were almost all French. This time, Lutèce came in first again, along with 14 French restaurants of various styles, including a few doing *la nouvelle cuisine*. But remarkably, this time six Italian restaurants made the list—Parioli Romanissimo, Il Nido, and Felidia in New York; Valentino in Santa Monica; and two in Los Angeles: one, the art deco extravaganza called Rex il Ristorante; the other, an upgraded pizzeria owned by a 35-year-old Austrian, born Wolfgang Johannes Topfschnig, who later changed his name to the sprightlier Wolfgang Puck.

After the results came in, it was my good fortune to dine at *Playboy*'s expense at all of the restaurants before writing the story. Many I already knew, including several of the superb French winners. I was also a devotee of the Italian restaurants, which I certainly ranked as equal to any of the French. It was good to go back to them all and see what was cooking.

Parioli Romanissimo, on New York's Upper East Side, was among the most ex-pensive—dinner could easily run $75 per person. It was run by Rome-born Rubrio Rossi, who was noted for serving the finest ingredients he could possibly obtain, including 40 or more cheeses, which were offered each night on a cart. There was lamb carpaccio with a red pepper puree and ravioli with *funghi porcini* in a cream sauce; a *tamarillo* salad one night, and on another, the Venetian dish *vitello tonnato* (veal with tuna sauce); lusty *cotechino* pork sausage in a rich black truffle sauce; and for dessert there might be a Campanian chocolate-chestnut torte.

It was a kind of Italian food that was rare anywhere, especially in New York, winning the *Times*'s first four-star review for an Italian restaurant (the only one for the next 36 years), ironically from the *Times*'s art critic, John Canaday. His successor, Mimi Sheraton, later demoted it to two stars, saying Parioli Romanis-simo was "on a par with half a dozen Italian restaurants in town."[1] When it relo-cated to an elegant Fifth Avenue townhouse, the paper's next critic, Bryan Miller, kept it at two stars, calling it "an urbane setting, [with] pampering service and Italian fare that is generally pleasing but hardly provocative."[2]

Il Nido, Adi Giovanetti's Tuscan-style *ristorante,* had been awarded three *Times* stars in the 1970s as the paragon of the New York–style Northern Italian cuisine then dominant in the city. It was a surprise, then, that Felidia made the *Playboy* list, because its focus was the wholly unfamiliar region of Istria, on the Yugoslavian border. Lidia Matticchio Bastianich, who owned the restaurant with her husband, Felice, was born in Istria, a peninsula jutting out from Trieste into the Adriatic. The area was controlled by various countries during its history, including Yugoslavia, which took control after the World War II. The result was the removal or emigra-tion of three hundred thousand Italians suddenly caught behind the Iron Curtain.

With the help of Catholic charities, the Matticchio family was placed in a refugee camp in Trieste. Two years later, they moved to New York, where Lidia met and married Felice Bastianich, a waiter at Romeo Salta. They were able to open two successful Italian-American restaurants in Queens, where Lidia began serv-ing a few of her grandmother's Istrian dishes, which brought her to the media's attention. Eventually, in 1981, the Bastianiches opened Felidia, on East 58th Street, a stretch already teeming with Northern Italian *ristoranti*. But Felidia was immediately distinguished from the rest by offering more Istrian-style dishes and by using ingredients native to the region.

"By then, we were just starting to get the kind of ingredients that made all the difference in our cooking," she said. "So I could reproduce the taste of my grand-mother's food and educate my guests about it; it was really all I knew beyond Italian-American food. After a while I traveled extensively throughout Italy and discovered how diverse Italian cuisine was, and I incorporated what I learned into my cookbooks."[3] Felidia was immensely popular, and Lidia herself was a trove of information for the media. Still, it took a decade before the *Times* would move Felidia from one- to two- to three-star status.

Like others on the *Playboy* list, Valentino was a very personalized, signature restaurant of a fervent crusader for fine Italian food. Piero Selvaggio, born in Sicily and raised in a boarding school, had his first restaurant experience at a truck stop. Plus, he admitted, "My mother was a mediocre cook."[4] Valentino emi-grated to the United States to earn a college degree in Romance languages at UCLA. He supported himself by working in local Los Angeles restaurants and found that he was a natural restaurateur: young, passionate, handsome, and full of Italian charm.

Together with Venetian chef Gianni Paoletti, Selvaggio opened Valentino in 1972, "on a very thin shoestring," as a fairly typical high-end Italian-American restaurant of its day, with black booths and paintings of cavorting Italian peas-ants.[5] He was 27 years old, had little actual background in the business, and knew little about Italian gastronomy north of Sicily.

That December, *Los Angeles Times* restaurant critic Lois Dwan included Valentino in a column on three wonderful restaurants for the Christmas holi-days, and overnight the restaurant was packed, serving more than a hundred cus-tomers. "We couldn't handle that many customers," he recalled. "We had no idea what to do. All we *did* know was that we were hot. Los Angeles at that time didn't have a good trattoria, a middle-of-the-road place where people could eat good food and feel comfortable. The movie business people weren't very sophisticated in their tastes, either. So we were it. Valentino was like a circus."[6] Selvaggio was certainly aware, however, that the food at Valentino was neither distinctive nor authentic, staying close to clichés of the day—baked macaroni, sea bass *piccante,* stuffed clams Naples style, and the ubiquitous Cobb salad. "I could kiss ladies' hands, and I was charming and warm, but it was a façade. Behind it was empti-ness: no real knowledge of food, wine, or business. . . . We called our food *Con-tinental Cuisine* because 'made in Italy' was not yet popular, and Italian food did not yet have a college degree. During those first years, we realized how much we needed to increase our education in food. . . . We learned the hard way. We survived the trends, the dark nights, and the bad times."[7]

In an effort to learn more, Selvaggio accepted the invitation of Pino Khail, director of *Civiltà del Bere,* to dine at some of the best new restaurants in Italy. "He took me to Giannino in Milan," recalls Selvaggio, "and I ate the most wonderful food—fettuccine with fresh porcini, a true *cotolette alla Milanese,* and carpaccio with white truffles—I didn't even know what they were, and they were served raw! After dinner, Khail said to me, 'You know what these dishes all have in common? They were all made with three ingredients of perfect quality and prepared in perfect balance.' After that I went home to Santa Monica, and the smell of rancid parmesan cheese in my kitchen at Valentino sent me running from my own restaurant."[8]

Selvaggio vowed he would try to replicate the flavors and the three-ingredient rule he had learned in Milan, but not until the late 1970s was he able to obtain quality Italian ingredients. When fine extra virgin olive oil, Prosciutto di Parma, fresh *porcini,* and white truffles did become available, Selvaggio was among the first to introduce them to his menus at Valentino. Soon he was offering his guests focaccia with sausage and zucchini flowers and smoked *scamorza* cheese; fresh tuna with cannellini beans; pasta with cuttlefish and calamari; *involtini* of duckling with caramelized onions, raisins, and a Barolo wine reduction; and a mousse of sun-dried tomatoes, pesto, and spinach.

Selvaggio, along with his new chef, Pino Pasqualato (and later, Luciano Pellegrini), realized that making the most of the increasingly high quality of California products and Pacific seafood could set him further apart from his competition and place him at the vanguard of Southern California cuisine. Thus, he incorporated corn into risotto cooked in red wine; he used shiitake mushrooms rather than Parisian; he served his guests sand dabs, abalone, and Pacific crab. He also built one of the world's finest wine cellars, the range of which included the best bottlings out of Italy, the finest crus of France, and the best wines made in California. The list spanned 27 pages.

By the time Valentino made the *Playboy* list in 1984, it was widely recognized as not just at the vanguard of Italian cuisine *and* California cuisine but as one of the world's most creative restaurants. Selvaggio had wiped the slate clean and challenged other restaurateurs to do the same. By 1980, *Gourmet* magazine's Caroline Bates could write, "With a menu that ranges more imaginatively than ever over the map of Italy and a phenomenal cellar of wines from vineyards all over the world, Valentino has truly come of age."[9] As the restaurant's cuisine evolved to greater heights, Lois Dwan would write in 1986, "Valentino is always a new experience. We take notes and never finish. We are never bored. Owner Piero Selvaggio is one of the few tuned to and in step with what is happening in Italy. Evolution, *aromi* (meaning aromatic), and, I think, love are the key words."[10]

Rex il Ristorante was by far the most extravagant and theatrical of the *Playboy* winners, set in downtown Los Angeles within the historic Oviatt Building, a former art deco haberdashery; inside, with its vast, two-story space, done with 30-foot colonnades, gilding, and Lalique sconces, it did indeed resemble an Italian liner of the *Rex* era. The captain of it all was an irresistible force, a former Cinecittà film producer-cinematographer named Mauro Vincenti, who looked like a Roman version of the rotund American comedian Jackie Gleason. Vincenti's flourishes began with his *basso profondo* voice, thick black eyebrows, and flailing hand gestures that would continue throughout an evening that could feel as much like a scene in a movie by Fellini (with whom Vincenti had worked) as a gastro-lecture on what the guests did not know, needed to know, and needed to forget about Italian food forever.

To say Vincenti was an iconoclast was to award him faint praise. He refused to have a freezer in the kitchen because he wanted everything to be fresh every day. He loved breaking all the rules except that of his own good taste. Price was no object; money—investors' money—was there to be spent; linens and glassware were to be handcrafted. The china was by Ginori; the Murano wineglasses were stemless, very thin, with six facets, the most elegant and expensive pizzeria tumblers ever created. Rex carried Champagne, but Vincenti also would insist you try a great sparkling wine from Franciacorta, along with hundreds of other *vini italiani* no one else carried or could get.

The food was always a revelation—true *scampi* dotted with beluga caviar; "Venus's bellybuttons" (*tortellini* with asparagus, truffles, and sliced vegetables); *triglie,* red mullet with orange slices; a carpaccio of mushrooms, and *tortelli* with chicken livers. The $20 main courses and six-course dinner at $55 were extravagant for an Italian restaurant at that time, but no one could say no to Mauro's entreaties to taste this and try a morsel of that. He won over the media by force of personality, charisma, intelligence, and a touch of the commedia dell'arte. Lois Dwan was obviously smitten by the effusions, writing boldly in 1986, "There is no other restaurant quite like it anyplace, not even in Italy whence the excitement emanates, but must be searched for in little towns between the big cities. . . . That Italian food is not the same in Los Angeles as it is in Italy is a frequent

lament. True, of course, and for many reasons, beginning with a serious difference of ingredients; ending, perhaps, with love."[11]

And then there was a new restaurant called Spago, a name that was Italian for
"string," but that really meant nothing at all; Wolfgang Puck just liked the sound
of it.

Puck had earned a considerable reputation as chef at Ma Maison, a French restaurant set in a ramshackle bungalow with Astroturf floor coverings, but so reeking
of L.A. cool that it had an unlisted phone number. Puck's employer, Patrick
Terrail, a tall, handsome Frenchman with thick black eyebrows who wore boldly
striped suits, a red carnation, and clogs, courted Hollywood movie society the
way Sirio Maccioni of Le Cirque courted New York high society, and Ma Maison
counted among its demanding regulars Orson Welles, Elizabeth Taylor, Cary
Grant, Jack Lemmon, Johnny Carson, and Frank Sinatra.

Puck, who had been trained in resolutely classic French restaurants such as
L'Oustau de Baumanière in Provence and Maxim's in Paris, brought to Ma Maison an exceptionally rich cuisine, with plenty of bloody-rare foie gras, "duck two
ways," and the fussy signature dish, whole fish *en croûte* stuffed with a rich mous-
seline. When he suggested that they might even have some fun serving pizzas,
Terrail categorically refused.

Though he was raised in the tradition of French chefs who never even peeked
out of their kitchens, Puck took on his own dining room persona, sporting a red
baseball cap rather than the traditional tall white toque, and he developed his
own relationships with Ma Maison's stellar clientele, many of whom would tell
him, "If you ever decide to open your own place, call me."

When Puck did obtain backing to open his own place, in 1982, the result was
180 degrees away from the lavish French cuisine of Ma Maison and other top
L.A. restaurants. He and his wife, Barbara Lazaroff, a pre-med student, took over
an old Armenian restaurant set above Sunset Strip, decked it out like a white-
washed barn—he originally planned on red-checkered tablecloths but switched
to white—filled it with huge displays of flowers and dramatic lighting, and fired
up the mesquite-wood grill. Andreas Vollenweider's "Caverna Magica" played in
the background. He had even installed a pizza oven, having seen one at Alice
Waters's café upstairs from Chez Panisse.

Spago's location, in less-than-chic West Hollywood, was certainly not a propitious setting for an important restaurant, but then Puck had never dreamed it would be. Still, the reputation preceding him from Ma Maison brought Puck immediate celebrity attention: The first day, two hundred people came through the door; soon, guests such as Kirk Douglas, Warren Beatty, Jack Nicholson, and Sidney Poitier were coming in to eat and to see "Wolf." Before long, Spago was the most sought-out restaurant in Los Angeles. As Ma Maison faded and died, Spago thrived. Patrick Terrail sniffed that Spago was a step backward for Los Angeles restaurants.

When I arrived at Spago that spring of 1984, I was made well aware that I was not among Spago's most important customers. Rows of paparazzi stood outside the restaurant to snap those Hollywood stars who flocked to the place nightly. Inside the door, I was met, reluctantly, by the withering gaze of the maître d', a slender Frenchman who dressed in a Gallic rendition of 1950s Ricky Nelson style and who had a very deep voice without a tinge of affability in it for those he did not know and air kiss personally.

He seemed wholly oblivious to me, dressed in an East Coast suit and tie, and then had to acknowledge with a sigh that, yes, I did indeed have a reservation. The maître d' shunted me and my wife off to a bench seat out of the way, along with others who looked completely crestfallen at being seated there, knowing they would soon be pitchforked into the Siberia of the rear dining room.

But then Puck's wife, Barbara, blew into view—a whirlwind of flailing arms, bejeweled fingers, and wide, dark-rimmed eyes, with a jet black hair cascading down the back of what looked like an extravagant kimono. She looked like a cross between Isadora Duncan and Cher.

"Are you John?" she asked, with a big smile.

I nodded sheepishly that I was, having phoned her in advance because I wanted to interview her and Puck about the Spago phenomenon. She then grabbed my wife and me by the arms and, with all the gaiety of Loretta Young seating dinner guests, gave us an "A" table a yard or two from the open kitchen, where Puck was cooking.

"You want Wolf just to send things out to try?" she asked.

"Sure," I said, "that would be great."

What came out first was one of Puck's pizzas—a textbook-perfect *pizza alla margherita,* with a crust that was thin but not *too* thin, with charred bubbles of dough that had been in a seven-hundred-degree oven for mere minutes, the tomato and mozzarella oozing together in ideal harmony, with a smoky, wheaty aroma that put me in mind of the best pizzas I had ever had in Naples and New York. Never had I seen one served on a Villeroy & Boch plate.

Puck himself, gap-toothed and stocky, speaking in an Austrian accent larded with L.A. slang, brought out a second pizza, this one topped with smoked salmon, golden caviar, sour cream, and chives. "Dis is vat I call my Jewish pizza," he said with, well, puckish glee. "I haf a lot of customers who are Jewish, you know, so I make dis for fun. Now it's become my number vun best seller."

Spago served terrific food—much more Italian and Mediterranean than French, and nothing like the haute cuisine at Ma Maison—and the ingredients Puck used were those that the so-called New California Cuisine chefs were hyping in the media: Sonoma baby lamb, Chino Farms tomatoes, Laurel Chenel goat's cheese—all the best that money could buy back in 1982. Puck's freshly made pastas were sumptuous, not the same old tomato-sauced clichés but imaginative dishes that took advantage of all those fine ingredients, along with newly imported Italian extra virgin olive oil, balsamic vinegar, and Parmigiano-Reggiano. And the wine list had plenty of Italian bottlings along with the best new California labels.

"You mind if I sit down a liddle?" asked Puck, joined by Barbara, who had just as much to say but was constantly jumping up to greet new guests.

Puck told me he would try anything to stay exciting. "I never considered myself a trendsetter," he said. "I just get bored easily." He dismissed critics who said his food veered too far from traditional restaurant fare. "I'd rather make a great pizza than make some dish vit canned truffles."

Upon hearing that shrugged, offhanded remark, I realized that Spago was already having repercussions in American food: The fact that an Austrian chef with a Jewish-American wife could turn pizza—long regarded as a low-class item that Italian restaurateurs should distance themselves from—into the chic food of the moment, and in so doing shower celebrity glamour onto the whole idea of simple, good Italian food, was the beginning of a sea change in world gastronomy.

All of a sudden, with the benediction of Alice Waters and the chutzpah of Wolfgang Puck, the food that Italian restaurateurs had thought they had put behind them—pizza—was threatening to come back with a glitzy vengeance.

And no one would ever take Italian food for granted again.

# Chapter 14

# No More Excuses

It is no coincidence that Italian food improved everywhere at the same time FedEx began service to Europe in 1984. Just as the jet plane had transformed Italy's tourist industry in the 1960s, so, too, did Federal Express's jets radically improve the availability of ingredients, food, and wine products. Its main competitor, DHL, out of San Francisco, concentrated at first on Asian destinations, but by the mid-1980s, it, too, was servicing Europe and the Americas. Everything was now within reach—at a price.

All those Italian ingredients—meat, fish, and fowl included—once impossible to obtain were now within 24 hours' reach. A phone call to a market in Rome could produce beautiful radicchio from Treviso. A fax to Naples might mean Mediterranean fish would leave the seaport immediately and arrive in New York's fish markets the next day. A white truffle collector could call a restaurant in London or Los Angeles, Houston or Tokyo, and have his product showered over fettuccine the following evening. Spoilage, damage, and rot were suddenly things of the past, so the excuses given at the 1983 GRI convention as to why Italian food could never taste as it does in Italy were dashed. Now the restaurateurs and chefs had to show they could cook as well as the Italians themselves.

By the mid-1980s, more and more Italian products were being shipped around the world than ever before, though, of course, not all of them required transport on an expensive overnight flight. By the same token, Italians were now importing ingredients from the rest of the world that had previously been denied, which affected the direction high-end Italian food would take. Restaurateurs could now get fresh foie gras from France's Périgord region and the best Russian and Iranian caviar.

Italy began shipping its most familiar products abroad in new forms. *Artigianale* (artisanal) pastas easily brought twice the price of regular dry pasta. Whereas, since the early 1970s, Americans had had access to only one kind of Italian rice, *arborio,* suddenly they had a choice of *vialone nano, Sant'Andrea, Roma, Europa,* and *canaroli.* The real Parmigiano-Reggiano, with its distinctive official stamp branded into the rind, replaced Reggianito coming out of Argentina.

For decades, Italian prosciutto was banned for export to the United States by the Department of Agriculture, as were most other uncanned, uncooked ham products, ostensibly to protect American livestock from trichinosis and hoof-and-mouth disease but primarily to protect U.S. pork producers from competition. A few American companies had long been producing prosciutto-style hams and enjoyed a legal advantage until 1989, when, after intense lobbying, Prosciutto di Parma and Prosciutto di San Daniele were allowed into the country. (Other hams available throughout Europe were still banned in the United States.) Eventually, in 2000, the USDA would also allow Italian *mortadella,* a cooked salami product, to come in, as well as *Speck,* the dried smoky bacon from Alto Adige, and other dried sausages such as *soppressata* and *pancetta,* while others, like *cotechino* and *zampone* continued to be banned.

Certainly the greatest boon to cooks everywhere was the availability of fine Italian olive oil, starting in the 1970s. Before then, olive oil was certainly imported, usually in one-gallon tin cans, but most was of mediocre or inferior quality, often made from pomace (the olive solids after pressing) or mixed with other vegetable oils. The cooking fat of classic cuisine and even everyday cooking was butter, butter, and more butter: The 1964 edition of the bestselling American cookbook *The Joy of Cooking* mentions olive oil only to explain why it may become cloudy in the bottle. Julia Child's *The French Chef Cookbook,* published in 1968, did not waste a word on olive oil.

Although Italy produced one-third of the world's olive oil, many bottles and cans carried the label "packaged in Italy," which did not necessarily mean the oil was made there; cheap Greek and Spanish oils were often mixed in or used instead. No wonder, then, that Marcella Hazan wrote in her 1973 *Classic Italian Cook Book,* "Unlike peanut oil or other vegetable oils, olive oil has a decided taste, which should not be used indiscriminately. The recipes in this book reflect the current trend of Italian cooking by using olive oil only where its presence is essential."[1]

Prior to the 1970s, few Americans—and few Italians—had ever heard of virgin olive oil and extra virgin olive oil, terms created by the International Olive Oil

Council, based in Madrid. While virgin olive oil had a wholesome ring to it and was clearly superior to the high-volume commercial brands, it was really a very basic oil made to conform to the council's directives regarding acidity, provenance, and refining. Italian authorities further narrowed the definition of what constitutes a quality oil using the designations DOP (*Denominazione di Origine Protetta*) and IGP (*Indicazione Geografica Protetta*).

Much of the reason olive oil became so popular in Europe and the United States was that studies suggested it had health benefits, in contrast to the unhealthy aspects of cooking with butter or lard. The ideas promulgated by the counterculture of the 1960s and 1970s about healthful eating coincided perfectly with new evidence that the diet of the Mediterranean region was more sensible than the fat-rich, high-cholesterol diets of northern Europe and of America in particular.

By the middle of the 1980s, cookbooks were reflecting the changeover from butter to olive oil, so that by 1986, Hazan could write glowingly—as part of a four-page section on the subject—in *Marcella's Italian Kitchen,* "No other ingredient is so critical [as olive oil] to the good taste of Italian cooking. I happen to like butter and I use it more liberally than many Italian cooks, but if I were commanded to eliminate either butter or olive oil from my kitchen, it's butter I would drop."[2]

The real astonishment about olive oil's soaring popularity in the mid-1980s was that French master chefs began using it—albeit French olive oil, at first—with abandon. Before then, to peruse a book such as *Great Chefs of France* (1978), by Anthony Blake and Quentin Crewe, which focused on the up-and-coming *nouvelle cuisiniers* of the late 1970s, was to come away thinking that olive oil was some exotic ingredient to be pulled from the larder only in exceptional circumstances, like making a dish from the French Riviera. Even in the cooking of Roger Vergé olive oil was rarely used, despite the fact that his restaurant Moulin de Mougins was located in the heart of Provence, where the use of olive oil is widespread.

Yet by the 1990s, French cuisine—especially haute cuisine—was awash in olive oil, so that in 1998, three-Michelin-star chef Alain Ducasse would write that olive oil was "the essence of the cooking," at the restaurant Louis XV, in Monaco's Hôtel de Paris in Monaco, where he became chef in 1987.[3] There he even developed a technique in which he set a bottle of extra virgin olive oil into an ice bucket filled with water and froze it, later using the cold oil to finish plates with a final drizzle. He explained, "The ice makes the oil thick and viscous so that it keeps form on the plate."[4] For his French colleagues, such admissions and benedictions were countenance to do the same. Almost sheepishly but knowing quality when he tasted it, Paul Bocuse told his friend Sirio Maccioni, "In my kitchen we have always cooked with butter, butter, butter; now it's olive oil, olive oil, olive oil—and most of it comes from Tuscany!"[5]

By the 1990s, however, extra virgin olive oil and other Italian products then entering the world markets needed no blessing from the French. The foodies of America and Great Britain had already adapted Italian foods—as well as Spanish, Greek, Middle Eastern, African, and Asian foods—to modern recipes. A magazine such as *Food & Wine,* founded by Michael and Ariane Batterberry in 1978 and bankrolled by the American Express credit card company, was just as likely to run an article on the varieties of prosciutto as it was on the types of semolina used in Tunisian couscous. *Gourmet* magazine was covering Northern Italian cheeses as well as Greek feta and kasseri. Highly authoritative cookbooks, written by young American and British writers who immersed themselves in foreign food cultures, began appearing with regularity, from Claudia Roden's *Mediterranean Cookery* (1987) and Joyce Goldstein's *The Mediterranean Kitchen* (1989) to Mary Laird Hamady's *Lebanese Mountain Cookery* (1987) and Diane Kochilas's *The Food and Wine of Greece* (1990).

The most important book of the era on Italian food was *The Fine Art of Italian Cooking* (1977), by Tuscan cooking teacher Giuliano Bugialli, whose comprehensive knowledge of Italian food history lent a great deal of weight to his subject; the title alone seemed to justify a new look at Italian food. Short and wiry, with a full beard and a *consigliere*'s grin, Bugialli was as passionate as he was professorial, insisting that his was not a book of Mama's recipes or a collection of trattoria favorites. "The problem arises when *trattorie* attempt to become *ristoranti*," he wrote, "and they decide to add a touch of the 'continental.' Or what they think is French cooking. Then they cease to be honest."[6] These he dismissed, drawing instead on the cuisine of "certain old Italian families,"[7] by which he meant, as did his hero Pellegrino Artusi, Tuscan cuisine.

Twelve years later, in the preface to a second edition, Bugialli was able to counter those critics who called him a Tuscan chauvinist by showing how Tuscan cuisine had triumphed over Continental and Italian-American cuisine. Gloating a bit, he wrote, "I hope you can pardon my satisfaction for the role that this book played in that evolution." By then—1989—he could write matter-of-factly about olive oil, detailing its components, its regional differences, *and* the fact that "this delicious oil is now considered to be extremely healthy."[8]

This triumph of Italian cuisine in America coincided with a proliferation of the ingredients that made it possible, the demand for which grew as the cuisine became more and more popular. Little by little, these Italian grocers brought in more cheeses from more regions—many of them pasteurized under U.S. law: goat's milk *robiola*, Piedmontese Taleggio, Gorgonzola *dolce* that was much milder and less salty than American versions, and creamy *mozzarella di bufala*, made from water buffalo's milk.

As more people began to learn about the products, more wanted to try them. *Aceto balsamico* (balsamic vinegar) was largely unknown outside of Modena—where it was so cherished that tiny vials of it were given as Christmas presents to relatives—until San Francisco's Chuck Williams (of the Williams-Sonoma kitchenware and foods empire) began selling it in his Beverly Hills store in 1973. The vinegar had a small success among well-heeled customers, for it was very expensive and a commodity people had to be coaxed to try.

Five years later, Giorgio DeLuca, the partner of Joel Dean at the upscale grocery Dean & DeLuca in New York's downtown SoHo district, took an order for 150 cases of lower-grade *balsamico* and called the *New York Times* to see if they would run a story on the novelty. It turned out to be a four-column story, which noted that the vinegar was so intense in flavor that only a drop or two was required, and that it was good for the diet-conscious consumer. The day the story appeared, Dean & DeLuca's phone was ringing off the hook with people desperate to buy a product they had never even heard of before that morning.

The irony was that Dean was against focusing solely on Italian products in their store, but soon, Italian exporters, food companies, and wineries were begging to get their products into the store. By the end of the 1970s, *aceto balsamico,* almost always in its inexpensive, commercial form, had become a requisite in every foodie kitchen and every Italian restaurant. Prior to that time, even Bugialli's and Hazan's cookbooks ignored it, though Hazan would spend more than a page in her 1986 cookbook extolling its virtues.

It is well worth noticing that Dean & DeLuca, along with other well-established New York Italian grocers like Balducci's, were located in downtown Manhattan, near the Italian neighborhoods. Balducci's was founded in Brooklyn in 1917 by a family from Bari. It relocated to Greenwich Village in 1947, and then expanded to larger quarters in 1970. (As too often happens, a family feud forced Grace Balducci to open her own store uptown, called Grace's Marketplace.) By the 1980s, Balducci's was regarded as the finest market of its kind, comparable in scope and offerings to the famous Peck in Milan, which opened in 1888.

At Balducci's, one could find scores of cured meats and hams, hundreds of cheeses, barrels of olives, dry-aged beef, fresh *porcini* mushrooms, and new items like purple-red *radicchio* and sun-dried tomatoes. Then there was "Mama's Corner," the prepared foods section of the store, with everything from an olive pie to osso buco and roast chicken and lasagna and baked ziti.

At Balducci's everything was expensive, but that was not the case on Arthur Avenue in the Bronx. There, the markets had been moribund for years, until the media began writing about this remarkable haven of Italian seafood markets, butchers, and grocers. Though you would not find every international item carried at Balducci's, you would find all the Italian and Italian-American favorites—more of them year by year as new products came in from Europe. As interest in the Bronx grew, the Italian-American Belmont neighborhood grew more profitable, cleaned up its gutters and aisles, and showcased the best that was becoming available, from stiff-as-a-board *baccalà* to soft shell crabs, from *culatello* salami to snow-white tripe, from jars of truffle butter to imported *gianduja* chocolate cream. And the purveyors, for the most part, not only let you try a sample of the prosciutto or cheese you were buying, they would give you a slice or morsel of something brand new to try and fall in love with—a piece of Italian bread with fresh ricotta and a drop of *aceto balsamico,* or a slab of grilled *mortadella* with mozzarella just out of the warm water.

Another legendary market was Corti Brothers, in Sacramento, California. There were similar places in other Little Italys around the United States, and, increasingly, in London, but few had as great a commitment to carrying the unusual or the novel ingredients as did Corti Brothers. The store was founded in 1947 by Frank and Gino Corti, who adopted the motto in their ads, "At Corti Brothers we just don't hand people products, we also talk food with them." Corti Brothers combined a butcher's shop with a wine store of extraordinary depth and breadth. They offered more than 200 beers, 250 pastas, and 70 olive oils. They also carried hundreds of Italian wines at a time when nearly every bottle needed to be explained to the customer—especially since they were in the wine country of Amador County, California, where they had helped the local wineries tremendously to get a foot in the door. The Cortis intended to change that, year by year, product by product, and their son Darrell took it upon himself to learn as much about every product as possible—not just where they came from but who grew them, tended them, bottled them, improved them. Darrell spoke several languages and was never one to mince words if he felt a product was overrated or overhyped. He would rage against a high-alcohol California wine as surely as he would about the lack of fat in an Italian sausage. A simple note in the company's newsletter on making cooked beans and serving them with tuna would turn into a dissertation on both ingredients, describing in detail their provenance, distinctiveness, and how to cook them—the beans were Caponi di Sartocchio (brought in from Pescadero, California) and the tuna from Consorcio Filetti di Bonito del Norte ("light pink-white color, firm, slender rectangles of outstanding flavor").[9] Corti Brothers had been beating the drum for Italian food and wine for decades, using their skills and connections to procure the very best of what were at the time very small amounts of products available to them. They were willing to pay for what they wanted and to tell their customers it was worth every penny. By the mid-1980s, their pioneering efforts had paid off not just in profits but in their contribution to a great educational shift in American gastronomy.

The same gears had been set in motion in London, the only non-Italian city outside of America that showed a real interest in modern Italian food. One of the crusaders was Antonio Carluccio, who arrived in London in 1975 as an Italian wine salesman. It was Carluccio who coined the word "Britalian" to describe the mélange of British—really, Continental—food and Italian dishes that littered menus upon his arrival in London. Having achieved some recognition as a cook, he was asked in 1981 by design tycoon Terence Conran to take over management of a ten-year-old restaurant called Neale Street in Covent Garden, which Carluccio later took over and where he cooked as close to his Italian ideal as possible. He also published the influential *Introduction to Italian Cooking* (1985) and appeared often on BBC's *Food and Drink Programme* and in his own series, *Antonio Carluccio's Italian Feasts*.

By the mid-1980s, Italians had proven they could produce beautiful sports cars, actors and actresses. Now they were producing beautiful food and wine, but it would take something far more glamorous to convince the world they were serious about achieving true greatness.

# Chapter 15

# Flash in the Pan

As ever, Lord Byron put it succinctly: "All human history attests that happiness for man,—the hungry sinner!—Since Eve ate apples, much depends on dinner."[1]

Of course, Adam's quick acquiescence to join her might have had more to do with her being stark naked than with the succulence of the forbidden fruit. In any case, they were the first people ever to be thrown out of an eating place for gluttony and being underdressed. Upon leaving the Garden of Eden, Adam and Eve were also the first to adopt matching wardrobes—two fig leaves, a brief fashion that gave way to the colored silks worn by Delilah when she drugged Samson's wine and by Salome when she performed her Dance of the Seven Veils as after-dinner entertainment for King Herod.

The connection between fashion, food, and sex—more or less in that order—is consistent in all civilizations, not least in ancient Rome and most assuredly in the Italian Renaissance, right up to the present day. By the 1950s the popular postwar Italian fashion for Capri pants, sandals, a blouse tied at the waist, gold jewelry, big sunglasses, and a scarf knotted behind the ears was made famous by women such as Sophia Lauren, Audrey Hepburn, and Jackie Kennedy. "Just like Chianti, Italy's fashions are becoming as well known as its table wines," wrote a reporter for *Life* magazine in 1952.[2] A few Italian fashion designers—Pucci and Gucci in particular—acquired worldwide reputations in the decade to follow, when *la dolce vita* was being absorbed into popular culture. As fashion loosened up in the 1960s, Italians were well poised to exploit their genius for color, cut, and cachet. Italian designers such as Missoni and Albini began holding their shows at the Pitti Palace, in Florence, while the Milan fashion shows "were like 'happenings' staged in a variety of venues, [so that] by the early 1970s, fashion magazines and newspapers in America focused much less on Roman couture and much more on ready-to-wear trends coming out of Milan."[3] The most important of the young Italian designers was Giorgio Armani, born in Piacenza, whose men's line featured aggressively bold shoulders that a Futurist could love, a slouchy roominess the modern athletic man could move in, and natural fabrics that wore like iron and barely wrinkled on an eight-hour flight to Europe. Armani's big breakthrough came when his clothes were chosen for the 1980 movie *American Gigolo,* the antihero of which is a Beverly Hills hustler named Julian Kaye (Richard Gere) who chooses his outfits each morning with a diligence and eye for color unfamiliar, even disquieting, to American men; of course, he dines with his clients at Perino's.

Two years later, Armani was on the cover of *Time* magazine. In the accompanying article, Pierre Berge, partner at France's Yves Saint Laurent company, was asked what impact he thought new Italian fashions were having. Except for pasta and opera, he sniffed, "the Italians can't be credited with anything."[4]

But by then, the Italians were already demolishing French fashion, especially couture, and the American media took full credit for the sea change. Editors at *Vogue* and *Harper's Bazaar* assigned the best young photographers to do fashion shoots on yachts off Capri, in piazzas in Florence, and in Rome's Trevi Fountain, mimicking the famous scene in *La Dolce Vita* when Anita Ekberg and Marcello Mastroianni cavort beneath the water spout. For retro-chic designers such as Dolce & Gabbana, photographers recreated the paparazzi's black-and-white flashbulb photos the 1950s and shot models straddling Vespas or driving Fiat 500s against a backdrop of Via Veneto cafés and al fresco trattorias, in front of open food markets. The layouts were aimed at a younger readership that had more designer jeans in their closets than couture gowns. *Newsweek* reported that the new Italian style was "for real people—albeit rich people—to wear to real places."[5]

And the places young, stylish people wanted to wear these new fashions were at more casual restaurants, which had by the mid-1980s become as much an entertainment as they were a night out. It was a simple equation: the woman who had just bought a Prada handbag wanted to show it off at a chic Italian restaurant, and vice versa—dinner at a chic Italian restaurant demanded she bring the Prada.

None of the Italian designers could have succeeded had it not been for the concomitant expansion of the women's movement in the 1970s. Literally wearing the pants, women entered the business world and paid their own clothing and restaurant bills. The more money and success they achieved, the less rigidity there was in their wardrobe. Women in business were now picking up the check, and they increasingly preferred to do it in an Italian restaurant where the owner showed none of the condescension entrenched at the traditional French restaurants where women in casual slacks were still not entirely welcome.

Before the mid-1980s, the arbiters of what constituted a fashionable restaurant were those who belonged to a clubbish minority of high society tycoons, and showbiz people who strutted to their tables wearing Chanel and YSL at the same French places, such as La Côte Basque in New York, Le Gavroche in London, and La Tour d'Argent in Paris. By the 1980s, such places had become passé, as casual bistros became more popular—hangouts such as Spago in Los Angeles, the Ivy in London, and downstairs at Fouquet's in Paris.

In the United States, the New American Cuisine movement was in full gallop and the French restaurants in full retreat as longtime institutions such as Le Chambertin, La Chansonette, and La Petite Marmite closed their doors. The growing food media industry expanded coverage of new restaurant hot spots where young celebrities from the film, art, and fashion worlds wanted to eat. Wine columnists proliferated—*HG* (formerly *House & Garden*) even hired Jay McInerny, who chronicled the decadent urban affluence of the 1980s in his novel *Bright Lights, Big City,* to write a column called "Uncorked."

In Italy, the restaurant landscape had not really evolved very much in the late 1970s and early 1980s beyond attempts by a handful of chefs to introduce *la nuova cucina.* More people than ever, though, were going out to eat. "It began with Sunday lunches, as of the 1970s," recalls Alessandro Grassi, a Florentine who works for several Italian style companies. "Before that, there really wasn't a weekend for most Italians. Sunday was the day to take off and relax, and eating out on Sundays was the real proof of a family's new status. During the week, the restaurants saw mostly the businessmen and tourists."[6]

When change came, it was not in the food or decor so much as the style of dining. This time period gave rise to those who came to be called the "fashionistas," a term coined by social chronicler Stephen Fried to describe "the army of models, photographers, designers, hair and makeup people, stylists and editors who toiled daily in the beauty trenches. It was a way of differentiating the traditional 'beautiful people' and their beautifying people."[7] Most of these innovations came from Milan, where the designers' shows were held twice a year. The Italians had so cunningly removed the starch from the fabrics, the petticoats from the dresses, and the drabness from men's suits, while providing softness, fluidity, color, and sexiness to it all, that it became irresistible. If Paris lingerie was naughty, La Perla's was downright sinful; if Savile Row suits fit impeccably, Armani's moved with the man.

The new casual Italian style needed desperately to be shown off in public, but not in the way fashion was so freakishly connected to the Champagne-and-cocaine-fueled glitz of the discos, where food was of absolutely *no* importance. The genteel Italianization of the late 1980s demanded a far more sophisticated approach to nightlife, to be played out in casual restaurants, in full view of one's friends and business colleagues. Nick Sullivan, now fashion editor at *Esquire* magazine, covered the shows in Paris and Milan in the 1980s, where he ate out for both lunch and dinner during the collections. "In Paris, only relatively few brands want to combine work and food," he says. "The French want to finish work then go eat with their friends. The Italians are more sociable because work *is* culturally social. Depending on how pretentious they were, they would take you a posh restaurant that signified global status, or take you to an unknown place with simple menu, which signified inside knowledge and expertise. In Italian culture, it's a signal of your in-ness that you get invited to places supposedly no one knows. This was a big joke, of course, as invariably there were usually ten other people you knew already there."[8]

A relaxed meal at home, cherished by Italians, was simply not possible during the fashion shows, so trattorias were more sensible and convenient than fine restaurants. Oddly enough, the Milan design houses seldom took their buyers and models to the *newest* trattoria on the block. One of the perennial favorites was Bagutta, which was opened in 1924 by Tuscan Alberto Pepori and became a central meeting place for journalists whose "fines" for arriving late went to fund a Bagutta Prize, a literary award for a chosen best author of the year, which, over eight decades, has included Italo Calvino, Silvio Negro, and Pier Angelo Soldini. Cartoons of regulars were drawn on menus and hung on the walls. So many artists and painters had their tables at Bagutta that in 1978 an exhibition of their work was held at Villa Simes-Contarini. Giorgio de Chirico was among them. "They were a noisy group who ate a lot and wanted to pay very little," wrote Orio Vergani of *Corriere d'Informazione,* in a 1956 obituary of Pepori's wife, Sora. "In that tiny place, Sora Pepori and her husband were used to serving the horsecab drivers whose stand was at San Babila, the flower-seller who after all these years is still there selling roses and gladiolas and peach blossoms in the shade of the old colonnade, and so they understood that that noisy band of little-known young men deserved affection and respect. . . . Before her eyes had passed half the history of Italian literature."[9] When a rumor got around that the restaurant might close, the media declared Bagutta "a center of outstanding cultural and historical interest." It was later given the benediction of the Ministero dei Beni Culturali.

After the war, Bagutta added to its cachet by drawing the new international movie stars, such as Gina Lollabrigida and Ingrid Bergman. By the 1980s, the fashion crowd arrived in droves, all to dine on Tuscan *casalinga* dishes such as beans and black cabbage, tripe *alla fiorentina,* and *fonduta* with truffles. During the June fashion collections, Bagutta's outdoor terrace tables became the toughest in town to get.

For seafood, the designers, buyers, and editors crowded the tables at Da Giacomo, owned by another Tuscan, Giacomo Bulleri, who hired decorator Renzo Mongiardino, the set director for Franco Zeffirelli's film *The Taming of the Shrew* and interior designer for Gianni Versace. The photographers would eat at Trattoria alle Le Langhe, near their studios.

But no restaurant was more important or more widely written of than Bice, yet another Tuscan trattoria, which was opened by Beatrice "Bice" Mungai in 1926 and has been at its present location on the Via Borgospesso within steps of the fashion houses and boutiques since 1939. Living above the restaurant until she died at the age of 97, Bice was known for her egalitarian approach to her guests, rich or not, famous or from nowhere, and she got along with everyone. Once, when Sophia Loren entered the room, everyone applauded.

During the collections, Bice was always packed. "Every table had someone I knew," says Nick Sullivan. "So one day my editor and I would have lunch with the designer from Gucci and the next day I'd be having lunch at another table with Burberry, while the Gucci people would be at the next table with another magazine editor."[10] Versace always sat in the room to the left of the entrance.

Long before Toulouse-Lautrec immortalized the Moulin Rouge in Paris, restaurants had benefited from the appearance of artists and models. In the 1980s, fashion models, not artists' models, became icons all their own, and their appearance at a restaurant would draw crowds eager to be reflected in the glow of women newly deemed "supermodels," along with their rock star boyfriends and flamboyant entourages. On a Saturday afternoon during the 1987 collections, young American designers Zoran, Michael Seroy, and Carlos Arias were dining at Bice, giddy to join a throng that included model Marisa Berenson, designer Carla Fendi, and Conte Camerama, a major stockholder in Fiat.

Such people had no time or desire to sit for three hours at an haute cuisine restaurant, preferring instead to wear their Dolce & Gabbana blue jeans, Armani T-shirts, and Ferragamo boots to a new hot spot where they would meet their photographer friends, colleagues, agents, and fashion editors. They still demanded French Champagne—in magnums—but they preferred to pick at a Caprese salad of mozzarella and arugula and a plate of fettuccine primavera rather than sup on *soupe à l'oignon* and roast pheasant. Never did the phrase *dolce far niente*—delicious inactivity—have so much meaning as when the fashionistas dined out in Milan's chic trattorias.

For these principal reasons—speed and hunger pains—fashion models would head to Paper Moon on Via Bagutta for its crisp, thin-crusted pizzas. The restaurant took its English name from the 1973 American movie of the same title, a favorite of owner Enrica Galligani, yet another Tuscan, who, with her husband Pio and daughter Stefania, opened in 1977 on Milan's main fashion street, the Via Montenapoleone, decorating its walls with photos of movie stars such as Clark Gable and Rita Hayworth from the Golden Age of Hollywood.

Like the jet set of the 1960s, celebrities and fashion people had their favorite places in Milan, Florence, Capri, Cannes, London, New York, and Los Angeles where they mingled with their own species. Paper Moon opened a branch in New York, which had by the 1980s secured its dominance as the world's fashion center. People involved in the industry needed restaurants that captured the style of the Milan trattorias such as Bice, Da Giacomo, and Bagutta—all of them, curiously enough, Tuscan in origin.

Still, that Tuscan food differed little from Milanese fare—in fact, all the Tuscan restaurants served a few Milanese dishes. What boosted the reputation of the Tuscan places in the 1980s was the fashion angle so attractive to the American and British food and wine media that drove the trends. As a result, they wholly ignored the food and restaurants of Southern Italy in favor of some vague notion of Tuscan cuisine, about which they knew little but assumed a **great** deal: Tuscan food was supposed to be lighter than other Italian food; the meats and fish were simply grilled, without sauces; Tuscan olive oil was deemed more refined; Tuscan wines were pronounced to be among the finest in the world. Suddenly, people whose first sip of wine was $5-a-bottle Lambrusco were now drinking $100 Brunello di Montalcinos and Super Tuscans.

It did not seem to matter much that many self-proclaimed Tuscan restaurants in New York had barely any Tuscan dishes on their menus. Two that did, Da Silvano and Il Cantinori, were very much a part of making New York's downtown arts and fashion scene neon bright.

In the mid-1980s, New York's run-down SoHo district—once called Hell's Hundred Acres—adjacent to Little Italy, had been developing rapidly as an inexpensive refuge for artists, who took over vast lofts that were as ideal for creating art and sculpture as for showing it. There were also a small number of boutiques—Comme des Garçons opened there in 1984—and a few places to eat, the best-known being the French haute cuisine restaurant Chanterelle.

Da Silvano was just on the edge of SoHo and Greenwich Village. It was opened in 1975 by Silvano Marchetto, a Florentine who had trained and worked in European restaurants until he moved to New York in 1968, waitering until he had enough money for his own place, a Greenwich Village bar named Bimbo's, which later became Da Silvano. Marchetto began with just four tables and a short menu that strayed from the red-sauce model of restaurants all around him. Several dishes, though not all, were Tuscan, such as *crostini* of chicken livers and *trippa alla fiorentina,* and it was novel enough at the time to compete with the highly popular Trattoria da Alfredo a few blocks West, where Alfredo Viazzi also served out-of-the-ordinary Italian food such as *cotechino* sausage with *salsa verde* and the Livornese seafood soup called *cacciucco.* Marchetto, who always insisted that his cuisine, while based on Tuscan tradition, was entirely his own idea and a lighter style than his competitors', was in the right place at the right time. SoHo's galleries were gaining traction and respect, especially after Italian-born Leo Castelli opened a downtown gallery a block away from Da Silvano, on West Broadway, and Mary Boone took a space in 1977 on the same street, where she represented up-and-coming neo-expressionists artists Julian Schnabel—then still driving a cab—and David Salle.

As the downtown art scene developed, so did Da Silvano's business, which he expanded to accommodate regulars like directors Michael Cimino, Martin Scorsese, and John Cassavetes, actor Robert De Niro, and artists Andy Warhol and

Jean-Michel Basquiat. A rapidly increasing number of fashion designers locating to SoHo in turn drew the midtown fashion editors downtown. None was more important than Anna Wintour, editor of *Vogue,* who made Da Silvano famous as much by her own presence as by whom she brought to the restaurant. As the most powerful woman in the fashion industry, Wintour had shifted the magazine's focus to younger designers, models, and photographers, which coincided perfectly with the edginess of the arts scene downtown, where she would hold photo shoots. Da Silvano was a place everyone wanted to be and be seen, including Madonna, who dined often at Da Silvano, and when she did, the diva wore Prada.

What Bice had achieved in Milan, Da Silvano achieved in New York, and the restaurant became a prime spot for gossip columnists and paparazzi to find fodder, in particular the *New York Post*'s notorious Page Six, which could always count on a good celebrity sighting at Da Silvano. So important was the gossip page to the restaurant's success that when the *Post* made Page Six into a magazine, Marchetto bought a full-page ad in an issue that proclaimed Da Silvano's one of New York's six "hot" restaurants.

The growing affection for Italian style's flair and food seemed easily tied in to Americans' view of *la dolce vita* as propagated in the movies, and no one seemed better suited to bring all those ingredients together than film producer Dino De Laurentiis. In 1981, De Laurentiis had declared, "There really are no Italian restaurants in the United States"; so he intended to open the biggest and best— a grandiose $3.5 million grocery and restaurant on New York's Upper West Side called DDL Foodshow, crafted in tile, glass, and brickwork. The place dazzled everyone upon its debut in the fall of 1982 with its extravagant displays of food; Murray Klein, of De Laurentiis's well-established but less showy competitor Zabar's, said of DDL's food, "It was so beautiful people were afraid to touch it. It looked like a display that said, 'Don't touch me. I'm not for sale.'"[11]

Like De Laurentiis, Arrigo Cipriani, the son of Harry's Bar founder Giuseppe Cipriani, was aware of the way Italian food, style, and celebrity were coalescing in the mid-1980s, but he had always avoided opening another Harry's Bar, a name that had already been appropriated, without the Ciprianis' permission. When London hotelier Lord Charles Forte approached Cipriani about opening a restaurant at New York's Sherry-Netherland Hotel, on Fifth Avenue and Central Park

South, Arrigo accepted his offer but refused to call the place Harry's Bar. The new $2 million restaurant, called Harry Cipriani, was run by Arrigo's son Giuseppe and opened in the fall of 1985. It was an immediate hit with fashionistas such as John Fairchild of *Women's Wear Daily,* actors Sean Connery, Michael Douglas, and Richard Gere, John F. Kennedy Jr., and Italian industrial titan Gianni Agnelli, who chose to sit in the less-than-desirable rear of the restaurant so he would be left alone.

The décor of Harry Cipriani closely echoed that of the Venice original, as did the menu, which was every bit as expensive, but failed to impress the tough New York restaurant critics. Not one to accept negative criticism lightly, Arrigo took out ads in the newspapers denouncing the *Times'* Bryan Miller, whom he refused even to seat in the dining room (Miller grew a beard and colored his hair to sneak back in), and said of *New York* magazine's "Insatiable Gourmet" Gael Greene, "I think it is possible that she forgot to remove the condom from her tongue before tasting the food."[12] Despite weak reviews, the restaurant grossed $7 million in its first year, causing the Ciprianis to think about immediate expansion. The next link in what would be a chain was Bellini, in a Theater District hotel—its proximity to Harry Cipriani infuriated Forte. On August 31, 1987, he sent a truck with a dozen men to close down Harry Cipriani and seize cash and credit cards, an event so astonishing that *New York* magazine dubbed it "the first hostile takeover of a kitchen in the annals of cuisine."[13] Much to the Ciprianis' delight, Forte's replacement restaurant flopped quickly, and the embarrassed Fortes asked them to return to the Sherry-Netherlands in 1991. When they did, the same international society crowd and fashionistas—though now a bit longer in the tooth—sashayed in immediately.

Harry Cipriani's amazing success with the fashion and society crowd in New York caused ripples of temptation all the way back to Milan, where Bice Mungai's son Roberto Ruggeri realized that their own little trattoria had become the glamorous symbol of Milan chic. Taking his cue from Harry Cipriani and sensing the time was right for Italian food, *and*—despite Bice's Milan address—Tuscan food in particular, to become fashionable, Ruggeri was coaxed by investors to open a branch in New York. Designed by Adam Tihany to evoke but not copy the ambience of the original, Bice New York opened in 1987, six blocks south of Harry Cipriani, on East 54th Street, right between Fifth and Madison Avenues, just around the block from Saks Fifth Avenue and all the new boutiques popping up nearby.

The buzz about Bice New York built up weeks in advance of its opening, and Ruggeri prayed he would attract the fashion crowd. By the time Bice did open, on a hot summer's day, when many in New York's glamour industries were out of town, the building above it was still under construction and the air-conditioning barely worked. Nevertheless, Ruggeri's hopes were rewarded: One of his first customers was designer Bill Blass, who proclaimed, "Pasta, salad and sparkling water. That's all you need on a hot day. And it appeals to people who are diet conscious. Even nouvelle cuisine didn't fit that bill. And the atmosphere . . . is also lighter and fresher somehow."[14] No restaurant review could possibly have been as persuasive as Blass's assessment of the way sophisticated people's eating habits had shifted in the late 1980s. Overnight, Bice's phone was ringing off the hook and tables were booked weeks in advance, with fashionistas claiming one table or another as their own, the most visible of which were up front, where the glass-paneled doors opened onto the street.

Favoritism is natural to every business, but in restaurants it creates antagonism. "Bice is the kind of restaurant everyone loves to hate," wrote the *Times'* Bryan Miller, "too chic, too crowded, too self-consciously European—yet everyone wants to visit. When this spinoff of a high-fashion trattoria in Milan opened last June in midtown Manhattan, it was immediately so jammed you would have thought they were giving away Christian Lacroix gift certificates with every carpaccio."[15] Miller gave the restaurant a single star, out of four; it mattered not at all.

With the success of the Bice New York, Roberto saw his mother's name in lights all over the world—Chicago, Beverly Hills, Mexico City, Miami, even Singapore and Dubai. Roberto's sisters Beatrice and Roberta, meanwhile, stayed in Milan, keeping their mother's flame alive and catering to their unfailingly loyal clientele, serving the same signature dishes of *pappardelle al telefono* with mozzarella and tomato to the models who arrived late at night after the shows. "They're starving by then," Roberta said, "and they eat like pigs."[16] Despite the high-end crowds packing Da Silvano, Harry Cipriani, and Bice New York, it was one of Silvano Marchetto's waiters, a former actor and fellow Tuscan named Pino Luongo, who would provide an even more potent mix of Italian food and fashion. Luongo had come to the United States in 1980 to escape being drafted into the Italian army. Looking for a waiter's job, he wandered around Greenwich Village "reading the menus in the restaurant windows to see if I could recognize anything. When I got to Da Silvano, I saw *ribollita, cibreo,* and other Tuscan dishes I loved."[17] Marchetto hired the handsome 27-year-old Luongo, and as time went on and his English got better, he was given more and more responsibility to manage the restaurant. After a falling out with

Marchetto, Luongo hooked up with two Da Silvano regulars, Steve Tzolis and Nicola Kotsoni, to open Il Cantinori in October 1983, on East Tenth Street, not far from Da Silvano.

Luongo decorated Il Cantinori to resemble a Tuscan home, with sepia-tinted photos of turn-of-the-century farmers; Puccini, Verdi, and Bellini rang from the speakers. At first, business was slow, until America's best-known food authority, James Beard, brought along a *Times* reviewer, who just before Christmas gave Il Cantinori a very positive two-star write-up. Within weeks, the restaurant was thronged with newcomers and old regulars from Da Silvano, including Andy Warhol, photographer Robert Mapplethorpe, and Keith Haring, who one night drove a Vespa right into the dining room so he could present it as a gift to *Vogue* fashion editor Elizabeth Saltzman. Keith Richards of the Rolling Stones came in, as did actors Tom Cruise and Richard Gere, all of whom lent the restaurant—and Luongo—a glamour that would carry on for years to come. And Tuscan cuisine had yet another outpost in America.

Then it had another, this time in the Hamptons, New York's summer playground for the very rich. There, in 1988, Luongo opened a seafood restaurant named Sapore di Mare (taste of the sea), one of the few Italian restaurants then in the area. On opening night, prepped for just 60 guests, Luongo was "besieged by customers who knew me from the city and to whom I simply could not say no."[18] It became impossible to get a table on weekends, especially since regulars would just show up after a day at the beach. One night, fashion tycoon Ralph Lauren showed up in shorts—then banned at Sapore di Mare—but with nonchalant aplomb simply donned a pair of checkered chef's pants borrowed from the kitchen and sat down to dinner without further ado.

But the most important of Luongo's customers, as it turned out, was Fred Pressman, patriarch of the Barney's men's store on 17th Street and Seventh Avenue, which was at the time expanding to become America's leading promoter of Italian men's fashions. Pressman wanted to open an Italian restaurant next to Barney's and originally asked Roberto Ruggeri of Bice to do so, but Ruggeri had legal problems back in Italy that prevented the deal. Pressman then turned to Luongo to create it and manage it—this at a time when the Chelsea neighborhood was mostly industrial. The restaurant would be built in the huge space where Macy's Thanksgiving Day Parade floats were once stored.

After selling his share in Il Cantinori, Luongo threw himself into the project, calling it Le Madri—the mothers—because he was going to have women chefs from various parts of Italy (along with one young Italian-American fellow, Alan Tardi, as a backup). "Food journalists hungry for the next big concept would eat up the idea that the restaurant's recipes came from actual, bona fide Italian mothers whom I would import from Italy and parade in front of them," Luongo wrote in his memoir, *Dirty Dishes* (2009).[19]

And he wanted a pizza oven. By serving pizza and having mamas cook their old recipes, Le Madri was both a throwback and an innovation, and it was all to be very stylish, backed by Pressman's money. What Pressman wanted was a place that would bring people to an unfashionable location, a place that reflected the sophistication of Italian style they were selling. Barney's ad campaign had long promised that since its clientele went out of their way to get there, they should be rewarded. Once, that referred to lower prices than at uptown stores; now, in 1989, they were selling the ultra-expensive, cutting-edge style coming out of Milan, and Le Madri was to function as a convivial culinary corollary.

Even before Le Madri opened, *New York* magazine did a five-page spread on the upcoming restaurant. "It made me feel like king of the city," said Luongo, "but I also heard rumblings about resentment from other restaurateurs; I could feel anger rolling down Seventh Avenue like hot lava."[20] The *New York* story and generally good food reviews put Le Madri into the front ranks of Italian restaurants and helped make Barney's a far more attractive destination. The mamas really *were* in the kitchen cooking *casalinga*-style food—*pappa al pomodoro,* fava bean *tortelloni,* stuffed suckling pig—along with higher-end items like risotto with lobster, ravioli with quail, and red snapper with blood orange vinaigrette. The hostesses were all beautiful, the waiters handsome, and the synergy of Italian restaurant and Italian fashion was complete—Luongo even found that bulimic models were ruining his Frette linen napkins by wiping their mouths after disgorging their lunch in the ladies room. Il Cantinori, even more than Da Silvano, put Tuscan food at the pinnacle of fashion, and, like Spago in Los Angeles, Le Madri helped make pizza chic.

# Chapter 16

# Trattoria Mania

Ironically, while new casual but very stylish restaurants in the Tuscan mode were opening everywhere else, Italian cities did not experience the same rush of new restaurants during the 1990s. The tried-and-true old-time trattorias got busier and busier, both with faithful regulars and with foreign tourists who wanted to eat only the most authentic cuisine within a region. The happy coalescence of Italian style, casual dining, first-rate ingredients, and authoritative cookbooks, and the recognition of Italian cooking's healthfulness had achieved so much attention and appeal that there was little impetus to raise the bar much further.

Travel and food magazines such as *Travel & Leisure, Gourmet,* and *Condé Nast Traveler* covered the old and the new, the former in feature stories about a city, the latter in the front of the magazine in flashy stories about hot spots where famous athletes or international rock stars had been spotted. Newspaper reporters, usually on smaller expense accounts, were more likely to ferret out a small six-table trattoria in an out-of-the-way section of Genoa or Bari as an insider's recommendation. *Tavola calda* eateries and *enoteca* wine bars were favored, the best pizzerias—by then ubiquitous throughout Italy—were anointed, and places thronged with tourists were assiduously avoided, even if they were also thronged with Italians who had been eating at them for decades.

New York was filling up with trattorias—Tuscan and otherwise, so that you could eat Venetian risotto at Remi, Roman baby lamb at Sandro's, Puglian *orecchiette* at i Trulli, *insalata di Caprese* at San Pietro, and Sardinian *malloreddus gnocchi* at Cala di Volpe.

French restaurants completely lost their grip in Los Angeles, where L'Ermitage, Le Dôme, L'Orangerie, and others went out of business as the restaurant scene became more casual and was inundated with Italian places like Madeo, Pazzia, Drago, and Locanda Veneta. Piero Selvaggio, finding his customers at Valentino most enjoyed the antipasti and pastas, opened Primi, where the menu was composed entirely of those dishes.

Other cities copied what they saw in New York and Los Angeles and made it all bigger and splashier, like the cavernous, boisterously loud 'Scoozi in Chicago, and the Sfuzzi chain out of Dallas (which Pino Luongo later took over). Marcella Hazan was hired as a consultant to Veni Vidi Vici in Atlanta. In Minneapolis, the chef at D'Amico Cucina indulged in *la nuova cucina* flourishes such as blackberry risotto.

San Francisco clung to its Chez Panisse-inspired passion for Mediterranean and Provençal food culture and its own Northern California cuisine, so that it had few notable Italian restaurants until the turn of the twenty-first century. Despite Italians' long agricultural heritage in Napa Valley, the region had become a bucolic refuge for very wealthy Californians longing to replicate the lifestyle of Provençal château owners. The symbiosis among wineries, hotels, and restaurants resulted in a slew of French restaurants such as Étoile, The French Laundry, and Pinot Blanc. So when chef Michael Chiarello, born and raised in Turlock, California, came to the valley, he found none of the Italian food he grew up eating. "My house didn't smell like other kids' houses," he said. "I grew up making cheese, olive oil, prosciutto, growing tomatoes, and making our own wine."[1] By the age of 24, he had already achieved a reputation at restaurants in Florida; he then moved back to California and put all he had learned from his immigrant mother's recipe into a casual, ivy-covered restaurant called Tra Vigne (among the vineyards) in St. Helena.

"When I opened Tra Vigne, I knew how to use the amazing cornucopia of ingredients from Northern California," he says. "It just seemed natural to do real Italian food rather than French, which was the rule back then."[2] Having opened during the week of the prestigious Napa Valley Wine Auction in 1989, the restaurant took off overnight. The setting, quite literally among the vines, had the ambience of a rustic country trattoria, complete with hanging sausages. Chiarello made his own olive oil for the restaurant and to sell commercially. And the food was very close to what one would then find in Italy—ravioli with spinach and red chard in sage butter, fettuccine with grilled artichokes and chervil, and thin-crusted pizza with caramelized onions and Gorgonzola cheese—but made with locally grown ingredients and enjoyed with Napa Valley wines.

"We tried to set ourselves apart in the eighties and nineties," says Chiarello. "It was the heyday of Alice Waters, Mark Miller, Jeremiah Tower, and restaurants like Stars and Zuni Café. So you had chefs who were half a generation ahead of me and had more experience; if I were going to separate myself from the pack, I chose to do it with ingredients rather than cook toe to toe with them. I started off trying to match technique for technique, but the talent pool was very narrow in the valley then. But I could pick a fig in the morning, make my prosciutto and olive oil, and no matter how busy I got, we had a recipe for success. The products were unique to Tra Vigne. I like to say that we were making salami before it was *salumi*, along with the mozzarella, olive oil, and the other things we did early on that were unique back then."[3]

Tra Vigne was a hit, but it was also an educational experience for its guests. "It was a slow, steady love affair," says Chiarello. "In the eighties, if you wanted to get people to know about your food, you had to do fancy benefits, cooking classes, get in front of people. You had to get in your dining room and tell people about sardines and lamb shank and share it all with an open heart. You gave away your first three hundred sardines. But people came to love it; they lapped it up. The hospitality of the Italian kitchen really captures the hearts of Americans."[4]

The food media adored Tra Vigne and places like it, especially when the chef was as movie-star handsome as Chiarello, who would go on to have his own TV cooking show. By the 1990s, Napa Valley was no longer being compared to Provence but instead was called the Tuscany of California. This shift was intensified by Frances Mayes's bestselling romantic memoir *Under the Tuscan Sun* (1996), which dampened the earlier influence of Peter Mayles's *A Year in Provence* (1989). Both books were reveries of wine, food, and cooking at a time when people's interest in those subjects had moved outward from major culinary cities like Paris, Rome, and Venice and into the country inns, auberges, osterias, tavernas, and vineyards, all beautifully photographed in food and travel magazines.

With its image already married to fashion and style, Tuscany, rightly or wrongly, continued to infatuate the media, and restaurants in America and London followed the scent. Some just appropriated the name, like Tuscany in Denver, Tuscan Steak in Miami Beach, Toscana in Dublin, and plenty of Tuscan Grills everywhere, all serving a version of *bistecca alla fiorentina* as proof of their seriousness. Even the low-end Olive Garden chain, owned by General Mills, performed its due diligence to Tuscany by sending its chefs to the village of Riserva di Fizzano to learn "authentic cooking secrets," although Tuscan-based items were but a small part of the Olive Garden menu, which was still loaded with old-fashioned Italian-American dishes like chicken parmigiana, fettuccine Alfredo, and spaghetti with meatballs.

Aldo Bozzi, who had been the head of Alfa Romeo in America since 1968, had begun to feel at home here rather than in Italy. So, when the company asked him to return in 1984, Bozzi quit and opened the Mezzaluna "Florentine trattoria" in New York. It was the first to serve the new thin-crust pizzas that had become fashionable because they were not as heavy as the traditional Italian-American versions heaped with ingredients. Bozzi commissioned Italian artists to paint *mezzalunas*—half-moon cutting knives—and put them on his walls. This brought him a more upscale, fashionable clientele than the usual pizzeria—Italian actor Roberto Benigni wrote a note to Bozzi (hung on the wall) that said, "If I had not found Mezzaluna, I would not have survived."[5] Before long, Bozzi opened a branch, Mezzogiorno, in SoHo, another in the Hamptons, and franchised others, including one in Aspen, Colorado. When Bozzi opened a unit in London's Covent Garden in 1992, Madonna debuted her book there, with nude photos of herself, and packed the place. "I prepared myself for jet trash, blown in on the tailwind of a millionaire's private charter," wrote a snarky writer visiting the restaurant for *The Independent*. "I found a handsome, moderately priced and warmly hospitable restaurant."[6] By 1995, there was a *Mezzaluna Cookbook*.

Most of these new Italian restaurants in the United States were run by non-Italians—a situation unthinkable a decade before. Italian chefs and restaurateurs, having insisted for decades that it was impossible to obtain the quality of ingredients found in Italy, now had access to the best, and it could be brought in overnight. Their insistence that only someone raised in an Italian kitchen could possibly have the taste to replicate the old dishes in American restaurants was blunted by changes they themselves had wrought: the Italians had been training young Americans to cook the correct way, and they had encouraged, even bankrolled, many to spend time living and cooking in Italy, and to bring what they learned back to America. Also, the people doing much of the cooking in Italian restaurants outside of Italy were immigrants from places such as Mexico as well as from the former Yugoslavia, where many families had fled to Italy, entered easily into the restaurants as waiters and cooks, and eventually emigrated to Europe and the United States, where they worked their way up the kitchen ladder, becoming cooks, then chefs, then, at a remarkable rate, restaurant owners. In New York, where most of the chefs had once been from Abruzzo, they were now coming from Croatia, Serbia, Montenegro, and Albania. "We were familiar with the food, worked in Italian restaurants, and learned Italian and English," says Montenegro-born Nick Vuli, owner of an Italian steakhouse named Flames in Briarcliff, New York. "It was hard work, but it was still the American Dream come true for us."[7]

In the 1990s, there also emerged a whole new generation of highly trained, passionately committed young chefs who were not born in Italy but who fell in love with Italian food after visiting or working there. Frank Stitt III opened Bottega in Birmingham, Alabama; Chris Bianco was widely credited as making the best pizza in the United States at his Pizzeria Bianco in Phoenix, Arizona; Todd English worked out of a tiny storefront in Charlestown, Massachusetts, called Olives that diverged from the formulaic Italian-American menus of Boston's North End. Marc Vetri brought fine Italian food to Philadelphia.

In Providence, Rhode Island, in 1980, a photographer named Johanne Killeen and her husband, George Germon, a sculptor, architect, and teacher at Rhode Island School of Design's European Honors Program in Rome at Palazzo Cenci, opened a miniscule eatery called Al Forno (from the oven), which they considered "simply an art project that keeps evolving. The kitchen is our studio, and the food we cook is like a canvas that is continually being repainted, changed, and refined. Food is eaten the way art is perceived; it is digested and recorded. Given the right circumstances, a connection is made and communication takes place, which is what art is all about."

At Al Forno they also perfected a technique they had seen in Italy: grilled pizza, which established a whole new style for an old favorite (see page 203 for recipe). Despite its very humble beginnings, Al Forno was named the best place for casual dining among the *International Herald Tribune*'s pick of the "World's Best Restaurants."

In Los Angeles, Mark Peel and his wife, Nancy Silverton, opened Ca'Brea, serving "country Italian food" such as roasted chicken and pork sausage with braised Napa cabbage. Silverton, once the vegetarian cook in her dorm at California State University, had studied at London's Cordon Bleu and spent several years as Spago's pastry chef. Next door to Ca'Brea, the couple opened La Brea Bakery in

1989, because Silverton felt she could not give her restaurant guests the true Italian experience if the bread was not every bit as good as in Italy. The bakery developed its own wild yeast starters and created more than a hundred bread varieties, supplying so many Los Angeles restaurants that it became unusual *not* to find La Brea bread on the table. Later on, Silverton developed a method of half baking then flash-freezing breads for sale nationally. In 1990, the James Beard Foundation voted her Pastry Chef of the Year.

These new Italian restaurants also brought with them a new kind of service. The service staff was now largely composed of young Americans whose affable, easy personalities invested the dining experience with a relaxing style that contrasted with the Italian-accented service of the past. Americans had, of course, always served as waiters in restaurants, and the idea of a struggling actor, musician, or model biding his time as a waiter had long been a cliché. But then, in 1985, a young Missourian came on the scene and set a new standard. Danny Meyer, who had once dreamed of becoming a professional baseball player, took a space off New York's downtown Union Square and opened a bright, two-level restaurant decorated with Italian murals and modern art with food as its theme. He hired an Italian-American chef named Michael Romano (formerly of the French restaurant La Caravelle) along with American waiters and managers he imbued with a highly focused sense of hospitality, a deft balance of familiarity, knowledge of the menu and wine, and professionalism.

The menu at Union Square Café was advertised as "American cuisine with Italian soul," with excellent bread and dishes such as *ditalini* with Gorgonzola and cream, *lombatina* of marinated veal, sage-perfumed rabbit with polenta, and a good American lemon meringue pie. The food was delicious and innovative, the prices very fair, the wine list impeccably selected, and the service set a standard for respectful friendliness that was noted by all the media and, just as important, by Meyer's customers, who spread the word that they had found a convivial Italian place with good food and really nice people. Union Square Café became famous as much for its food as for its ambience, and both aspects of it success were adopted around the United States immediately.

The Old World style of service was fading fast in Italian restaurants; the tuxedoes and red waiters' jackets were replaced by Armani suits, Oxford button-down shirts, and colorful ties. Captains who always recommended the bestselling wines were pushed aside by well-trained wine stewards who sought out small Italian estates and good value. The reception at the front desk was no longer a mix of condescension and deference; instead, the smile was genuine, the concern for every guest egalitarian, and guests' preferences were duly noted for the next time they made a reservation.

The shift was well underway, and the old style of layered, over-sauced, daintily garnished Italian food was fading along with French haute cuisine. The appeal of the new Italian restaurants in both London and the United States was, however, every bit about casual style as it was about the food, though chefs still took care not to stray too far into rustic exoticism. As Charles Scicolone, then owner of New York's Apulian restaurant i Trulli said, "We put Pugliese dishes on the menu—oxtail, stewed rabbit, tripe—but nobody wanted to eat it, so we had to take it off."[8]

There was even a minor backlash among some media suggesting that the new Italian trattorias' style and menus had snobbishly neglected the improvements wrought in traditional Italian-American food as a result of increased access to better ingredients. Italian-American chefs either were wholly ignored by media or were told that the red-sauce dishes were dated, heavy, greasy, and boring.

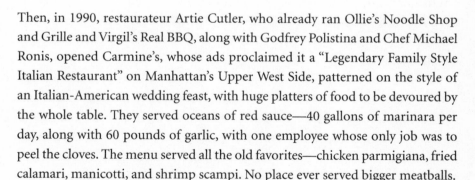

Then, in 1990, restaurateur Artie Cutler, who already ran Ollie's Noodle Shop and Grille and Virgil's Real BBQ, along with Godfrey Polistina and Chef Michael Ronis, opened Carmine's, whose ads proclaimed it a "Legendary Family Style Italian Restaurant" on Manhattan's Upper West Side, patterned on the style of an Italian-American wedding feast, with huge platters of food to be devoured by the whole table. They served oceans of red sauce—40 gallons of marinara per day, along with 60 pounds of garlic, with one employee whose only job was to peel the cloves. The menu served all the old favorites—chicken parmigiana, fried calamari, manicotti, and shrimp scampi. No place ever served bigger meatballs.

The food at Carmine's was also cheaper than at the midtown trattorias—the average check was about $20—at a time New York was going through a recession. The place looked cunningly old from the day it opened, with dark, varnished wood, immigrant photos, wood-beamed ceiling, and red-checkered tablecloths.

What guaranteed Carmine's success from the start was not rave reviews from New York's idiosyncratic critics—in various articles, the *Times* wrote, "This is not subtle or sophisticated cuisine but party food intended for boisterous groups who want to shovel it in while enjoying the convivial atmosphere,"[9] and, "Think about the standard pre-risotto, pre-arugula dishes that Italian food authorities like Tony May and Giuliano Bugialli detest, and they're probably on Carmine's menu."[10] Instead, it was a half-page article in *New York* magazine the month after it opened that described its old-fashioned theme and menu as a throwback before *la nuova cucina* and Tuscan trattorias stole the spotlight.

The article, by Richard David Story, was titled "That's Italian" and sighed with nostalgia: "Imagine the Little Italy restaurant of your dreams—black-and-white photos, dark wood floors, friendly waiters, big, steaming platters of sausage and pasta and chicken served family style—move it 100 blocks uptown, and you get the idea. And here's nothing *nuova* about the *cucina*. This is food old-fashioned grandmother cooking—chicken with peppers, linguine with clam sauce, veal Milanese, and ravioli with that famous tomato sauce."[11]

Story was signaling that perhaps too much style and sophistication had blinded people to the basic goodness of Italian-American cooking, winking at readers, Isn't this *really* the way we like our Italian food to be? Deep down in many people's minds, the article reminded them of how tasty the old food really was, and the next day Carmine's had long lines out the door, with a 45-minute wait for a table.

Carmine's might have seemed like a gamble in 1990, but Cutler went on to open a branch of Carmine's in the Theater District—he insisted his restaurants were as much theater as they were places to eat—then expanded to Atlantic City and the Bahamas.

So, too, at the long-established Patsy's in the Theater District, chef Sal Scognamillo asked his father, Frank, if they could try putting meatballs, tripe, and stuffed calamari back on the menu. "I told him we used to make a thousand meatballs a week but took them off in the eighties because people stopped ordering them," said Frank. "They wanted only Northern Italian cuisine. But I told Sal, 'Okay, go ahead, try it.' We sold thirteen hundred meatballs by the end of the first week."[12]

It may have been *retro*-chic, but it still sold plenty of meatballs and spaghetti.

This same interest in Italian food was gaining momentum in London, where, well into the 1980s, Italian restaurants had pretty much followed the pattern set by Mario Cassandro and Franco Lagattolla at La Terrazza and Alvaro in the 1960s. Then, in 1987, Rose Gray, daughter of an RAF pilot, and American Ruth Rogers

opened a very modest canteen in the London suburbs that would become as famous as it was beloved. Given Gray's and Rogers's backgrounds, it was hard to
imagine at the beginning that they would be so successful. Gray was an art teacher
and lampshade maker with scant restaurant experience, but she had developed
a passion for Italian home cooking while living in Lucca. She was a chef at a Manhattan nightclub called Nell's for some time, followed by a stint at Carluccio's
restaurant. Rogers, whose husband, architect Richard Rogers, owned the ware-
house that would house the restaurant, had no professional cooking experience
at all but shared Gray's love for Italian home cookery, which she knew from her
husband's Italian mother.

At first, the eatery was simply there to serve the architecture studio's staff
members, and the women opened with just one waiter and one dishwasher. This
was the River Café, and as it grew, it garnered a reputation for serving honest,
simple, light Italian fare of the kind already in place in the New York restaurants
Gray knew well. The River Café's stark, sleek combination of long windows overlooking the garden and river, the blue marine colors, and luminous graphics created a much fresher atmosphere than that of any Italian restaurant in London,
and the fashion magazines and food press brought a very posh, very regular
crowd out to Thames Wharf in Hammersmith, where guests sat at close-set tables within view of the stainless steel kitchen and were able to see everyone coming and going.

The guiding principles of that kitchen—to use the freshest possible ingredients and to cook them as simply as possible so as not to cover their essential flavors—were evident in dishes such as rice and potato soup, *porcini* risotto with
sage and orange, polenta with *borlotti* beans, and roast chicken cooked in Pinot
Grigio wine. The menu changed every day, according to what was found to be
best in the market. Little by little, they added cured meats, smoked fish, and baked
fruit desserts and focused far more on vegetables and soups than was then usual
in Italian restaurants. They had vegetables grown for them, planted their own
gardens, and plucked zucchini flowers within minutes of frying them up in extra
virgin olive oil.

Critical opinion was near unanimous that the River Café had brought something truly fresh and new to Italian food in London. The London *Times* gave it
five out of five stars. *Square Meal* wrote, "Their simple, meticulously sourced Italian cuisine was a forerunner of the return to simplicity that has marked culinary
trends in recent years, while the open-plan layout of the kitchen was a design
first for the capital."[13] And the *Telegraph* gushed, "This is a restaurant for food

lovers, not lovers. Dining here, even Room with a View natives could not claim 'mama cooked it better.'"[14]

Still, not everyone agreed: Antonio Carluccio sniffed, "It's very, very good food, but not Italian, never was. The Italian food that Rose serves is her and Ruth Rogers' interpretation of Italian food. The Italian Academy of Food have been there and they say, 'No way is it Italian food.'"[15] Rogers, in turn, sniffed back, saying that there never *was* any authentic Italian food in London before they opened the River Café. "We wanted to make bread soups, very simple food, we didn't want to make the slightly poncy Italian foods which started with Mario and Franco."[16]

Given the success of the River Café—with reservations difficult to get a month in advance—and a slew of new Italian restaurants at the turn of the twenty-first century, poncy restaurants were roundly being trumped by what Londoners took to calling "the trats."

## GRILLED PIZZA

Grilled pizza was the creation of Johanne Killeen and George Germon of Al Forno restaurant in Providence, Rhode Island, who had seen a similar technique of cooking pizza not in an oven but on a charcoal-fired grill.

*1–2 packages yeast*
*2 teaspoons sugar*
*4 cups of flour*
*1 teaspoon salt*
*¼ cup olive oil*
*1 ½ cups of warm water*

1.   Proof yeast in 1 cup warm water.
2.   In a large bowl add sugar, flour, olive oil, yeast with its water, and ½ cup more water to form a soft dough. Add more flour or water if necessary. (This step is easy in a food processor.)
3.   Knead dough until it can be formed into a ball. Place in bowl and cover rim with plastic wrap. Allow dough to double in size, about 1 ½ hours.
4.   Punch down the dough, return to bowl, and let rise again for 40 minutes. Pour dough onto floured board and knead till pliable, and stretch to rounds about 6–8 inches. Let rest under plastic wrap for 15 minutes.
5.   Heat a grill to medium-high and when the grill rack itself is hot, brush pizza pieces with olive oil and place on grill for about 1 minute. Turn over, brush with olive oil, and place toppings on the pizzas, e.g., tomato, mozzarella, sausage, etc.
6.   Remove from grill when toppings begin to melt or meld.

Serves about 8.

# Chapter 17

## *Salute!*

Just at the moment Italian food was gaining real stature, status, and class in the 1990s, it was also achieving something more enduring: a recognition of its healthfulness, which was quite a turnabout for a cuisine once associated with enormous platters of heavy, cheese-rich, oily pastas and meat and fish swimming in thick sauces. Indeed, Italian food outside of Italy became so popular precisely because it had always been reliably cheap and filling. Italian restaurateurs lavished their plates with ingredients and sold them to people who associated the portions with an Italian love of abundance.

In America, the single-serving, thin, eight-inch pizza on a plate as served in Naples had grown over time into a thick, 14-inch pizza on a pan or a two-inch-thick square topped with six or seven ingredients. In Italy, a three-ounce portion of pasta was about average; in America, the average was twice that size—and that was often as a side dish next to the main course. Italians would finish their meal with fruit or a morsel of cheese; in America, the meal ended with a three-inch-high wedge of cheesecake, sometimes topped with strawberries.

Like the rest of the American diet, such excess was a celebration of the country's largess and efficiency in producing large amounts of food cheaply, and reflected a belief that, in a world of deprivations, all kinds of food and lots of it had to be a good thing. It was called bounty. Pizza was lumped with fast foods such as hamburgers, hot dogs, French fries, and doughnuts. The frozen food sections of supermarkets swelled with portions of lasagna that contained the number of calories recommended for an entire day. Pasta sauces contained sweeteners, thickeners, and chemical preservatives.

Restaurant food, whether it was Italian, French, or Chinese, was by its very nature supposed to be filling and satisfying, and a night out was a break from culinary routine. People went off their diets on the nights they dined out, and any restaurateur who offered small portions would be out of business within a week.

America had always had its temperance and nutrition advocates, going well back to the nineteenth century. Pellegrino Artusi had criticized gluttony—something that was not a temptation for most Italians at the time. Jeremiads against alcohol in America were motivated far more by morality than by nutritional concerns, and there was so much pseudoscience and pure hokum behind the claims of early nutritionists that their recommendations rarely rose above the level of hucksterism.

Health and nutrition were taught in the public schools, but since there was so much hunger during the Depression, little heed was paid to home economics charts about what constituted a healthy diet. After World War II, rationing remained in effect throughout most of Europe; then, when prosperity came in the 1950s, Europeans gorged on the blessings of the new economy—blessings that by then had become taken for granted in the United States. Overindulgent Americans ran for the Bromo Seltzer; Italians for the Brioschi.

The counterculture of the 1960s lashed out against the fat-rich, meat-driven American diet, although advocates of change, such as Alice Waters, were more concerned about people eating food that came from good, healthy, natural sources, meat included. *La nouvelle cuisine* lightened up the traditional French diet, but there was plenty of *beurre blanc* and foie gras in the recipes. There had, of course, always been diet books, some weirder than others—*The Drinking Man's Diet* (1964) was one of the worst—but few were intended as guides to better overall health.

While vegetarianism had always been practiced in the United States, it was ignored by the wider public as suspiciously radical. Then, in 1971, a graduate student in social work at the University of California at Berkeley named Frances Moore Lappé published a cookbook sponsored by the Friends of the Earth organization called *Diet for a Small Planet*—"High Protein Meatless Cooking"— in which she said she had "discovered the incredible level of protein waste built into the American meat-centered diet," concluding that "feeding the earth's people is more profoundly a political and economic problem which you and I must help to solve."[1] The book was an astounding bestseller, eventually selling three million copies, and *Gourmet* magazine pronounced Lappé one of 25 people who had changed the way Americans eat.

The U.S. Department of Agriculture had by the 1970s taken a more active role in monitoring food additives, banning the injection of antibiotics in livestock, ordering recalls of canned tuna containing high levels of mercury, and reducing levels of nitrites in cured meats such as bacon. In 1971, activist Michael Jacobson founded an official-sounding but wholly private organization called the Center for Science in the Public Interest that regularly published hyperbolic warnings about the dangers of eating movie popcorn, enchiladas, Campbell's soups, and most Italian food, in 1994 calling fettuccine Alfredo a "heart attack on a plate"[2] and suggesting a consumer consult his cardiologist before ordering it.

However vague, terms such as "organic," "healthful," and "natural" were bandied about in whole grain cookbooks, vegan pamphlets, and even on labels for commercial boxed cereals. Ads proclaimed that *some* studies *suggest* that *some* forms of cancer *may* be prevented by eating this or that product. The best-selling *Last Whole Earth Catalog* recommended commune leaders buy cooking equipment, because cooking and serving good food was the best way to attract good people.

None of this sounded particularly beneficial to Italian food, at least in America, where, by the early 1980s, the more sophisticated consumers were beginning to watch their diet. "There is a definite new trend," Alfredo Viazzi of New York's Trattoria da Alfredo told the *Times* in 1982. "These days people prefer pasta with sauces made with vegetables instead of meat. They still buy a tremendous amount of pasta with cream, but they have fish and vegetables as a main course. I remember times when people would have eaten a whole basket of bread and butter before the waiter had had time to take their order. You don't see that."[3]

In Italy, many of the precepts of counterculture foodism had already been in place for decades, even if the peasants so lovingly embraced by the health food movement had barely enough food to sustain a family. The Italians of Il Boom were, of course, enjoying their new abundance and even warming to the commercial food products coming from their factories. Still, in every region, Italians continued to pride themselves on the purity and traditions of *i nostrani* (our food), from true Prosciutto di Parma to the capers of Pantelleria. They would endlessly argue about what goes into making an authentic Tuscan *ribollita* soup or a Roman *spaghetti all'amatriciana*. A *consorzio* was founded to come up with the ten regulations that make a true Neapolitan pizza (among them, the height of the dough ring, diameter, type of oven used, baking temperature, etc.), and a committee of Bolognese formed a Learned Confraternity of the Tortellino, which later went on to decide the exact width of *tagliatelle* (eight millimeters).

Except for the number of calories they consumed, Italians did not change what they ate very much over the past half century. There was more meat and fish, of course, less polenta by choice, and a good portion of vegetables. Wine was enjoyed daily. Bread at every meal. Cheeses were eaten in moderation. Desserts were an occasional indulgence on weekends. To Italians, "food is natural, eaten with gusto," wrote Frances Mayes, in *Every Day in Tuscany* (2010). "It must affect your digestion if you think the first quality of pasta is fattening [or if] the word 'sin' is attached to dessert. I've never heard of a dish referred to as 'your protein' or 'a carb,' and there's no dreary talk at all about glutens, portion control, fat content, or calories."[4]

The defenders of Italian food would argue that the way Italians ate was far different from and healthier than the American diet of fast food, snack food, junk food, and processed food, and many Italians were repelled by the intrusion of American fast food restaurants into Italian cities. That intrusion was cause for yet another learned confraternity to burst out in rage against it. Perhaps inspired by Parisian shopkeepers who in 1955 protested in response to a rumor that Coca-Cola had bought Notre Dame cathedral and planned to put a billboard on the façade, Piedmontese journalist Carlo Petrini, outraged by the imposition of a McDonald's next to Rome's Spanish Steps, formed an organization called Agricola in 1986, which quickly acquired the more digestible name Slow Food.

At first, the movement was embraced by the media as a typically romantic Italian response to what seemed inevitable to the rest of the world: that American fast food companies were deliberately going to market themselves as icons of American youth culture, as much as blue jeans, T-shirts, and rock 'n' roll were. Like these, McDonald's, Burger King, and Kentucky Fried Chicken were highly appealing to young people in Paris, London, Berlin, Moscow, and even Beijing when they opened, and Slow Food feared that Italian food would be compromised by the global expansion of the American brands—and that Roman monuments would be blighted by their presence.

Slow Food grew quickly from its original designs and manifestos, and the group found they were hardly alone in their contempt for American fast food (even if Italians had been eating their own versions of fast food, including pizza, for ages). Initially, the movement was simply a reminder that the slow enjoyment of good traditional food is a pleasure not to be lost in a modern world that increasingly rushed through meals with little regard for taste or quality. The organization published scores of pamphlets and magazines, helped found chapters around the world, and held a wine fair called the Salone del Gusto in Turin, where they also sponsored Terra Madre, a symposium attended by members of the world's food cultures. As the organization gained more support and credibility, there was a Slow Fish festival in Genoa and a cheese festival in Bra. To promote studies in nutrition, they opened a University of Gastronomic Sciences at Pollenzo, in Piedmont, and at Colorno, in Emilia-Romagna. In 2004, *Time* magazine named Petrini one of the world's heroes of the year—quite an honor for a man who started out by inveighing against Il Big Mac.

Today, Slow Food counts more than a hundred thousand members with eight hundred chapters in 132 countries. It has offices in Switzerland, Germany, New York, France, Japan, the United Kingdom, and Chile. In its philosophy statement, the group says,

> We believe that the food we eat should taste good; that it should be produced in a clean way that does not harm the environment, animal welfare or our health; and that food producers should receive fair compensation for their work. We consider ourselves co-producers, not consumers, because by being informed about how our food is produced and actively supporting those who produce it, we become a part of and a partner in the production process.[5]

Its mission includes defending biodiversity and food heritage, while supporting initiatives such as school gardens, which give children the experience of eating food they grow themselves.

As Slow Foods expanded, it seemed to proliferate in ways that were more polemical, to the point of sidestepping the fact that most people in the world could not afford the kinds of foods the organization was promoting. Their advocacy of seeking out the finest artisanal producers and crops grown as close as possible to the kitchen door had costly ramifications most of the world's people could not bear.[6]

Nevertheless, Slow Food was crucial in restoring the belief that Italian food can be among the healthiest in the world, if good products are chosen with care, if cooking is done with respect, and if people take their time eating and enjoying a glass of wine. The philosophy was not just sound but delectably persuasive at a time when Italian food was already loved all over the world.

Concomitant with Slow Food's influence was the carefully mounted campaign to prove that something called the Mediterranean Diet was superior to most others in the world and most specifically to America's. Conceptualized by the Oldways Preservation Trust, which was established by K. Dun Gifford in Boston in 1988, the Mediterranean Diet drew upon pioneering work done by American scientist Ancel Keys and his wife, Margaret, in the 1950s. Trained in everything from economics and social science to oceanography, biology, and physiology, Keys published a study of malnutrition diets entitled *Biology of Human Starvation* (1950) and was one of the first to warn of the dangers of high cholesterol levels in the blood, which he said were worsened by the consumption of saturated fats in milk and meats but not by unsaturated fats of vegetable oils.

Using data compiled in an epidemiological study of the isle of Crete conducted by the Rockefeller Foundation, Keys began his own investigations of coronary risk factors in seven countries, including Italy, concluding that the diet of the common people of Naples in the early 1950s was far healthier than the American diet. He found the Italian diet of that period was low in fat and high in cereals, breads, fruit, vegetables, and other foods that seemed to keep their coronary disease low. He also found that olive oil, not animal fat, was the principal fat used by the people throughout the Mediterranean. Another study, conducted from 1963 to 1965 by the European Atomic Energy Commission, confirmed the Rockefeller and Keys findings.

The Oldways Preservation Trust began promoting their version of the Mediterranean Diet in January of 1993 at a conference held by the Harvard School of Public Health and the World Health Organization. The nostalgic name Oldways traded on the same wholesome connotations as Slow Food and derived from K. Dun Gifford's 1987 trip to Qufu, birthplace of Confucius, where he learned of the Confucian ideal of harmony among earth, body, and spirit, albeit while feasting on 36 courses over a three-hour meal. He decided the next day to found the nonprofit Oldways "to research and promote a harmony of traditional food patterns, sustainable agriculture, and healthy eating and drinking. It would combine 'the best of the old ways' with 'the best of the new ways,' and stand in strong contrast to what I like to call 'techno foods' that, oxymoronically, remain 'fresh' for months on grocery store and kitchen shelves."[7]

Later that same year, Gifford traveled to Italy with food writer Nancy Harmon Jenkins, beginning in Piedmont, heading northeast, then on to Tuscany. They ate and drank well and lavishly, tasting Super Tuscans and artisanal grappas, marveling at white truffles, and cooking game birds in a farmhouse in Cortina. "This Italian culinary adventure was an exhilarating immersion into a second of the world's great traditional 'oldways' cultures," he later wrote, "where the sensory elements of the foods and wines are inseparable from a joyous way of living. It was a sensual Italian yin to the intense Chinese yang in Qufu, and strong validation of my image and purposes for Oldways."[8]

With early funding from the International Olive Oil Council and other companies that saw great value in promoting the Mediterranean Diet, Oldways grew quickly in stature, gaining support from the Italian Trade Commission, the American Italian Pasta Company, Barilla, the Consorzio Parmigiano-Reggiano, Goya Foods, the Latino Nutrition Coalition, the National Fisheries Institute, the United States Potato Board, the Mediterranean Foods Alliance, and even Campbell's Soup, Domino's Pizza, and Pizza Hut. Like Slow Food, Oldways held symposiums, led Culinaria food tours, and published books and recipes.

The diet's principles, as laid out in Nancy Harmon Jenkins's *The Mediterranean Diet Cookbook* (1994), called for food that was "nourishing to the body because it's wholesome and to the soul because it tastes so very good," using a graph that directly imitated the well-known USDA food pyramid of 1992.[9] In contrast to the USDA's pyramid, however, which indicated that eating up to nine ounces of meat a day was perfectly healthy, meat was at the narrow top of the Mediterranean Diet pyramid graph; breads, pastas, couscous, polenta, bulgur, and other grains were at the broad bottom. Nowhere on the USDA graph was olive oil mentioned; on the Mediterranean Diet pyramid, olive oil got its own layer, just above beans, legumes, and vegetables.

The Mediterranean Diet took flight with a global media that recognized the romantic and historic allure and appeal of those countries ringing the Mediterranean Sea—those ancient cultures already popular with tourists, who could now glide down the Nile and the Dalmatian coast, sail the blue waters to Capri and Sardinia, and sit in a Tuscan trattoria and eat their fill, contented now that what they were eating and drinking was actually very, very good for them.

Food editors, always desperate for a way to make their readers believe they could lose a few pounds, began promoting more and more Mediterranean foods, especially the most familiar, Italian. Book publishers scrambled to get out volumes on Mediterranean food each season, and the majority were about Italian food—*Flavors of the Riviera*, by Colman Andrews (1996), *A Passion for Piedmont*, by Matt Kramer (1997), *Naples at Table*, by Arthur Schwartz (1998), *Food and Memories of Abruzzo,* by Anna Teresa Callen (1998), and dozens more. One publisher even thought it was time for a comprehensive reference guide to Italian food, *The Dictionary of Italian Food and Drink* (1998), which I was privileged to write.

Combined with the joy of eating as promoted by Slow Food, the Mediterranean Diet took the wind out of those critics who decried Italian food as heavy and unhealthy. One could hardly blame the Italians for gloating that they had known it all along.

Chapter 18

# Alta Cucina

By the mid-1990s, all the stars were aligned for Italian food to dominate global gastronomy; it was not only fashionable, but now there was the good news that it was also healthy. The concept of the chic trattoria had turned out to be an easy sell outside of Italy, but convincing people—even *in* Italy—that expensive, stylishly designed *ristoranti* were worth the same money paid out at French restaurants was much more difficult. Expensive Italian restaurants such as Valentino in Santa Monica and Rex il Ristorante in Los Angeles continued to be ranked among the best fine dining spots in the United States, along with a few other high-end attempts, such as Galileo in Washington, D.C., and Spiaggia in Chicago, which brought a wholly new idea of Italian food to the conservative dining scene of the Midwest.

Galileo, opened in 1984, was the creation of Piedmontese chef Roberto Donna, whose highly personalized, authentic *cucina italiana* immediately made the Northern Italian menus and staid décor at established places such as Cantina d'Italia and Tiberio look dated. Like Mauro Vincenti in Los Angeles, Donna was a flamboyant promoter of *la dolce vita,* ever ready to lead excursions to Italy, always a good interview for a TV spot. He had won everything from the Chef of America Award from the Master Chef's Society in 1991 to the Caterina de' Medici Award that same year from Federazione Italiani Cuochi. His cooking was sumptuous and expensive, his wine list huge, and his clientele the politicians and Washington media that kept him in the spotlight.

Spiaggia was the creation of Levy Restaurants, founded in 1978 by Larry Levy, whose first entry into food service was D. B. Kaplan's Delicatessen, followed by eateries at Chicago's Comiskey Park. Levy said the idea to do an upscale Italian restaurant came to him while he was in Italy to buy marble for a new building on Chicago's Magnificent Mile. Dining exquisitely on fresh seafood at Ristorante Bistrot on the beach in Forte dei Marmi, he began fantasizing over "having a jewel box of an Italian restaurant" in his new development, where he would try to reproduce the flavors and feeling of *la dolce vita* he so enjoyed that day. "As I observed these rituals, this way of life, and the joy of the Italian people, I wanted to bring it all back home with me," he said. "I have always been passionate about all things Italian: the food, the wines, the cars, the clothes, the cities, the people and their culture. I am as passionate about my hometown of Chicago as I am about Italy."[1] Once again, it was not only the wonderful food but an entire package of Italian culture that drove the concept.

Levy chose the name Spiaggia (beach) for the new restaurant, where he "envisioned delicious, authentic Italian meals with fantastic regional Italian wines being served to Chicago's leading locals and visitors in a tiered setting where every guest could view Chicago's own *spiaggia*. . . . I imagined romantics proposing marriage, families celebrating special occasions, and investment bankers toasting their biggest deals. . . . Whenever I am asked which is my favorite 'dream become reality,' I always answer with Spiaggia."[2]

What his dream needed was a chef in tune with all Levy sought to reproduce from his time in Italy. He therefore hired Tony Mantuano, who had been chef at a contemporary pasta place called Pronto. To prove how serious he was, Levy sent Mantuano and his wife, Nancy, to Italy, all expenses paid, for a full year, where they learned to cook with the reigning masters of the day at restaurants such as Dal Pescatore in Canneto sull'Oglio and Romano in Viareggio. Upon his return, Mantuano was brimming with enthusiasm for the new *ristorante*. "We wanted to totally avoid what was going on around us in Italian restaurants," he said. "And we were told by other restaurateurs, 'Look, kid, you're never going to make it if you don't serve meatballs.' But we never did and we were packed from the day we opened in 1984."[3]

The menu at Spiaggia was an amalgam of all Mantuano had learned about authentic taste, great ingredients, and elegant presentation, which would include dishes such as black pasta with prawns, fettuccine with walnuts and cream; beef-filled *tortellini* in an arugula-tomato sauce; octopus with fava beans; *mascarpone torta;* and, in the adjacent Café Spiaggia, pizzas made with fresh mozzarella from Texas.[4]

Chicago—home of Pizzeria Uno and scores of red-sauce eateries—had never seen an Italian restaurant like Spiaggia, not least because of its polished décor, spectacular panorama over the Magnificent Mile, and its wine list with hundreds of the finest Italian labels at prices that reflected the upward spiral of *vini italiani* in the mid-1980s. Spiaggia was an immediate hit, receiving the ultimate four stars from both the *Chicago Tribune* and *Chicago* magazine and drawing a culinary and celebrity clientele that ranged from Princess Diana and President Bill Clinton to Paul McCartney (for whom Mantuano prepared an Italian vegetarian meal) and Alice Waters. Recognizing that Spiaggia was a crucial place to showcase Italian wine, illustrious winemakers such as Angelo Gaja, Maurizio Zanella, Marchesi di' Frescobaldi, Piero Antinori, and Silvio Jermann made frequent pilgrimages to the restaurant.

Spiaggia's success was a wake-up call for Italian restaurateurs in Chicago, not least the Capitanini family, which had for decades run the beloved, old-fashioned Italian Village. Within the same cavernous building they now put Vivere, designed by trendsetting architect Jordan Mozer in a riot of colors and De Chirico-esque forms and spirals, with a menu that reflected the modernity of Italian cuisine. The wine list grew and grew to be one of the most comprehensive in the world, with 45,000 bottles, including six hundred Italian labels, three hundred French, three hundred Californian, and two hundred from other countries.

Without the fussy French-influenced eccentricities of *la nuova cucina, alta cucina* was faring well in Italy, where a few more Michelin stars were awarded each year to expensive restaurants such as La Pergola in Rome, Cracco in Milan, Il Pellicano in Porto Ercole, and Don Alfonso 1890 in Sant'Agata sui Due Golfi. Even if these were *ristoranti* for rich people, they garnered international respect and a higher status among the world's cognoscenti. Their cellars were filled with huge inventories of the best Italian and French wines, Champagnes, and spirits—and their parking lots with Mercedes-Benzes, Maseratis, and Aston Martins. If they were rarely full, they seemed to be kept open by their own celebrity, with owners who had learned quickly to capitalize on their international renown to get lucrative book deals, consulting jobs, and media appearances.

By the same token, Italian-American food had far more success abroad than did the Italian originals. Pizza—not least in its associations with the youth culture of California—had become so popular that California Pizza Kitchen opened dozens of units in China, Guam, Indonesia, Japan, Malaysia, South Korea, and the Philippines, as well as in the United Arab Emirates. By 1988, Pizza Hut had already opened its first unit in Beijing.

More eager than ever to get out the message that Italian food had moved beyond the regional trattoria level, Tony May set out to spread the gospel of both authenticity and *alta cucina*. Building on the efforts in the 1980s of the Gruppo Ristoratori Italiani, which had been sending young Americans to study in Italy, May believed it was time for America's culinary schools to recognize Italian cuisine's advancement beyond the Italian-American models still entrenched throughout most of the United States and those countries outside of Italy that had begun opening Italian restaurants.

Since the 1980s, schools such as the Culinary Institute of America (CIA) in Hyde Park, New York, Johnson & Wales College of Culinary Arts in Providence, Rhode Island, and the French Culinary Institute in Manhattan had devoted little or no class time to Italian food. "When I attended the Culinary Institute of America, Italian food instruction was a week and a half program during a two-year certification," says Michael Chiarello of Tra Vigne. "I had as much time with Italian food as I did with Chinese."[5]

May, who was on the board of the CIA, vowed to change that formula, so, with a $35,000 grant from the Gruppo, in 1984 he helped the school build the Caterina de' Medici restaurant and teaching program, where students would get far more rigorous training in Italian cooking. The Caterina de' Medici restaurant had five student-staffed areas, from its formal main dining room to the casual Al Forno dining room with an antipasti bar and wood-fired oven. All the furniture and fixtures were researched and purchased in Italy.

"The idea was really a slam dunk," says Ferdinand Metz, then president of the CIA. "The GRI had been regularly sending Italian chefs as lecturers to the students, but we did not have good attendance. But we needed another restaurant for the students to learn in, and there was a new emphasis on nutrition, so Italian food seemed the most natural way to go. Tony added a lot of energy to make it all happen."[6]

Later, John Profaci, founder of the Italian food importer Colavita USA, which had been instrumental in introducing extra virgin olive oil to America, donated money to open the Colavita Center for Italian Food and Wine at the CIA, which, as part of the school's baccalaureate program, offered Italian as a language, along with studies in Italian culture.

With the help of Lucio Caputo's Italian Wine & Food Institute, May also compiled a comprehensive cookbook titled *Italian Cuisine* (1990), which I edited. *Italian Cuisine* covered everything, from the classifications of olive oil and *aceto balsamico* to the myriad ways of making *salumi* and *salsicce*, with detailed explanations of white truffles and species of Mediterranean seafood and a full glossary of Italian culinary terms, from *abbacchio* to *zuppa pavese*. May wanted it to be so authoritative that he even included a recipe for cooking donkey, which I convinced him to delete.

May was insistent that the image of Italian food was still too bound by regionalism, which he felt was perfectly apt within those regions, but that, given the overnight transport of foods from Sicily to Tuscany, one could easily find creditable Sicilian food in Florence and convincing Tuscan food in Palermo, especially since better-trained cooks were relocating to various cities throughout Italy. He further asserted that, despite FedEx and DHL, the very best local products from a region did not find their way into foreign kitchens. "Outside of Italy, you find Italian food, not regional Italian food," he said, "and the only way to obtain the ultimate people's respect is to create restaurants that serve modern *cucina italiana* that is as refined and innovative as any in the world."[7]

Having left the Rainbow Room in 1984, May was already running two restaurants in New York, the traditional La Camelia and, with chef Sandro Fioriti, a lusty Roman trattoria named Sandro's. Then, in 1985, the principals of the Equitable Life Insurance Company, who were building a skyscraper in midtown Manhattan, approached May to open an Italian restaurant across from the French seafood restaurant Le Bernardin, which they had already signed up. May agreed to manage the new restaurant, to be called Palio, after the colorful historic horserace that takes place each year in the piazza in Siena.

It was a spectacular place, with a downstairs bar wrapped in a 124-foot mural of the Palio race by leading Italian modernist Sandro Chia. Upstairs was a serenely beautiful, large dining room decorated with banners from the Palio, slatted mahogany woodwork, and exquisite table settings from the finest Italian designers. Massimo Vignelli did all the graphics.

May brought in a chef from Alto Adige named Andrea Hellrigl (who soon changed his name to the more Italian-sounding Andrea da Merano), whose own restaurant, Villa Mozart in Merano, was considered one of the finest in Italy. A perfectionist, Andrea had no patience for anything less than the best quality, and food costs added measurably to the astounding $12 million cost of building and maintaining Palio. Everything was made on premises, from the breadsticks to the pastas. An array of impeccably ripe cheeses was offered, along with a wine list of great breadth and depth. The menu was singularly inventive and expressive of Andrea's personality, which was decidedly Northern Italian with a streak of the Germanic. He would spread marinated salmon with truffle paste. Foie gras was

sliced over beef carpaccio. Mussels came in a saffron broth, and risotto was studded with morsels of rare, roasted quail. Gnocchi was tossed with garlic-scented
frogs' legs. The signature dessert was a "black polenta," made with cornmeal and
rich, bittersweet chocolate.

There were always more traditional Italian dishes on Palio's menu, such as
*risotto alla Milanese, ziti all' amatriciana,* and a *timballo* of macaroni with eggplant, but all of it was finessed by Andrea's imagination. Thus, May and Andrea
were stung when more than one New York food critic insisted the food was not
really very Italian. "At the beginning they had no understanding of modern Italian cuisine," said May. "It was lighter, for one thing; you didn't feel like you'd just
eaten a cow when you left Palio. Eventually the critics came around, but it was
tough at the beginning."[8]

Palio certainly won points on style, however, which was further evidence that
Italian designers were leading the way by the late 1980s, a time when French
restaurants were still weighted down with heavy curtains, brocade linens, and
crystal chandeliers. Palio was a place interior designers took their clients, colleagues, and students to see the direction of modern restaurant décor.

A major lease dispute caused May to leave Palio in 1988. Andrea stayed on but
passed away in 1993, at the age of 61, and the restaurant eventually closed. But
May's next project was intended to improve upon all he had worked to achieve
up until then. Taking over a defunct Italian restaurant at Columbus Circle in
1988, May acquired the right to transfer the idea, components, menu, and chef
of a two-Michelin-star "worth a detour" restaurant in Imola, outside of Bologna,
named San Domenico. Opened by banker Gianluigi Morini in 1970 with the in-
tention that profit would come second to quality, San Domenico was everything
May wanted to show off to New Yorkers and the world. He reproduced even the
bright orange linens, terracotta floors, leather chairs, and hanging lamps of the
original location. Waiters donned red blazers; waitresses wore black dresses with
white aprons and lace bonnets. The wine list ran to nine hundred labels. And
Morini's 34-year-old chef, Valentino Marcattilii, came to New York for the first
year to replicate his cuisine, bringing along a 28-year old American sous-chef
named Paul Bartolotta.

Trained under the great Nino Bergese, personal chef to Italy's Victor Emmanuel III, Marcattilii was rigorously grounded in classic technique, which included the use of expensive ingredients such as foie gras and lobster, along with
white truffles and 50-year-old *aceto balsamico.* "Food for the nobility had to be
light but inventive and stimulating, because chefs like Mr. Bergese were cooking

for the same people day after day," Marcattilii told the *Times*. "These were people who never knew hunger and who could afford the finest ingredients."[9]

His cooking was lighter than that of others in Italy, but he did not shy away from richness: he was already famous in Italy for his tour de force signature dish called *uovo in raviolo*. His was truly *alta cucina* of the kind May had been so intent on showing to sophisticated Americans accustomed to the Northern Italian trattoria style represented by Il Cantinori, Bice, and others. As did his French colleague Gilbert Lecoze at Le Bernardin, Marcattilii marinated raw fish in olive oil as seafood carpaccio. He placed saffron risotto in a moat of highly reduced beef glaze, while at the same time he could render the humblest of Italian home dishes—*pappa al pomodoro,* a stew of tomatoes, bread, olive oil, and Parmigiano—into a triumph of bursting flavors. Tripe was braised with carrots and tomato; suckling pig and baby lamb were simply roasted; and he would even make a cake of *struffoli*—the Neapolitan holiday favorite of tiny fried dough balls glazed with honey and served with ice cream.

It was a cuisine that was both sumptuous and delicate, like no one else's, and San Domenico, along with Palio in New York, Spiaggia in Chicago, and Valentino and Rex Il Ristorante in Los Angeles, was proving that Italian food had many faces, from the rustic to the *raffinato*, from pizza to chocolate polenta. When Marcattilii felt the New York kitchen was in true control, he and Morini returned to Italy, leaving Minneapolis-born Bartolotta in charge of the kitchen, and made periodic trips to New York.

The media's reaction was all that Tony May had hoped for; even the *Times* was pleased and awarded San Domenico three stars. The paper's critic Bryan Miller wrote, "At the rate Italian cuisine is invading this town, the celebrated New York cheesecake may soon be supplanted by tiramisù. Few of the new restaurants, however, offer distinctive food from Italy's exciting regional repertory. San Domenico is a felicitous exception." Miller heaped praise on the pastas and wrote that "the kitchen respects fresh seafood, never obscuring its flavor by oversaucing."[10]

Such remarks drew customers, but it was Miller's closing paragraph that was most telling of a period when the reputations of such Italian restaurants were rising so high: "San Domenico's exemplary performance can only fuel the Italianization of New York. I tremble at the possibility of wrestling with pesto fettuccine at Yankee Stadium—although a frosty Orvieto might be a nice change of pace."[11]

But New York was hardly the only city in America where Italian food had taken such a firm grip in the low- and mid-level categories of American gastronomy.

According to the 1986 results of the annual "Tastes of America" poll by *Restaurants & Institutions* magazine, 70.3 percent of consumers said they ordered Italian food when eating out, and the bestselling items were lasagna, pasta salad as an entrée, and fettuccine. Of all the restaurants surveyed, 83.1 percent said they had an Italian dish on the menu and 75.3 percent said they served pasta. Chains such as Olive Garden, Grisanti's, and Macaroni Grill proliferated throughout the United States, even opening branches abroad.

The French, well aware of how Italian cuisine, wine, and restaurants had shattered their once comfortable culinary world, reacted in various ways: All maintained, correctly, that French classicism was the basis for all modern European and American cuisine, and *alta cucina* restaurants such as San Domenico borrowed heavily from its example. The less enlightened French chefs would continue to maintain the glory of all that had gone before; the more reasonable came to the conclusion that Italian cuisine, even American and Asian cuisine, had a good deal to offer and to embrace. What had once been anathema in a French kitchen was now regarded as a way to adapt the plethora of new ingredients coming not just from Italy but from the whole world. If chefs had no problem using Japanese *shiitake* and *enoki* mushrooms, why not use Italian *porcini,* which were, in any case, part of the same genus, *boletus?* If other chefs had brought spices such as ginger, saffron, and *peperoncini* into their larder, why could the French not do the same and still maintain their food's Frenchness? After all, even Alice Waters had added Italian dishes to her Provençal menus for her 1984 cookbook *Chez Panisse Pasta, Pizza, and Calzone.*

The first and most important concession the French made was easy enough: olive oil, which had always been a staple of kitchens in southern France. But when chefs all over France began cooking with olive oil in dishes where butter had once been sacrosanct, it was an astonishing shift—one that was quite acceptable to gourmets who not only wanted to eat lighter cuisine but wanted great flavor from it. By the mid-1990s, French chefs were cooking a wide range of dishes with olive oil, as well as drizzling it over their seafood and vegetables. Choose any French cookbook of the 1990s and the ratio of dishes requiring olive oil over butter is probably better than two to one. By the time a revised *Larousse Gastronomique* arrived in 2000, olive oil had more than a column of information, recommending it with arugula, even noting the pungency of Tuscan olive oil. Also in this updated edition, which was translated into English the following year, *Larousse* gave Italy's gastronomy five whole pages, acknowledging that "Italian cuisine is one of the best known outside its country of origin. Pasta, risotto, fritto misto and pizza are enjoyed practically worldwide, together with excellent charcuterie (including mortadella, salami, Parma ham and zampone) and cheeses, notably Gorgonzola and Parmesan, which goes so well with all pasta dishes. The fine quality of Italian ice cream and water ices is also widely acknowledged."[12]

And there it was: the low-key but tacit admission by France's greatest culinary authority that Italian food had become more familiar than and, by extension, was preferred to, French cuisine. Few noticed the statement, but there should have been riots in the streets of Paris and jubilation in the streets of Rome and Naples.

Sensible French chefs came to realize that the global appeal of pasta in so many forms, including Chinese and Japanese noodles, could be put to good use in their restaurants. A decade before, putting ravioli, cannelloni, and fettuccine—the "eenie" foods!—on a French menu would have been appalling. By the 1990s, it would be difficult to find a French menu *without* some form of Italian pasta. Of course, to uphold the luxury of haute cuisine, those pastas had to be stuffed with foie gras, cuddled in a béchamel, and showered with black truffles. But they were there: whether it was at a restaurant by Alain Ducasse, Joël Robuchon, or Pierre Gagnaire, pastas played an increasingly large part of the menu. "The French chefs only really make stuffed pastas like ravioli and cannelloni," says Marco Maccioni of Le Cirque. "They needed it to be 'conceptualized' along French lines; they couldn't just make simple spaghetti."[13]

Ducasse in particular saw the advantages of offering pasta at his myriad restaurants around the world, and even consulted on an Italian restaurant in Paris called Il Cortile, where he served *vitello tonnato,* pasta with a sauce of squid's ink, shellfish, and arugula, and a spit-roasted lamb with garlicky Sicilian eggplant. He then ventured into Italy itself to open a resort and restaurants named L'Andana near Grosseto. At the august Hôtel Plaza Athenée in Paris, he serves house-made pasta with cockscomb and white kidney beans. At Louis XV in Monaco, he offers a Provençal salad with black truffles and olive oil from Liguria, and a breast of squab with foie gras and polenta. And at the Dorchester in London, the menu lists artichoke ravioli with calamari and shellfish with black olives.

In London and the United States, where French masters were busy opening branch restaurants, pasta was to be found on every French menu. At the rigorously classic Le Bec Fin in Philadelphia, chef-owner Georges Perrier followed suit by serving foie gras ravioli with truffle sauce, and in New York, at the posh Lespinasse in the St. Regis hotel, Swiss chef Gray Kunz offered a first course of *pappardelle* with white truffles.

The acceptance of pasta in particular gave the go-ahead to Sirio Maccioni of Le Cirque and Tony Vallone of Tony's to bring their love for and expertise in Italian food to their flagship restaurants. In fact, both were already running full-fledged Italian restaurants: Maccioni had Osteria del Circo on Manhattan's west side, where he served everything from true Tuscan *cacciucco* to his wife Egidiana's 40-ingredient soup. Circo, which opened in a blinding New York snowstorm in 1996, was to be a place where his three sons, Mario, Marco, and Mauro, could also better learn the business. While Egidiana was not the chef, she was the driving force in the kitchen, and she directed the cooks to make dishes from her own childhood and those her husband loved, such as *ribollita* bread soup, tuna and beans, and individual thin-crusted pizzas.

At Le Cirque, Maccioni had always offered daily "*classiques,*" but increasingly in the 1990s they were Italian: *pot au feu* became *bollito misto,* and *cassoulet de Toulouse* on Tuesday was joined by osso buco Milanese on Thursday. In that decade, he still had French chefs in the kitchen, some a bit more willing than others to add an occasional pasta or two, such as the foie gras ravioli with black truffles in bouillon and the gnocchi with black truffles, asparagus, and vegetable *jus,* even on the same menu. Later there would be a separate section for pastas, which included *spaghetti alla chitarra,* foie gras ravioli, and lobster risotto.

Maccioni would also hold special Italian dinners, like the lavish white truffle menu from 1994: slices of *lardo* and white truffles on *crostini,* a scallop salad with white truffles, a risotto with white truffles, sautéed *noisettes* of veal with *porcini* and white truffles, plus cheese and desserts, along with fine Italian wines.

In 1997 Le Cirque moved to much larger quarters in the Palace Hotel's landmarked Villard Mansion. As time wore on, Maccioni wanted the food at what was now called Le Cirque 2000, to be as modern as it was balanced with classicism. One signature dish, prepared by Cambodian-born, French-trained chef Sottha Khunn, was consommé with foie gras ravioli—a recipe that required three pages of instructions.

Tony Vallone, meanwhile, had branched out in Houston during the 1980s with the more casual Grotto, then La Griglia, along with an Italian steakhouse named after his son Joey. But as he got access to the better Italian and Mediterranean ingredients he wanted to create a true *cucina italiana,* so he added more and more dishes to the menus at Tony's. By the end of the 1990s, his menus were almost entirely Italian and his wine list heavy with Italian bottlings. "Little by little my clientele was being educated," says Vallone. "They'd ask me where to eat Italian food in New York and Italy. By 2005, I started playing to my heart and made my menu what I call 'progressive American' with a heavy Italian accent and world-class cooking."[14]

Like Maccioni, Vallone relocated, forsaking the dated furnishings of the old Tony's for an arched dining room in a dramatic design suitable for the Houston Symphony, with a 12-foot free-form sculpture by Jesus Moroles, and works by Robert Rauschenberg and other artists. Upon opening in 2005, Vallone turned his menu from Continental-French to *alta cucina,* with dishes such as house-made *taglierini* heaped with Gulf Coast baby shrimp, tomatoes, shaved garlic, and basil. A captain would crack open the salt crust on a succulent red snapper, napped with a reduction of Barolo wine. And each day, Vallone would bring in Italian or Mediterranean foods almost no one else could find, including *moleca,* a tiny soft-shell crab netted only in springtime from the lagoons of Venice.

The menu was now in categories of *crudi* (tuna *tagliata* with blood orange and pomegranate), *passione* (Brunello risotto with Savoy cabbage), *primi* (*burrata panzanella*), and *secondi* (veal *piccata Milanese*), along with prime steaks, roasted sea bass with soy vinaigrette, and chicken *bigarade*. He called it a "European-style menu [that] shows its Italian roots with new creations that are developed each day, and rivals the best that you can find in New York, Milan, London, or Paris," then wisely noted for his faithful regulars, "but rest assured that your Tony's favorites are still available; we call them our 1801s (named after our previous address on Post Oak) and they are the classic dishes upon which our reputation for culinary excellence was built."[15]

*Chapter 19*

# Mondo Italiano

The death knell of French haute cuisine has been sounded about as often as for the demise of Broadway, not least in the plaintive title of Michael Steinberger's book *Au Revoir to All That: Food, Wine, and the End of France* (2009), which details how the decline in both standards and admiration for the glories of French cuisine has been long in coming, as Michelin-star restaurants go empty and master chefs go global rather than stay in their kitchens cooking. More troubling was that the French did not seem to care.

"The French, these days, are no longer eating like the French," moaned chef Bernard Picolet of Aux Amis du Beaujolais in Paris. "They are eating like the English. Younger French people today don't understand or care about food. They are happy to gobble a sandwich or chips, rather than go to a restaurant. . . . They know all about the internet but they don't know where to start to eat a fish."[1]

Perhaps, but such assertions look at the issue from the wrong end: Haute cuisine as represented in ultra-expensive dining salons with crystal chandeliers and gold bathroom fixtures did indeed suffer by being out of kilter with the way people wanted to eat by the turn of the twenty-first century. But the true spirit of haute cuisine was still very much intact, and, in fact, it was more widespread than ever, as the restaurants of the *alta cucina* movement demonstrated in a more appealing way. By 2000, Italian food had become fully entrenched in cities from New York to Berlin, but classic French cuisine and techniques were the ballast for it all. The heart of haute cuisine had always really been about the excellence of product, the care in cooking it, and the richly flavorful result that distinguishes it from food that is merely tasty. And under that definition, haute cuisine, like *alta cucina* and Mediterranean cuisine, lives on, and at a global level.

Not surprisingly, French haute cuisine rallied in the late 1990s—but in Las Vegas, where billions were being spent to remake Sin City into a sophisticated entertainment citadel showcasing the best of everything on earth, even if it was in the middle of the scruffiest part of the American desert. Nearly all the highest-end new restaurants at hotel casinos such as Bellagio, MGM Grand, and Mandalay Bay were haute French, with names like Guy Savoy, Joël Robuchon, Picasso, and Le Cirque. With one exception—a branch of Piero Selvaggio's Valentino, at the Venetian—all the Italian restaurants in Las Vegas were notched below the *alta cucina* level. There were chain eateries like Maggiano's Little Italy and four California Pizza Kitchens, branches of New York restaurants such as the upscale Fiamma and Il Mulino, even an extravagant, 200-seat version of Rao's at Caesars Palace, where they even reproduced the Harlem restaurant's red storefront façade.

In 2005, Valentino was joined by another entry in the *alta cucina* mode, Bartolotta Ristorante di Mare, which entrepreneur Steve Wynn located in his $2.7 billion Wynn Las Vegas casino-hotel. The Bartolotta in question was Paul Bartolotta, who had been appointed chef at San Domenico after Marcattilii returned to Italy. Trained at San Domenico in Imola, Bartolotta had also learned his craft at Michelin-star restaurants in France such as Moulin de Mougins, Paul Bocuse, and Taillevent. After leaving San Domenico New York, he took over the kitchen from Tony Mantuano at Spiaggia in Chicago, where he won the 1994 James Beard Award for Best Chef in the Midwest.

At his namesake restaurant in Las Vegas, Bartolotta had no desire to repeat his menus from San Domenico or Spiaggia; instead, drawing on Wynn's carte blanche, he could order any kind of seafood he wanted from anywhere in the world—*seppie, scamponi* (Sicilian langoustines), true *scampi, cicala di mare* (slipper lobster), and *triglie* (mullet), all just arrived from the Mediterranean that morning. His cooking was pristine, never masking the essential flavors of the seafood, always dressed or sauced with the finest olive oil and herbs. Bartolotta won raves from every quarter, local and national; still, the Michelin Guide gave the restaurant zero stars, while awarding three to Joël Robuchon and two each to Guy Savoy and Picasso.

Everywhere else in America, Italian food, wine, and restaurants were more popular than ever and at every level. Even lower-end, non-Italian family restaurants listed Italian dishes as separate menu categories: Cheesecake Factory, based in California, lists 13 pizzas, 14 pastas, shrimp scampi, and chicken parmigiana sandwiches among its two hundred menu items. The menu at Applebee's, "the largest casual dining chain in the world," includes "spicy shrimp diavolo" over penne with shredded Parmesan; *asiago* chicken with roasted garlic, tomatoes, and basil; and four pastas, such as "chicken broccoli pasta Alfredo bowl" and "three-cheese chicken penne." Families could go to Romano's Macaroni Grills, with scores of units around the United States, to enjoy tomato bruschetta, *mozzarella alla Caprese* (with vine-ripened tomatoes and buffalo mozzarella), Amalfi chicken, six kinds of pizza, and lobster ravioli—all available on the menu at the unit in Lincoln, Nebraska.

London's restaurants at the turn of the twenty-first century were still gripped by Francophilia, with young British chefs using as many British ingredients as possible on classic French bistro and brasserie recipes, what I call "BBC" (braised beef cheeks) cuisine. Not surprisingly, all of the Michelin Guide's two- and three-star choices (as of 2010) in London are French, most with British chefs. Only six Italian restaurants, including the River Café, have received even a single star.

By 1998, about five thousand Italian restaurants were operating throughout Great Britain, though 60 percent of them served only pasta or pizza. London had plenty of Italian restaurants, but few were among the city's most fashionable. The owner might be Italian, but his cooks and waiters were usually British. One of the "smartest" restaurants in the city was Zafferano, opened in 1995 by Giorgio Locatelli, a native of Lake Maggiore, who had learned to cook at his family's restaurant—"I was too clumsy to work in the front of house, always banging into chairs and dropping glasses,"[2] he said. He trained in Milan then worked in London at the Savoy, though he did not speak English, and at Laurent and La Tour d'Argent in Paris. Along the way, he came to the conclusion that "France has haute cuisine, but Italy doesn't. Each region tends to keep to its own style. I've always thought that Italian cooking had the heart, it had the palate, but it lacked technique."

Returning to London, Locatelli became head chef at a small Sardinian trattoria named Olivo, where he honed a simpler Northern Italian style of cooking than was then conventional. While there, he met restaurant entrepreneur Claudio Pulze, who, with star chef Gordon Ramsay, offered to make Locatelli a partner at Zafferano in tony Belgravia. The restaurant started off slowly, with modest prices, and then began drawing London's society and fashion crowds. With manager Enzo Cassini as ringmaster, Zafferano catered to—and put up with—a clientele for whom social clout was at least as important as the food. When the unabashed snob/movie producer/food critic Michael Winner saw that his preferred table at Zafferano was occupied one afternoon, he exited the door and refused ever to return.[3] In 1998, it won Best Italian Restaurant from the Carlton Restaurant Awards and earned a Michelin star.

Locatelli left in 2002 to open his own place, Locanda Locatelli, which became even more popular than Zafferano (where he was replaced with a series of British chefs) and won its own Michelin star. The new restaurant, with its vanilla cream, gray, and brown colors, burnished cherry wood, soft leather banquettes, and glass panels, looked nothing like a trattoria but was from the start stylishly convivial, with the handsome Locatelli and his beautiful wife, Plaxi, making the table rounds. A groveling media reported on every socialite, lord and lady, press titan, actor, and actress who filled those banquettes, and Locatelli became one of London's celebrity chefs, hosting his own TV shows called *Pure Italian* and *Tony and Giorgio,* and writing a massive, 624-page cookbook and memoir titled *Made in Italy* (2006).

Italy had for centuries been very attractive to the cold-climate British, and by the late twentieth century, Italian cuisine had become a true comfort food in Great Britain. Italian restaurants began to nudge the Anglo bistro-brasseries for attention. Working in an Italian kitchen was no longer considered inferior to working in an Anglo-French kitchen, so that by 1990, the staffs at most London Italian restaurants were devoid of Italian captains or waiters, with British, French, or Eastern Europeans far more likely to be serving the food.

London's Italian restaurants did not follow the *alta cucina* line but instead aimed for a mix of casual style and regionalism. One exception was the Connaught hotel's venerable Grill Room, which contracted London's star chef Gordon Ramsay to turn it into a high-end, very expensive Italian-Mediterranean restaurant, with an Essex-born chef named Angela Hartnett. Hartnett was the daughter of a hard-drinking English sailor and a long-suffering Italian mother, Giuliana, who is eulogized in Hartnett's book *Cucina: Three Generations Of Italian Family Cooking.* Giuliana's family had escaped from Mussolini's Italy to settle in Wales and run a fish and chips shop.

At 18, Hartnett went to Italy for a year to work as an au pair and then attended Cambridge Polytechnic. She began working in restaurants, among them, Ramsay's Aubergine, and developed a style of cooking which she described as modern European with an Italian influence. Eventually, Ramsay installed her at the Connaught and named the dining room after her. In its first year, Angela Hartnett at The Connaught won the Square Meal Guide's Best New Restaurant award, and in 2004 a Michelin star.

After his contract ended at The Connaught, Ramsay and Hartnett opened Murano in Mayfair, where the coincidence of Italian tradition and English ingredients showed how fussily different Italian cooking in London was from that in Italy or America: Hartnett would steam Dover sole with crab and scallop, hand-rolled linguine, vichyssoise and poached oyster; Cornish turbot came with crab tortellini, spiced carrot purée, and Swiss chard, in a smoked red wine reduction; and apple black pudding and octopus salad was served with onion purée and potato cake.

Much closer in spirit to New York Italian restaurants, Sartoria was launched by Sir Terence Conran, who had pioneered the modern London brasserie in the 1980s at Bibendum. Sartoria was located near London's most upscale fashion boutiques, and right on the city's premier street for men's fashion, Savile Row. Even the media-savvy chef Marco Pierre White (whose mother, Rosa Gallina, was Italian and whose father, Frank White, was a chef in Leeds) eventually opened an Italian restaurant after a string of elegant and expensive French ones. Having retired from the kitchen, White became a restaurateur, opening a St. James trattoria, named after his son Luciano, where the walls were hung with erotic black-and-white photos from White's own collection. The menu stressed simplicity—White said he was going back to his Italian roots—with dishes such as *risotto alla milanese,* liver *alla veneziana* with polenta, *bistecca alla fiorentina,* and tiramisù. The London *Times* called the menu "tourist-board Italian: that is, a compilation of easy-eating Latin favorites without a particular regional purpose . . . like a CD of sing-in-the-bath arias."[4] Luciano did not fare well and closed in 2009.

The music at White's chain of Frankie's restaurants, opened in mid-decade with Frankie Dettori, was more in the style of Frank Sinatra and friends, and the retro décor featured twirling glitter balls on the ceiling, mirrored walls, and an atmosphere billed as "reminiscent of the American clubs of yesteryear, radiating an ambience of lavish decadence."[5] The menu featured old and new favorites such as grilled halibut steak *alla Siciliano, gnocchi alla Sorrentina,* and *spaghettini* of lobster Americano.

By the turn of the twenty-first century, if Italian food had not taken London entirely by storm, it was certainly moving in like a warm fog, settling in every corner of the city.

Italian cuisine was also embedded in the fabric of American cookery. The acceptance of Italian food on the basis of its flavor, its style, and its association with *la dolce vita* was complete enough so that its healthfulness was simply an added bonus. It was wholly ironic, then, that the next step in the evolutionary process was actually *away* from the cuisine's supposed healthfulness toward a far lustier, fattier style of cooking pioneered in the United States by a Seattle-born Italian American named Mario Batali, a major figure in Bill Buford's bestselling 2007 book *Heat: An Amateur's Adventures as Kitchen Slave, Line Cook, Pasta-Maker, and Apprentice to a Dante-Quoting Butcher in Tuscany.* Buford described the rigors of working as a "kitchen slave" at Batali's Greenwich Village restaurant Babbo but also gave an extensive profile of Batali himself, a big, red-haired mixture of Wallace Beery, Falstaff, and Gargantua.

Always bellowing with a breathy, high-energy torrent of information, not without its expletives, Batali was America's corollary to London's Marco Pierre White. A hellraiser and motorcycle enthusiast, Batali, whose great-grandfather was a coal miner and whose father had a salami and sausage store in Seattle, studied Spanish theater at Rutgers University. He then shifted to Le Cordon Bleu in London but soon dropped out from a lack of interest. He apprenticed with the demanding White, but his true culinary epiphany came while he was cooking at a small family restaurant named La Volta in the Northern Italian village of Borgo Capanne. There he found the religion of *cucina italiana casalinga.*

Back in the United States, in 1993, Batali opened the miniscule restaurant in Greenwich Village named Pó, where he was first recognized for cooking up hearty Italian food. Five years later, in partnership with Joseph Bastianich, a former stockbroker and the son of Lidia Bastianich, he took over the two-story premises that had been the venerable Coach House and launched Babbo Ristorante e Enoteca. Babbo opened to enormous acclaim, winning three stars from the *Times,* which called the food a "radical departure with sure footing,"[6] and one star from Michelin.

In an *Esquire* article on Babbo titled "Keeping the Faith—Italian Style," I wrote that Batali was nothing if not evangelical. Rotund, wearing a scraggly red beard, ponytail, khaki shorts, and sneakers, Batali had a tenor to his voice that makes clichés like "awesome" and "killer" seem fresh and believable. He wanted everyone to eat well and also to understand what they were eating and why it was made that way.

Batali never held back in letting you know the provenance of a dish or ingredient, nor in criticizing the poor quality Italian food elsewhere. He crafted his menu to be expressive of his own extravagant personality, and if people did not want to eat sardines, cockles, tripe *alla parmigiana,* lamb's tongue, headcheese, duck prosciutto, squab livers, oxtail, rabbit, and sweetbreads as much as he did, that was *their* problem; the menu had plenty more to choose from, most of it uncompromisingly rich, little of it light, with no discernible health benefits. Among the restaurants of its day, Babbo was closest to serving the kind of familial cooking then being enjoyed in Italy.

Being in New York, however, Babbo was extremely loud, the decibel level heightened by Batali's choice of music by Radiohead and Guns N' Roses, and if anyone complained, he would just shrug. Impossible to book even weeks in advance, Babbo was both the most successful and the most influential restaurant of the late 1990s.

Batali and Bastianich soon went on to open several more restaurants: a tiny rustic trattoria called Lupa in 1999, serving just antipasti and pastas; a year later, an Italian seafood place called Esca; in 2003, a tapas bar called Casa Mono; a cubbyhole-sized place called Bar Jamón that sold Spanish ham; and a huge pizzeria called Otto with a two-hundred-label wine list. Their biggest gamble was an *alta cucina* restaurant called Del Posto, opened in 2006 near Manhattan's Meat Packing District. Costing $15 million, Del Posto had the three-tiered look of an Italian ocean liner's dining salons, with a grand staircase, graphic tile work, and made-to-order carts that captains would wheel tableside for carving *cotechino*, pheasant, and loin of veal. Joseph's mother, Lidia, was their partner at Del Posto, and she stood behind a mahogany station whipping up zabaglione while a captain prepared a tasting of Italian chocolates for dessert. The food was elegant and, Joseph Bastianich said, evoked grand dining rather than the gutsy *casalinga* style of their other restaurants. And it was very expensive—a rack of veal for two went for $95.

By the time Del Posto opened, the Batali-Bastianich partnership was already golden; Del Posto was booked for weeks in advance, eventually winning four stars from the *Times*—its first four-star rating for an Italian restaurant in 36 years. In the fall of 2010 Batali and Bastianich opened a 32,000-square-foot Italian grocery called Eataly in New York, complete with raw bar, eating counters, and an Italian steakhouse.

As time wore on and his commitments to books and television grew, Batali became further and further removed from the actual cooking in his restaurants. He became a fixture in the ever-roving celebrity chef's crowd, complete with foodie entourage, which separated him from those Italian restaurateurs and chefs who stayed and cooked in their restaurants. With a constant flow of personal appearances, Batali insisted he was not betraying what he had learned from his time with the family that ran La Volta, where Mama was out front, Papa was in the kitchen cooking, and the children were busing plates; he said he had no desire to live such a life. Nevertheless, in 2010 Batali told a TV interviewer that his dream for the future was to live in Trastevere or Testaccio in Rome and run a trattoria open just three days a week, serving 35 people a night.

Batali's absence from his kitchens did not seem to hurt his bottom line. His importance to the development of Italian food in America was in convincing people that the Italian cuisine went far beyond the dishes that had become totems on others' menus. Those who had once felt virtuous and smug about eating light Italian fare either had to admit that Babbo's food was unbelievably good but maybe not all that healthy, or stay clear of the kind of food Italians had been happily eating ever since Il Boom. Or they could eat less of it.

Other young New York chefs followed Batali's hearty lead—Andrew Carmellini at A Voce and Locanda Verde, Scott Conant at Scarpetta, Marco Canora at Insieme, and many others. One of the best and most innovative chefs to combine the most robust elements of the *casalinga* style with the more refined aspects of *alta cucina* was Michael White, another huge fellow like Batali but with a far less intimidating demeanor.

White had none of Batali's Italian-American blood, either. He was born in Wisconsin to parents who were aghast at their son's announcement that he wanted to become a chef. Like Batali, he went to Italy after high school to learn how to cook, spending years there before returning to the United States, where he worked alongside Paul Bartolotta at Spiaggia. In 2004, White hooked up with a wide-ranging restaurant group called B. R. Guest in New York as chef at a two-story Greenwich Village restaurant called Fiamma, not far from Babbo; White got three *Times* stars and helped open a Fiamma branch in Las Vegas, but soon had a falling out with B. R. Guest. That led to his partnering with veteran restaurateur Chris Cannon, who already ran two restaurants in New York: L'Impero near the UN and Alto in midtown. Cannon and White changed the name of the former to Convivio to reflect a more casual approach, while they refashioned Alto away from an unfamiliar Trentino-Alto Adige-style menu to *alta cucina* befitting its name.

Their most ambitious venture, however, was Marea, opened in 2009 on the former premises of San Domenico New York. Here, in a sleek bi-level dining room done in modern Italian design, White sought to capture the kind of pristine seafood he had enjoyed in Italy, particularly at the restaurant Romano in Viareggio.

Only because he was able to depend on daily deliveries of great seafood from around the world—as Bartolotta did in Las Vegas—could White dream of capturing such an ideal. "I eat, sleep, and die Italian," he says, "and over the years I've developed relationships with fishmongers so I can get the best wild fish available anywhere, overnight. In the past, we American chefs had to work much harder than the Italians do because they have the product right at the shore. I remember when I cooked with Paul [Bartolotta] in Chicago, we'd be so happy just to get fish shipped in overnight from Maine. Now I e-mail brokers every day. That is a radical change."[7]

The results were indeed stunning, and usually stunningly simple, such as a beautifully lighted seafood *crudi* bar. The antipasti included a warm mackerel tartlet with a marmalade made from shallots and a fresh salsa. Pasta involved spaghetti with crab and sea urchins with basil; ravioli was stuffed with tuna belly, and *cavatelli* came in a shrimp *ragù* with beans. "I have so many Italians who tell me that it's hard to find pasta in Italy as good as ours," said White. "I don't want to be boastful, but there are now very few restaurants in Italy where you can eat as well as here. In Italy, when Mama is still in the kitchen, the food is great, but Italians are not letting loose of tradition enough, while others are copying molecular foams and other nonsense."[8]

White's reference to "molecular foams and other nonsense" was to the kind of highly experimental, often deliberately off-putting food first developed in the 1980s by Spain's master chef Ferran Adrià, whose influence on young chefs was actually far, far less than the media that idolized him suggested. The few chefs who, like the Italian Futurists of the last century, tried deliberately to manipulate food into new forms, textures, and sensations were media darlings, topping many best-restaurant lists from London's *Restaurant* magazine awards to America's *Gourmet*. A few chefs tried novelties such as making gelato with dry ice; others were like Gennaro Esposito, of Torre del Saracino in Vico Equense, who was deliberately iconoclastic, as when he combined shellfish with cheese, *baccalà* marinated with apple and molasses, and called dishes by names like "egg in purgatory."[9]

But the impact of molecular cuisine was very limited, even in Spain, and only two or three chefs in Italy had appropriated the idea; neither had any of the London chefs, with the exception of Hester Blumenthal of the Fat Duck in Bray; in the United States, a mere half dozen, most in Chicago, fiddled with such concepts.

Chefs such as Batali and White, among so many others in the 1990s, had eschewed culinary trendiness for both a return to the wholesome goodness of Italian food and a highly personalized cuisine that came as much from their hearts as from their training. And White was right: by the time he opened Marea in

2009, Italian food in America, and to a lesser extent in other countries, was as good as the best in Italy itself.

It was a triumph Batali and White's predecessors had dreamed of, from the immigrant cooks who could never reproduce the flavors of the Old Country, to Tony May and Piero Selvaggio, who had to battle the bias that Italian food and service was something less than haute cuisine. Italians—and all the American, British, and Japanese chefs who were making Italian food—had come to share a vision and knowledge that theirs was now truly a global cuisine.

Indeed, the popularity of low-end and high-style Italian restaurants had become international, from Brazil to Berlin, from Vancouver to Victoria. Marchesi Antinori modeled Cantinetta Antinori trattorias on his Florence original and opened branches in Zurich in 1994, Vienna in 1995, and Moscow in 2004. Giorgio Armani branched out from fashion design to design hotels and restaurants, putting a namesake Italian *ristorante* into his flagship store in New York, as well as developing the Armani Hotel Dubai, to be followed by Marrakech, Marassi, Shanghai, and London. (Ironically, in Milan, Armani opened a branch of the Japanese sushi restaurant Nobu, with the help of actor Robert De Niro.) Dolce & Gabbana launched Gold in Milan, with glittering bar benches, gilded bamboo, and gold-leaf-coated chocolate desserts, with the music from the James Bond movie *Goldfinger* playing in the lounges. Gold had a "Bistrot Italian Menu" and a "Gourmet Menu," but hedged its bets with its American guests by also offering hamburgers and crème brûlée.

Maniacally label conscious, Japanese consumers embraced Italian style big time—Armani launched a store in Tokyo in 1987 and pledged to open two hundred more in Japan—along with Italian cuisine at the high, middle, and low end. Japan has thousands of pizzerias, including American chains such as Pizza Hut, which provides English-speaking visitors phonetic pronunciations of Japanese pizza words, like "cheezo crusto" (cheese crust), "napoorio" (Napoletana), and "karamatti furitti" (fried calamari).

Upscale trattorias such as La Granata and Granata Moderna in the basement of the Tokyo Broadcasting System Garden Building cater to media who come to sit at tables with red-checkered cloths in a room of Italian brick archways to eat *tagliolini* with *porcini* mushrooms and mozzarella-stuffed zucchini blossoms. In the Four Seasons Chinzan-so Hotel, Il Teatro is a Milanese-inspired *ristorante* serving *alta cucina* such as ravioli filled with shredded braised duck in a Norcia black truffle sauce with Taleggio cheese. Tokyo is also home to a branch of the illustrious Florentine restaurant Enoteca Pinchiorri, with a 12,000-bottle wine cellar. There is also, of course, an Italian-American place called Carmine, where veal Marsala is a specialty.

China, too, with its historic noodle culture, easily assimilated Italian food. Va Bene Shanghai opened in October 2001 in the city's fashionable Xintiandi entertainment district; four months later it was voted the city's "Top New Restaurant" by *Shanghai Entertainment Guide.*

Even in India Italian restaurants have gained a strong foothold. "It's only since the past few years that this Foodie wave has washed ashore in Mumbai," wrote Rashmi Uday in the *Times of India* in 2009. "In the past few years, world class Italian restaurants (Vetro, Celini, Mezzo Mezzo) in five star hotels jostled for attention with the standalones (Giovanni, Mia Cucina, Flamboyante). . . . Please notice how not a single new French restaurant has opened even in the distant past."[10]

The Italian food gospel was being spread more enthusiastically than ever by the media in the twenty-first century, not least among book publishers, who brought out dozens of Italian food and wine books each season, including single titles on risotto, pasta, bread, *panini,* and gelato. Every region of Italy was explored between book covers, with individual titles on the food and wine of Sardinia, Liguria, Piedmont, Abruzzo, and the rest. After publishing comprehensive, scholarly volumes such as *The Oxford Companion to Food* (1999) and *The Oxford Encyclopedia of Food and Drink in America* (2004), the company came out with *The Oxford Companion to Italian Food* in 2007.

There was a momentary dry patch for Italian food books in the United States after the low-carbohydrate "Atkins Diet" craze became a frenzied fad upon the publication in 2002 of *Dr. Atkins' New Diet Revolution.* At the height of its popularity, one out of every 11 Americans were said to be on the diet. Pasta sales dropped nearly 10 percent in the United States, and book publishers, more myopic than usual, decided that Italian cookbooks were no longer worth publishing because no one was eating carbohydrate-rich pasta anymore. The death of Dr. Robert Atkins in 2003 (he slipped on ice) and his company's bankruptcy two years later slowed the diet's momentum to a halt, and pasta sales shot back up quickly afterwards. So did the publication of Italian cookbooks.

Television also jumped on the Italian food bandwagon, both in Italy and abroad. Italy's TV stations, under RAI, programmed numerous cooking shows by well-known chefs such as Gianfranco Vissani and a generation of young ones; the Italian food and wine magazine *Gambero Rosso* even had its own channel through RAI from 1999 to 2009.[11]

Cooking shows were also immensely popular in Great Britain, including the 12-part series *The Italian Kitchen,* by Ruth Rogers and Rose Gray of the River Café, which ran from 2002 to 2004. As popular for her voluptuous movie-star beauty as for her cooking, journalist-turned-food writer Nigella Lawson sold 300,000 copies of her first book, *How to Eat* (1998) and followed up with *How to Be a Domestic Goddess* in 2000, the same year she began her TV show *Nigella Bites,* which drew nearly two million viewers. This led to a similar show on the American E! Channel, and another, *Nigella Feasts* on the Food Network, further expanding her global recognition. While Lawson cooked all kinds of simple-to-make home recipes, as often as not they were Italian or Mediterranean based.

Well into the 1990s, the only Italian cooking show on American TV was the PBS series *Ciao Italia* with host Mary Ann Esposito, who seemed to be everyone's lovable Italian-American aunt, the one who never ran out of wonderfully savory recipes for everything from meatballs and spaghetti to all kinds of regional Italian dishes. Esposito grew up in western New York with two Sicilian grandmothers, who passed on their culinary skills. With a Master's degree in food history from the University of New Hampshire, Esposito cast a scholar's eye on regional *cucina italiana* and self-produced the *Ciao Italia* series, which is now in its twenty-first year. While the show was mostly set in the TV studio kitchen, Esposito would also take her cameras to Italy to meet the cheesemakers, the vineyard owners, the hog farmers, home cooks and restaurant chefs, cooking along side of them, chatting in sing-song Italian, and translating it all into an easy-to-digest American TV idiom. With 11 cookbooks tied in to the show, *Ciao Italia* is the longest-running cooking series on television.

If Esposito at first represented a proud Italian-American tradition, another PBS cook, Lidia Bastianich, introduced viewers to Italy's regionalism on her series *Lidia's Italy,* which began in 1998 and was filmed in her own family kitchen. PBS had approached her about a series after she had appeared on segments of Julia Child's *Cooking with Master Chefs.* She proved to be a natural teacher, patient and maternal; on each show she would bring her family onto the set, including her mother Erminia, her son Joseph, who co-owned Babbo and with whom she opened other restaurants in New York, Kansas City, and St. Louis, and her daughter Tanya, a Renaissance art history graduate who worked on her mother's shows and cookbooks.

By the time *Ciao Italia* was well established, the Food Network began, a cable channel created in 1993 by a former journalist from Providence, Rhode Island, named Joe Langham. The network started out clumsily enough by using old TV cooking shows, some in black-and-white, which included Julia Child's original French Chef series and Graham Kerr's *The Galloping Gourmet,* but nothing Italian. As live and videotaped formats evolved, the network developed shows around the carefully crafted and coiffed personas of their hosts, such as Louisiana chef Emeril Lagasse, New Yorker Bobby Flay, Austro-Californian Wolfgang Puck, and Italian American Mario Batali, each a very different personality but all soon to be major TV stars and very wealthy men. Batali, on his show *Molto Mario,* was the only one doing Italian food. Dressed in his nightly uniform of rolled-up shirt-sleeves, khaki shorts, and orange Crocs, the rotund chef spoke as fast as he cooked, instructing on-camera guests in the small details of why following tradition was so important for both flavor and spirit. He was, with the others, also part of a ridiculous samurai-like cooking challenge show called *Iron Chef,* which pitted him against colleagues to come up with dishes from mystery ingredients, the results to be judged by a panel of slurping food media notables.

Seeking its own Nigella Lawson, Food Network hired the diminutive beauty Giada De Laurentiis. Born in Rome with a show business pedigree that included producer Dino De Laurentiis and actress Silvana Mangano, Giada grew up in New York and Beverly Hills, trained at Le Cordon Bleu in Paris, and worked for Wolfgang Puck. She was a food stylist in 2003 when Food Network hired her to host *Everyday Italian,* which had a solid six-year run. She followed with cookbooks, a two-part TV series called *Giada in Paradise,* about Santorini, Greece, and Capri, won a Daytime Emmy Award for Outstanding Lifestyle Host, and became a spokeswoman for Barilla pasta.

As the network intended, De Laurentiis became as famous for her ingenuous sex appeal as for her culinary talent, and her friendly, Beverly Hills girl-next-door demeanor contrasted with the sensual photo shoots she did for magazines. As with Lawson, the absurd media term "food porn" became attached to De Laurentiis because she wore deep necklines and posed for suggestive magazine spreads, including one in *Esquire* that showed her lying seductively in a pool of tomato sauce.

An even bigger success for the network was Rachael Ray—also a girl-next-door type but less Beverly Hills than Glens Falls, New York—who hosted *30*

*Minute Meals* and parlayed her success into her own magazine, *Every Day with Rachael Ray,* and a syndicated talk show. Her Food Network show was not specifically Italian in nature, but the concept of creating a meal in 30 minutes caused Ray, a former caterer, to turn most often to Italian recipes; just as important, her constant urging of her viewers to use what she called "EVOO"—extra virgin olive oil—for everything from salad dressing to sautéing did more for that ingredient's sales than anything else in its seven-thousand-year history.

Ringing endorsements of olive oil and Italian food had also been heard among the food magazines of the 1990s, when the time-consuming, ostentatiously sophisticated meals of a kind found in *Gourmet* magazine had gone the way of the duck press. Instead, *Gourmet, Bon Appétit, Food & Wine,* and *Saveur,* as well as women's lifestyle magazines such as *Good Housekeeping* and *Family Circle,* were publishing simpler recipes that would appeal to two-career couples with less time than ever to cook. Columnists earnestly explained the differences between one Italian rice and another. And Italian wines were always in the pictures, having achieved a status equal to French wines, whose sales, especially abroad, had been dropping as Italian wines were rising.

In 2000, for the first time in its 25-year-history, *Wine Spectator* gave its Wine of the Year Award to an Italian label—the 1997 Antinori Toscana Solaia. The next year, the award went to the 1998 Tenuta dell'Ornellaia Bolgheri Superiore Ornellaia, and in 2006, to the 2001 Casanova di Neri Brunello di Montalcino Tenuta Nuova. In addition, 13 Italian wines have achieved the magazine's top score (100 points) for excellence. Robert Parker's highly influential *Wine Advocate* newsletter, which began in the 1970s with reviews of mostly Bordeaux and Burgundy, expanded coverage in the 1990s to include Italy, hiring full-time associates to cover the region.

It was not wholly surprising, then—although it would have been difficult to imagine a decade before—that *Gourmet* magazine put a photo of meatballs and spaghetti on its cover for January 2009, calling it "the ultimate Italian-American classic" and explaining that "while this famous duo is thought to have originated in southern Italy, it transcended its roots long ago and has come to occupy as cherished a place in the American psyche as the hamburger."[12]

Four months later, with a line that sang out "New American Classics," *Bon Appétit* put on its cover a photo of whole grain spaghetti with beef and sausage *ragù*. In the feature story, the editors posed an earnest question about just how far American, Italian, and Italian-American had come.

> Just what is American food? Pizza? Fried chicken? A great big juicy T-bone steak? Or is American cooking in the 21st century more likely to be *mole*, Asian-inspired curry, or an organic, artisanal, locally sourced main-course salad? We've selected a dozen iconic American dishes and replaced them with their modern culinary counterparts. It wasn't easy—one man's spaghetti and meatballs isn't necessarily another man's whole grain spaghetti with slow-cooked beef and sausage *ragù*—and there were plenty of arguments along the way. . . . Do you agree? Do you think we're out of our ever-loving minds?[13]

The kind of gusto that caused Italian food to become the world's most popular, enticing, healthful, and accessible is something competitive cuisines such as sushi, Spanish tapas, molecular, and avant-garde have never achieved. The universal comfort level of Italian food is beyond any other cuisine's, so that while a Frenchman might weep over his beloved *boeuf bourguignon* and a Moroccan swoon over his mother's couscous, Neil Simon has been proven right when he called the love of Italian food a law of the universe.

The fits and starts, fads and trends, tastes and styles that have brought Italian food and wine to its present state of global admiration now form the basis of passionate discussions of what is in and what is out, and just keeping up with what's stylish. Bloomingdale's fashion director, Kal Ruttenstein, said that a major source of inspiration in his work comes from dining regularly at Da Silvano in New York, Bice in Milan, and Le Stresa in Paris. "Restaurants are the discothèques of the first decade of the new century," he told the menswear publication *DNR*. "I have to be out there to see what everyone is wearing. I don't feel like I'm doing my job if I'm not out at night."[14]

So dominant had Italian food and restaurants become by the turn of the century that even New York's French Culinary Institute acknowledged its importance by establishing the Italian Culinary Academy, designed by Tuscan chef Cesare Cassella, which offers students the opportunity to study in Parma.

At the moment, the lusty culinary style Mario Batali fostered at Babbo is paramount among the network of foodies in the media and the blogosphere who gossip instantly about the newest trattoria in Rome or Greenwich Village. Newspaper food sections and magazines publish in-depth articles on Italian exotica, from *lardo* to *fregola,* from thin Sardinian *carta da musica* bread to the peppery, hot Calabrian spreadable pork and chile condiment '*nduja,* which a 2009 *New York Times* article called "the Lady Gaga of pork products."[15]

Meatballs—the prototypical symbol of Italian-American excess—made an astounding comeback in the century's first decade, appearing on Italian menus around the United States. One Houston restaurant, the Rockwood Room, began making them with Kobe beef, and spaghetti and meatballs was named "Dish of the Year" on the cover of *Bon Appetit*'s January 2010 issue, which included five meatball recipes inside. When a Brooklyn restaurant announced a "Meatball Slapdown" competition among leading New York chefs in January 2010, it sold out within days.

But no dish soared as high into the culinary stratosphere in the past decade as pizza did. Once dismissed as an old-fashioned, cheap, oily, garlicky Italian-American snack food sold out of storefronts, pizza rose to faddish eminence in the 1980s, beginning with the California models at Chez Panisse and Spago, so that Italian restaurateurs who had removed their pizza ovens in order to move up in culinary class were now putting them back so they could serve pizza right alongside with *penne alla vodka* and fettuccine and white truffles. Indeed, even those truffles, or truffle oil, now graced the new pizzas, which were taking different, thinner forms as flatbreads. And even though few people ever attempt to make pizza at home (unless it is frozen), Food Network now offers 50 pizza recipes on its website.

If America led the pizza revolution, the world followed quickly. In 2005, Ed Levine published *Pizza: A Slice of Heaven,* with history, lore, ratings, essays, even poems, by authors as disparate as Nora Ephron, Roy Blount Jr., and Calvin Trillin. Noting that there were more than sixty thousand pizzerias in America, Levine asked, more or less seriously, "Could pizza be the catalyst for world harmony? A candidate for the Nobel Peace Prize? The appeal of pizza crosses all ethnic, racial and class lines. Everybody, from working class families to college kids to multi-billionaires, loves pizza."[16]

The so-called artisanal pizza craze began in New York around 2004, when well-established pizzerias such as Totonno's in Brooklyn, John's and G. Lombardi's in Manhattan, and Mario's in the Bronx were joined by new contenders like Franny's in Park Slope, Una Pizza Napoletana in Greenwich Village, and Zero Otto Nove on Arthur Avenue. According to a 2010 *New York* magazine piece, "you can't walk two blocks without getting pied in the face by a Neapolitan these days."[17] The article went on to describe a new pizzeria named Co. (with backing from French chef Jean-Georges Vongerichten) in Chelsea, where owner Jim Lahey used the Neapolitan model for his crust but challenged all the traditional rules. "Tomatoes aren't even indigenous to Italy," said Lahey in 2009, "so where do we get off saying it has to be tomatoes on top of the bread? [Mozzarella is] a cliché. I'm going to have to control the use of what is an overused ingredient."[18] Lahey's menu, then, includes a pizza with zucchini-anchovy purée and zucchini blossoms; another with *honshemeji* mushrooms, *guanciale,* quail eggs, *béchamel,* buffalo mozzarella, Parmigiano, and garlic; and one with radicchio, red onion, chiles, and three cheeses, which *New York* said looked like "a nest built by a slightly deranged bird."[19]

Pizza had become so ubiquitous in New York restaurants of any kind that a review in *The New Yorker* posed the question, "Can you procure a restaurant license without a pizza oven these days?"[20]

Along with the once humble pizza, many Italian foods associated with the lowest class have been brought into the gastro-sublime. Fava beans, spelt, *cavolo nero,* tripe, chickpeas, rabbit, even breadcrumbs—the "poor man's grated cheese"—are now on contemporary menus. The rich, hearty Roman *spaghetti alla carbonara,* made with eggs and pancetta or *guanciale,* is now so popular that it may well fulfill the role Calvin Trillin once envisioned for it: to replace turkey at Thanksgiving.

Perhaps no contemporary dish better demonstrates just how far Italian food has come as does a very beautiful creation of chef Fortunato Nicotra of New York's Felidia: On a warm plate, he places a round of soft, golden polenta, enriched with cream-centered *burrata* cheese, and on top of that he sets a swirl of American caviar. Such a thing was once unimaginable for anyone but the richest Italian nobility, who would not in any case eat polenta, which was so commonly associated with the poor; now, for a price of $21, anyone can have it (see page 243 for recipe).

Nicotra, who is from Sicily, says he first thought of the dish when good *burrata* from Puglia began coming into the United States eight years ago. "I wanted to do something with caviar like the Russians and French do with sour cream, but make it Italian, so I use the *burrata,* which, when you cut it, the cream oozes out. The polenta is poor people's food from the north of Italy and *burrata* is from the south. The caviar is rich people's food, but the Italians have started to use their own locally produced caviar in dishes. I use caviar from California, because this is America and it's very good. So the dish is a combination of so many influences, but it is also very much Italian. It is also mine."[21] And for all that, Fortunato's simple antipasto dish explains the charm of contemporary *alta cucina,* which can now compete with the finest cuisine in the world.

## POLENTA WITH BURRATA AND CAVIAR

At Felidia restaurant in New York, Chef Fortunato Nicotra created this dish in 2009 from the once-humble polenta together with creamy *burrata* mozzarella and caviar as a way of combining the traditional with the new internationalism of Italian cuisine.

*4 cups water*
*1 fresh or dried bay leaf*
*1 tablespoon salt*
*1/2 tablespoon extra virgin olive oil*
*3/4 cup coarse yellow cornmeal*
*2 tablespoons butter*
*12 ounces burrata*
*3 ounces domestic caviar*
*1 tablespoons chives, chopped*
*6 slices country bread, toasted*

1.  Pour cornmeal into a 3- to 4-quart cast iron, enameled cast-iron or other heavy saucepan, and add 2 cups water, the bay leaf and $1/2$ tablespoon salt and bring to a boil over medium-high heat. When boiling, add the olive oil.
2.  Stir until the cornmeal thickens, adding more water as necessary to keep a porridge-like consistency. When the polenta starts to pull away from the sides of the saucepan, it is ready.
3.  Divide the hot polenta evenly into six warm bowls. Add 2 ounces of burrata directly on top of the mound of polenta. To the burrata, add $1/2$ ounce of caviar. Garnish with chives, and finish with a drizzle of extra virgin olive oil. Serve with toasted bread.

Serves 6.

# Coda

Trends in Italian and Italian-American food have waxed and waned, ebbed and flowed, but they continue to evolve. It is important, therefore, to bring up to date the stories of those people and places in this book that had such influence on that evolution.

The last of the nineteenth-century **Delmonico's** restaurants closed in 1923, a victim of Prohibition, but at various times different owners opened one or another of the units. The restaurant at 56 Beaver Street was reopened in 1993 by Milan Licul of the Ocinomled Group, which owns several fine dining Italian restaurants including Murano, Arno, and Scalletta.

**G. Lombardi's**, the first documented pizzeria in America (1905), closed its doors on Spring Street in New York in 1984, but it was reopened a block away in 1994 by John Brescio and is still operating at 32 Spring Street.

In the **Arthur Avenue** section of the Bronx, many of the old-time groceries, food stores, and restaurants still thrive, including Mario's, Dominick's, and Tony and Anna's restaurants, Madonia and Addeo bakeries, Mike's Deli, Calandra & Sons Cheese, Cosenza's fish market, and Biancardi's butcher. In recent years, the neighborhood has received a large influx of immigrants from the Dalmatian coast who have purchased a good deal of the real estate and opened their own restaurants there.

**Barbetta**, opened in 1906, still occupies its original brownstones in New York's Theater District and is run by the founder's daughter, Laura Maioglio.

Vincent Sardi Jr., whose father opened **Sardi's** in 1921 in the Theater District, took over the restaurant in 1947 and ran it until 1985, when he sold it to Detroit producers Ivan Bloch and Harvey Klaris and restaurateur Stuart Lichtenstein, who declared bankruptcy in 1990 and closed. Vincent Sardi resumed ownership a year later with partner Max Klimavicius. Sardi passed away in 2007. Klimavicius still runs the restaurant.

**Mamma Leone's** was sold to Restaurant Associates in 1959. The new owners changed its location and later, in 1992, closed the restaurant.

**Elaine's** has barely changed in menu or clientele. Its owner, Elaine Kaufman, died in 2010, but the restaurant is still at its original premises at 1703 Second Avenue in New York.

**Mercurio, Romeo Salta, San Marino, Orsini's,** and **Il Nido** have all closed.

**Trattoria,** in New York's Pan Am Building (now the MetLife Building), was transformed by Patina Group into a pizzeria-trattoria named Naples 45.

**Patsy's,** owned by the Scognamillo family in its third generation, is still at its West 56th Street location in New York's Theater District, with grandson Sal now acting as chef.

**Amerigo's** in the Bronx closed in the mid-1990s.

The original **Palm** steakhouse is at its original location at 837 Second Avenue in New York. It is now an international corporation with its own wholesale meat company and 25 branches in the United States, along with units in London and Mexico City.

After running San Domenico for 20 years, **Tony May** closed the restaurant on Central Park South (it is now Michael White's Marea) and moved south to 26th Street to open a much larger, more contemporary restaurant called SD26 with his daughter Marisa. He is still very active with the Gruppo Ristoratori Italiani.

**Sirio Maccioni,** with his wife, Egidiana, and sons Mario, Marco, and Mauro. still runs Le Cirque in New York, along with Le Cirque, Circo, and Sirio in Las Vegas.

**Piero Selvaggio,** owner of Valentino restaurants in Santa Monica and Las Vegas, opened another branch in Houston at the Derek Hotel in the fall of 2009.

Long after Pino Luongo sold his share in **Il Cantinori,** the Tuscan *ristorante* still thrives as one of the most fashionable in New York. After the HBO series *Sex and the City* filmed an episode in which the character Carrie Bradshaw celebrates her thirty-fifth birthday at the restaurant, business got even better.

After leaving Le Madri, **Pino Luongo** opened a series of Italian restaurants, including Tuscan Square, Cocopazzo, and a restaurant in Barney's uptown Manhattan location. He bought the Sfuzzi chain out of Dallas, and when it foundered, he attempted unsuccessfully to replace them with branches of Cocopazzo. He has published several books, including *A Tuscan in the Kitchen* (1988), *Simply Tuscan* (2000), and his memoir *Dirty Dishes* (2008). Today Luongo owns just one restaurant, Centolire, on Madison Avenue in New York.

**Lidia Bastianich** still owns Felidia with her family as well as restaurants in St. Louis and Kansas City, Missouri, and several in New York with her son Joseph and partner Mario Batali, including Del Posto in New York's Meat Packing District.

She has written five Italian cookbooks and produces her PBS programs *Lidia's Family Table* and *Lidia's Italy*.

**Danny Meyer**, under his Union Square Hospitality Group, now runs a dozen food operations, most based in New York, including Union Square Café, Gramercy Tavern, Tabla, the Modern, Blue Smoke, Shake Shack, and his latest, Maialino, a Roman-style restaurant with blue checkered tablecloths. He is the author of *Setting the Table: The Transforming Power of Hospitality in Business*.

**Mario Batali**, with partner **Joseph Bastianich**, now runs a wide range of restaurants in New York and Las Vegas. In 2008, with Nancy Silverton, he opened Pizzeria Mozza and Osteria Mozza in Los Angeles. Batali is the author of eight cookbooks.

**Pepe's Pizza**, which opened in New Haven in 1925, is still on the same premises and now has a branch in Yonkers, New York.

Chicago's **Pizzeria Uno**, launched in 1943, is now a corporation with more than 175 Uno Chicago Grill restaurants in 28 states, Puerto Rico, South Korea, United Arab Emirates, Honduras, Kuwait, and Saudi Arabia.

**Michael Chiarello** left Tra Vigne in California's Napa Valley in 2000 to create NapaStyle, a showcase of handcrafted home goods and artisanal foods, and Chiarello Family Vineyards. He has written six books and hosted shows such as *Season by Season* on PBS and Food Network's Emmy Award-winning *Easy Entertaining with Michael Chiarello*. He was named Chef of the Year in 1985 by *Food & Wine* magazine. In 2008, he returned to the restaurant business with Bottega in Yountville, California.

**Tony Mantuano** is still executive chef at Spiaggia in Chicago, which had $10 million in sales in 2009. He remains committed to *alta cucina* and still only serves pizza and meatballs in the adjacent Café Spiaggia.

**Mosca's**, outside of New Orleans, was damaged by hurricanes Katrina and Rita and closed for renovation. It is still in continuous operation in Avondale, Louisiana, and is still run by the same family. **Pascal's Manale** is also still in business, since 1913, at 1838 Napoleon Avenue.

**Musso and Frank Grill** in Hollywood is still open, with many longtime waiters who go back decades in the restaurant's history. In October 2009, the restaurant was bought by Jordan M. Jones, a fourth-generation descendant of one of the early owners.

**Perino's** in Los Angeles staggered through the 1970s and finally closed in 1983, then moved downtown. It was reopened on its original location on Wilshire Boulevard in 1985 but was soon padlocked by bankruptcy trustees. It was again resurrected in 1986, this time by Italian investors Carlo Bondanelli and Gualtiero Billi, who brought the menu up to date, but poor business caused them to close the restaurant in 1989, never to reopen.

**Wolfgang Puck** is one of the richest, most entrepreneurial chefs in the world. He has opened dozens of restaurants—several under the Spago name—created a line of food products, including frozen pizzas, written books, and had a show on Food Network, as well as making countless appearances on TV and at charity affairs. He is also famous for his Oscar Night parties.

**Fior d'Italia** expanded in size over the decades and is still in operation in San Francisco's North Beach area, now on Mason Street in the San Remo Hotel. The restaurant has had only three sets of owners over more than 120 years; currently it is owned by Bob and Jinx Larive.

**Caesar's Place**, where Caesar Cardini created the Caesar salad, is still open but is not associated with the Cardini family.

Keeping his focus on Houston, **Tony Vallone** opened and later sold the more casual restaurants Grotto and La Griglia. He continued to make the menus at his flagship Tony's more and more Italian, and in 2009, he opened a casual but sleek trattoria called Ciao Bello.

**Castello Banfi** still imports a wide range of Italian wines, including Riunite Lambrusco and those made at its estate outside of Montalcino, where the Mariani family now runs an elegant inn. It also owns estates in Piedmont. John Mariani Jr. and Harry Mariani are proprietors; John's daughter Cristina Mariani-May and Harry's son James are co-CEOs. Castello Banfi is the first winery in the world to be internationally recognized for exceptional environmental, ethical, and social responsibility. It was named "Winery of the Year" by both *Wine Enthusiast* and *Wine & Spirits* magazine.

The **E.&J. Gallo** wine company continued to expand its worldwide wine offerings, creating its own vintage-dated wines in 1983; Gallo Estate premium wines were launched in 1993, the year Julio Gallo died. In 1996, it introduced its first foreign brand, Ecco Domani. Ernest Gallo died in 2007, at the age of 98. E.&J. Gallo Winery is now the world's largest family-owned winery and the largest exporter of California wine.

The **Mariani Packing Company**, founded in Cupertino, California, after the 1906 San Francisco earthquake, is now the largest dried fruit company in the world.

**Robert Mondavi** maintained his importance to the winery that bore his name and published his autobiography *Harvests of Joy* in 1998. In 2004, Constellation

Brands took over Robert Mondavi winery at a cost of $1.36 billion. Mondavi established the Robert Mondavi Institute for Food and Wine Science and helped found COPIA: The American Center for Wine, Food, and the Arts in Napa now closed. He died at the age of 94 in 2008. His son Michael has gone on to launch his own winery, M by Michael Mondavi, as well as running a wine sales company, Folio Fine Wine Partners.

Italian Americans have continued to open wineries in California and other states, along with investments by Italians such as **Marchese Piero Antinori**, who has interests in Stag's Leap as well as in Washington State wineries. Napa Valley in particular has seen a good number of Italian Americans who have started wineries in the past two decades, including Fontanella Family Winery, Grassi Wine Company, Robert Biale Vineyards, Arger-Martucci Vineyards, and Francis Ford Coppola Winery, owned by the director of *The Godfather* and other movies.

**Mary Ann Esposito** continues to produce and host her TV show *Ciao Italia,* now in its twenty-first year, with 1.4 million weekly viewers on 270 PBS stations, while writing cookbooks connected with the show's content. She has been honored with awards from the National Italian American Foundation, the National Organization of Italian American Women, the Columbus Foundation, and the Pirandello Lyceum of Washington, D.C.

**Chef Boyardee** Italian canned foods was sold to American Home Foods, renamed International Home Foods, and later purchased by its current owner, ConAgra Foods.

**Rice-a-Roni** is now owned by Golden Grain Company of Chicago.

In 1998, the Swiss firm Lindt and Sprüngli Chocolate acquired **Ghirardelli Chocolate Company** as a wholly owned subsidiary of its holding company.

**Alfredo's Ristorante** still exists in Rome, now run by the grandson of the original owner, Alfredo Di Lelio. The Alfredo's franchise outside of Italy, now run by Russell Bellanca, expanded then shrunk to one, at New York's Rockefeller Center.

**Passeto** in Rome is also still one of the city's fine dining classics.

**Trattoria Giannino**, which opened in Milan in 1899, is still open, as are **Bice** (run by Bice's granddaughters), **Bagutta**, and **Le Langhe**, still drawing the fashion crowd during the Milan shows.

Arrigo Cipriani and his son Giuseppe Cipriani opened **Cipriani Downtown** in Manhattan's trendy SoHo neighborhood in 1996. They also bought a vast catering facility at 55 Wall Street for $28 million, took over the Rainbow Room in Rockefeller Center, put a trattoria into Grand Central Terminal, and set up restaurants in Hong Kong, London, and Porto Cervo.

The original **Harry's Bar** (unassociated with any others by that name) is still open in its original location on the Calle Vallaresso.

**Lucio Caputo** left the Italian Trade Commission in New York in 1982 and opened his own Italian Wine & Food Institute, a nonprofit corporation established to promote and further improve the image of Italian wines and foods in the United States. In 2003, he was awarded the Cavaliere di Gran Croce in the Order to the Merit of the Italian Republic.

In February 2010, the **Italian Trade Commission** held VINO 2010: Italian Wine Week, the largest Italian wine trade show held outside of Italy, uniting over four hundred Italian wineries with over 2,800 members of the trade and press. Kevin Zraly, press conference moderator, called it an event where "the world's number one producer [Italy] meets the world's greatest wine consumer [the United States]."

**Marcella Hazan** has settled with her husband, Victor, in Longboat Key, Florida, and continues to write cookbooks and teach. She retired from her cooking school in Venice in 1998 but went on to give classes at the French Culinary Institute in New York. She was knighted in 2005 by the president of Italy.

Italian food journalist **Luigi Veronelli** died in Bergamo, in 2004, at the age of 78.

**Roberto Ruggeri**, who expanded the Bice name around the world, took on Japanese investors in the 1980s, but the crisis in Japan's economy caused him to buy them out in 1994. In 1988, he opened a very successful Bice in Paris, with Middle Eastern investors, but closed it after five years when the lease ran out. Ruggeri closed several others branches, including those in Houston and Dallas, but today there are 25 Bices, including one each in Qatar, Beirut, Johannesburg, and Capetown, two in Dubai, and eight in Mexico. Ruggeri still runs the company from his headquarters in Miami.

**Gualtiero Marchesi** left Milan in 1993 to open a restaurant near Brescia in a country resort, the Ristorante Erbusco in the Albereta Hotel, where he forged a still more global cuisine rather than an Italian one. He returned to Milan to launch Gualtiero Marchesi di San Pietro all'Orto in 1998, then opened a restaurant in Paris and, in 2002, opened Osteria dell'Orso.

**Gianluigi Morini** still runs San Domenico in Imola with Chef Valentino Marcattilii.

The third and fourth generations of the Santini family still **own** and operate **Dal Pescatore** in Canneto sull'Oglio.

**Antonio Carluccio** is a consultant and operates food stores in 45 locations in the United Kingdom.

London's **River Café**, which reopened in 2008 after a kitchen fire, continues to be one of the most popular restaurants in the city. Owners Rose Gray and Ruth Rogers were honored in 2009 with a Members of the British Empire award for their contributions to the hospitality industry. Their ten cookbooks are among the bestselling of all time. Rose Gray died of cancer in 2010.

Peter Boizot, who had 80 **Pizza Express** eateries, still runs Pizza on the Park, which has also become one of London's premier jazz venues.

The **Michelin Guide** continues to increase its star rankings in Italy; as of 2010, there are 229 restaurants with one star, 37 with two stars, and 6 with three stars. The 2011 edition lists 233 with one star, 37 with two stars, and 6 with three stars.

Whether or not she ever actually said, "Everything you see I owe to spaghetti," **Sophia Loren** seems a gloriously apt symbol of Italy and of its food. Of good stature and real backbone, with a proud jaw and irresistible smile, voluptuous and inviting, sophisticated but down-to-earth, sensuous but refined, simple but complex, savory and sweet, salty and bitter, exquisitely modern but wholly grounded in tradition, Sophia is a fabled and fabulous image. Like a great pasta, that image can bring a man to his knees or lift him to the sublime. Like a sip of Italian wine, she can cure his thirst or make him ravenous for more. Luckily for all of us, La Grande Sophia and *la grande cucina* are two of so many artistic and cultural treasures *bella Italia* has for so long happily and graciously shared with a world of so many spoons.

# Notes

## Chapter 1 A Plate of Soup Surrounded by Too Many Spoons

1. *The Roman Antiquities,* Book One. Trans. Earnest Cary (Cambridge, MA: Harvard University Press, 2001), 31.
2. "The People of Rome," in *Readings in the Classical Historians,* ed. Michael Grant (New York: Charles Scribner's Sons, 1992), 603.
3. Felipe Fernández-Armesto, *Near a Thousand Tables* (New York: The Free Press, 2002), 165.
4. Angelo Pellegrini, *The Unprejudiced Palate* (New York: Macmillan, 1948), 25. A more romantic view of polenta-eating was provided by Marcella Hazan when she wrote in *The Classic Italian Cook Book* (1973), "It was made daily in an unlined copper kettle, the *paiolo,* which was always kept hanging at the ready on a hook in the center of the fireplace. The hearth was usually large enough to accommodate a bench on which the family sat, warming itself at the fire, making talk, watching the glittering cornmeal stream into the boiling kettle, encouraging the tireless stirring of the cook. When the *polenta* was done, there was a moment of joy as it was poured out in a streaming, golden circle on the beechwood top of the *madia,* a cupboard where bread and flour were stored. Italy's great nineteenth-century novelist, Alessandro Manzoni, described it as looking like a harvest moon coming out of the mist. The image is almost Japanese."
5. Goethe, *Italian Journey.* Ed . Thoms P. Saine and Jeffrey L. Sammons; Trans. Robert R. Heitner (New York: Suhrkamp Publishers, 1989), 33–34. Entry dated Sept. 17, 1786. Pellagra persisted even into the twentieth century among Americans in the Deep South, where 1,192 Mississippians died of the disease in 1913 owing to a diet principally made up of corn.
6. See Giovanni Rebora, *Culture of the Fork: A Brief History of Food in Europe* (New York: Columbia University Press, 2001), 46–48.
7. Alexandre Dumas, *Dictionary of Cuisine,* ed., abridged and translated by Louis Colman from *Le Grand Dictionnaire de cuisine* (New York: Simon & Schuster, 1986), 164.
8. In researching her *Encyclopedia of Pasta* (Berkeley: U. of California Press, 2009), Oretta Zanini de Vita identified more than 1,300 pasta names, both factory and homemade.
9. Giuseppe di Lampedusa, *The Leopard,* trans. Archibald Colquhoun (New York: Pantheon, 1960), 96–97.
10. Cited by Fernández-Armesto, 124.
11. Leigh Hunt, *The Autobiography of Leigh Hunt* (London: The Cresset Press, 1959), 392.
12. Ibid., 398.
13. Charles Dickens, *Pictures from Italy* (New York: The Ecco Press, 1988), 32, 56, 103.
14. Ibid., 155.

15.  Booker T. Washington and Robert E. Parker, *The Man Farthest Down* (New York: Double-
     day, 1912), 144.

16.  In her book *Why Italians Love to Talk About Food* (New York: Farrar, Straus and Giroux,
     2010), Elena Kostioukovich writes extensively about the myriad *sagre* held in Italy's
     provinces.

17.  As Gillian Riley writes in *The Oxford Companion to Italian Food* (New York: Oxford Uni-
     versity Press, 2007), 28: "Artusi's book made a greater contribution to the unification of
     Italy than all the efforts by politicians and linguists to bring a century of separate entities
     with their own dialects into a coherent nation."

18.  The best English translation of Artusi's book is by Kyle M. Phillips III (New York: Random
     House, 1996), from which these quotations are taken.

## Chapter 2   The Great Escape

1.   *London at Table, or How, When and Where to Dine and Order Dinner* (London: Chapman
     and Hall, 1851) and John Richardson's *The Exhibition London Guide and Visitor's Pocket
     Companion* (London: Simpkin, Marshall, and Company, 1851).

2.   Cited in John D. Folse, *The Encyclopedia of Cajun & Creole Cuisine* (Gonzales, LA: Chef
     John Folse & Company, 2004), 109.

3.   Madame Elizabeth Kettenring Dutreuil Begué, *Madame Begué and Her Recipes*, 194–
     195.

4.   Mariani Premium website, http://www.marianifruit.com/family/.

5.   Angelo Pellgrini, *The Unprejudiced Palate* (New York: The Modern Library, 2005), 22.

6.   Quoted in Allon Schoener, *The Italian Americans* (New York: Macmillan, 1987), 41.

7.   Novelist Mario Puzo described the arrival of the vegetable man: "'CHE BELLA IN-
     SALATA!'"—what beautiful salad . . . not asking anyone to buy, only asking the world to
     look at the beauty. Pride, not cajolement, in his voice, he repeated his cry each time his
     horse took a mincing step along the Avenue. In his wagon were boxes of onions dazzling
     white, great brown potatoes, bushels of apples, bouquets of scallions, leeks, and pars-
     ley sprigs. His voice rose rich with helpless admiration, disinterested, a call to lovers.
     'What a beautiful salad.'" In *The Fortunate Pilgrim* (New York: Ballantine Books, 1977),
     p. 48.

8.   Quoted in John Mariani, *America Eats Out* (New York: William Morrow, 1991), 65.

9.   Donna R. Gabaccia, *We Are What We Eat: Ethnic Food and the Making of Americans* (Cam-
     bridge, MA: Harvard University Press, 1998), 51–52.

10.  Quoted in Mariani, 65.

11.  Catherine Scorsese with Georgia Downard, *Italianamerican: The Scorsese Family Cookbook*
     (New York: Random House, 1996), 3.

12.  *Impressions du Voyage, Le Corricolo* (Paris: C. Levey, 1886), 94.

13.  Georges Auguste Escoffier, *Le Guide Culinaire*, trans. H. L. Cracknell and R. J. Kaufmann
     (New York: Mayflower Books, 1921), 30.

14.  Begué, 194–197.

## Chapter 3    Feeding the *Americani*

1.  Clementine Paddleford, "Pizza Pies Offer Savory Snack For Midnight Parties at Home," *Herald Tribune,* April 21, 1939.
2.  William Grimes, *Appetite City: A Culinary History of New York* (New York: North Point Press, 2009), 96.
3.  "Joe Guffanti's Victuals," *New York Times,* July 1, 1900.
4.  Niccolo de Quattrociocchi (of El Borracho restaurant), *Love and Dishes* (New York: Bobbs-Merrill, 1950), 165.
5.  G. Selmer Fougner, *Dining Out in New York* (New York: H. C. Kinsey & Company, 1939), 21.
6.  Lawton McKall, *Knife and Fork in New York* (New York: Doubleday & Company, 1949), 64–65.
7.  Ibid., 63.

## Chapter 4    The New Way of the Old World

1.  Filippo Tommaso Marinetti, *Gazzetta del Popolo,* Dec. 28, 1932, 395.
2.  Corrado Govoni, "Facciamo I conti," *Futurismo* vol. 2, no. 28 (March 19, 1933).
3.  From promotional copy for *Rex.*
4.  Despite their speed and modernity, *Rex* and *Conte di Savoia,* having been built to serve the less popular "sunny southern route," rarely sailed more than half full during the Depression, so first-class passengers were increasingly joined by emigrants going to America. A skewed sense of steerage class in those days can be seen in the rollicking scene in MGM's movie *A Night at the Opera* (1935), starring the Marx brothers, in which the zany trio stows away on a ship out of Italy and lines up to receive an enormous plate of spaghetti for dinner, then to watch immigrants in Hollywood-designed blouses, sashes, and head scarves dance and sing "Santa Lucia" with joyous abandon. When the war began, both the *Rex* and *Conte di Savoia* were painted in neutral colors and continued passenger service until Mussolini joined with Hitler, at which point the ships were considered by the Allies as prime targets, especially since there had been talk of converting the *Conte di Savoia* into an aircraft carrier. Before that could happen, U.S. Air Force bombers sank her in 1943, and the Royal Air Force fighter-bombers destroyed the *Rex* a year later.
5.  Martin Gilman Wolcott, *The Evil 100* (New York: Citadel, 2004), 69.
6.  Cited in John Dickie, *Delizia!: The Epic History of Italians and Their Food* (New York: Simon & Schuster, 2008), 261.
7.  John Mariani, "Harry's Bar: 'A Clean, Well-lighted Place,'" *The International Review of Food & Wine* (Sept. 1979), 61.
8.  Ibid., 60.
9.  Ibid., 67

## Chapter 5    The Good, the Bad, and the Delicious

1.  Cited by Margalit Fox in "Peg Bracken, 'I Hate to Cook' Author, Dies at 89," *New York Times,* Oct. 23, 2007.

2. Kathy Casey, *Retro Food Fiascos* (Portland, OR: Collectors Press, 2004), 40.

3. Angelo Pellegrini, *The Unprejudiced Palate* (New York: Macmillan, 1948), 7–8.

4. Elizabeth David, *Italian Food* (New York: Penguin Books, 1958), 14.

5. Culinary Arts Institute of Chicago, *The Italian Cookbook: 160 Masterpieces of Italian Cookery* (Chicago: Culinary Arts Institute of Chicago, 1954), 3.

6. Ibid., 26.

### Chapter 6    Il Boom and La Dolce Vita

1. Cited in Jerre Mangione, Jerre Morreale, and Ben Morreale, *La Storia: Five Centuries of the Italian American Experience* (New York: Harper Perennial, 1992), 233.

2. Interview with Dr. Lucio Caputo by John Mariani, Jan. 10, 2010.

3. The Di Lelio family still runs the restaurant in Rome, but they sold rights to franchise the name to Guido Bellanca, a one-time encyclopedia salesman, then multimillionaire automobile dealer, who lost most of his money in weak investments. He first opened a restaurant in Rome, then moved to the United States, where in 1978 he obtained backing from Citibank to open an Alfredo's branch in their new New York skyscraper. He called it L'Originale Alfredo di Roma Ristorante, using a caricature of Alfredo Di Lelio by Al Hirschfeld on his menu cover, then went on to open branches in Miami and at Epcot Center at Disneyworld in Orlando, Florida, where he served a thousand people or more every day. Today, Bellanca's son Russell runs the remaining restaurant of the franchise, across from New York's Rockefeller Center, where he, too, has photos of contemporary celebrities eating the famous fettuccine.

4. *Picture Cook Book,* Ed. Mary Hamman (New York: Time, Inc., 1958), 1.

5. Waverly Root, *The Food of Italy* (New York: Scribner, 1971; New York: Vintage Books, 1977), 12. (Citation refers to the Vintage edition.) In his book Root writes, "Curiously enough, you can travel through Italy itself and still come away with the impression that all Italian food is alike—if you eat in the restaurants frequented by tourists, as tourists often do. The give foreigners what they demand because it is what they are accustomed to, and what they are accustomed to is that emigrant Neapolitan restaurant proprietors abroad have put before them."

6. As Luigi Barzini, in *The Italians* (New York: Atheneum, 1964), 46, described the allure at the time it was at its strongest, "Foreigners come to Rome to taste *la dolce vita* in Via Veneto, in night clubs, in villas on the Via Appia, in film studios, or artists' ateliers in Via Margutta. . . . Others are longing for things that have kept their natural flavor, those simple flavors which industrial civilization is now supplanting with conventional ones. They like the guileless wines, the local cheeses which are unknown a few miles away, the freshly-picked fruit warmed by the sun; the sea urchins split in half with a rusty knife when still dripping with water, and eaten with a few drops of lemon; the *pane casareccio,* or home-baked bread; the passion of the hairy peasant girls smelling of healthy sweat. These people above all relish what they believe are the simple and genuine emotions of the Italians who are apparently unashamed of them and seldom try to hide them."

7. John Mariani, "Harry's Bar: 'A Clean, Well-lighted Place,'" *The International Review of Food and Wine* (Sept. 1979), 61.

8.  Ernest Hemingway, *Across the River and into the Trees* (New York: Scribner, 1950), 77.

9.  Cited in *The Quotable Cook* (New York: The Lyons Press, 2000), 201.

10. Mariani, "Harry's Bar: 'A Clean, Well-lighted Place,'" 61.

11. Ibid.

12. "Arthur Frommer on a Half-Century of Travel," Frommers.com podcast, May 4, 2007.

13. Ibid.

14. Ibid.

15. Ibid.

16. Quoted in "Europe on 5 Dollars a Day," Associated Press, April 30, 2007.

### Chapter 7   This Italian . . . Thing

1.  Ironically, some of those protests were mounted by a shadow front of the Profaci crime family called the Italian American Democratic Organizations. There was even an aborted plan to murder the show's producer, Desi Arnaz, but later episodes in the series did focus more on non-Italian criminals.

2.  Mario Puzo, *The Fortunate Pilgrim* (New York: Ballantine Books, 1997), appendix, "Mario Puzo on *The Godfather*," 279.

3.  Reprinted in Greene's "Vintage Insatiable," on Insatiable-critic.com.

4.  Ibid.

5.  "Classic TV Quotes: The Sopranos," http://www.classictvquotes.com/quotes/shows/the-sopranos/page_2.html.

6.  Italian-American writer Bill Tonetti explains the allure of "The Sopranos" by noting that all the men on the show "do what most men, in their hearts, wish they could do: spend time with one another out and about, idle and unrestrained by the civilizing presence of women in their workplace, free to drink, smoke, curse, eat thick sandwiches of meat and cheese and carry guns and fat rolls of large-denomination bills. They freely commit violence and fornicate, the very things men still do best but are most vigorously denied by contemporary codes of acceptable conduct. . . . . True, Tony Soprano's families (both of them) are deeply dysfunctional. But even that doesn't keep them apart: they've found the path we all seek, a way for family members to be alienated and estranged and bitterly at odds but still closely intertwined and unshakably connected. They still show up for dinner." "A 'Sopranos' Secret: Given the Choice, We'd All Be Mobsters," *New York Times,* March 4, 2001, http://www.nytimes.com/2001/03/04/arts/television-radio-a-sopranos-secret-given-the-choice-we-d-all-be-mobsters.

7.  Joseph Iannuzzi, "Mafia Cookbook," Simon and Schuster website, http://books.simonandschuster.com/Mafia-Cookbook/Joseph-Iannuzzi/9780743229357.

8.  Joseph Iannuzzi, "Cooking on the Lam," Simon and Schuster website, http://books.simonandschuster.com/Cooking-on-the-Lam/Joseph-Iannuzzi/9780743269803.

9.  Molly O'Neill, "The Surrounding Scene—Life of the Party; New York Invites the Delegates to Make Themselves at Home," *New York Times,* July 14, 1992.

10. "Dominick's Restaurant," *New York* magazine, http://nymag.com/listings/restaurant/dominicks-restaurant/.

### Chapter 8   Stirrings

1.   Interview with Tony May by John Mariani in New York, Feb. 12, 2010.
2.   Ibid.
3.   William Grimes, *Appetite City: A Culinary History of New York* (New York: North Point Press, 2009), 261–262.
4.   Ibid., 250.
5.   Deborah Moxham and John Schenck, *The Providence Guide to the 91 Best Restaurants . . . and More* (Providence: Providence Restaurant Guide, 2008), 14.
6.   John Mariani, ed. *Mariani's Coast-to-Coast Dining Guide* (New York: Times Books, 1986), 63.
7.   Spencer Morgan, "Elaine Kaufman," *New York Observer,* Dec. 18, 2005.
8.   Mimi Sheraton, *Eating My Words* (New York: William Morrow, 2004), 96.
9.   Ibid., 97.
10.  Ted Patrick and Silas Spitzer, *The Best Restaurants of America* (New York: Bramhall House, 1960), 97.
11.  Ibid., 221.
12.  *Forbes Magazine Restaurant Guide* (New York: Forbes, Inc., 1971), vol. I, 164–165.
13.  Ibid., 361.
14.  Patrick and Spitzer, 139.
15.  *Forbes,* 308.
16.  "The Princedom of Pasta," *New York,* Dec. 14, 1970, 86.

### Chapter 9   Simmerings

1.   Calvin Trillin, *American Fried* (New York: Penguin Books, 1974), 13.
2.   Luigi Carnacina, *Great Italian Cooking* (New York: Abradale Press, 1968), 366.
3.   Ibid., 7.
4.   Ibid., 8.
5.   Ibid., 9.
6.   Prosper Montagné, *Larousse Gastronomique,* trans. Nina Froud, Patience Gray, *et al.* (New York: Crown Publishers, 1961), 545.
7.   Craig Claiborne, *The New York Times International Cook Book* (New York: Harper & Row, 1971), 394.
8.   Marcella Hazan, *The Classic Italian Cook Book* (New York: Harper's Magazine Press, 1973), 5.
9.   Ibid., 8.

### Chapter 10   From Dago Red to Super Tuscan

1.   Horace, quoted in *The Fireside Book of Wine,* ed. Alex Bespaloff (New York: Simon and Schuster, 1977), 209.

2. Maguelonne Toussaint-Samat, *A History of Food,* trans. Anthea Bell (Cambridge, MA: Blackwell Publishers, 1992), 281.

3. Well after World War II, when Italian wineries were being rebuilt, most wines were still sold in bulk to restaurants. But the destruction of wineries during the war was the catalyst for vintners to adopt the more modern technology then developing in other nations' viniculture.

4. What Hanneke Wilson wrote in the *Oxford Companion to Wine* (Oxford: Oxford University Press, 2006), 365, about Italian wine drinking may sound rudely condescending, for it could also be said of the overwhelming majority of wine drinking people throughout the world, but it is still telling: "The Italian's relationship to wine is not necessarily a hedonistic one. The average Italian is far from a connoisseur of fine bottles, but is rather the heir of thousands of years of vineyard cultivation and wine-making. There are few Italians without some conception—though the conception itself may be naïve, foolish, banal, or simply wrong-headed—of how grapes are grown and transformed into wine."

5. As wine writer Tom Maresca made clear in an article titled "Why Chianti Is the Most Misunderstood Wine in the World": "[F]rom the beginning, the producers most interested in skirting the law, breaking the law, changing the law, were the ones most serious about making better wine. The ones who just wanted to sell a lot didn't care what the law said: They would make the same wine they always had, and sell it to the same markets they always had."

6. Leon D. Adams, *The Wines of America* (New York: McGraw Hill, 1978), 241.

7. Ibid., 246.

8. All quotations here and below from Caputo are from an interview by John Mariani, Jan. 9, 2010.

9. Burton Anderson, *Vino: The Wines & Winemakers of Italy* (New York: Little Brown and Company, 1980), 5.

10. Anecdote told by Biondi-Santi to John Mariani in an interview, Oct. 1976.

11. ItalianMade.com, official website of the Italian Trade Commission, http://www.italian-made.com/home.cfm?display=0.

### Chapter 11    Breaking Away

1. Jean Anthelme Brillat-Savarin, *Physiologie du Goût* (1825), aphorism no. 9, cited in *The Yale Book of Quotations,* ed. Fred R. Shapiro (New Haven, CT: Yale University Press, 2006), 104.

2. Craig Claiborne, "A Precious Moment Arrives for Luxury-Loving Palates," *New York Times,* Oct. 27, 1976, http://select.nytimes.com/mem/archive/pdf?res=F60717FC395B167493C5A B178BD95F428785F9.

3. Marilyn Bender, "Where the Cuisine Is Haute and the Atmosphere Haughty," *New York Times,* Dec. 24, 1968. http://select.nytimes.com/mem/archive/pdf?res=F00C13FD3F54157 493C6AB1789D95F4C8685F9.

4. Ibid.

5.   Laurie Johnston, "What Not to Wear For Haute Cuisine," *New York Times,* April 12, 1973. http://select.nytimes.com/mem/archive/pdf?res=F40711F739551A7493C0A8178FD85F47 8785F9.

6.   Sirio Maccioni and Peter Elliot, *Sirio: The Story of My Life and Le Cirque* (New York: John Wiley & Sons, 2004), 160.

7.   Ibid.

8.   Ibid., 161.

9.   Ibid., 17.

10.  Ibid., 30.

11.  Ibid. 174.

12.  Ibid., 174.

13.  Ibid., 177.

14.  Ibid., 176.

15.  George Fuermann, *Tony's: The Cookbook* (Fredericksburg, TX: Shearer Publishing, 1986), 6.

16.  Interview with Tony Vallone by John Mariani, Jan. 4, 2010.

17.  Ibid.

18.  Ibid.

### Chapter 12   Coming to a Boil

1.   Paul Levy and Ann Barr, *The Official Foodie Handbook* (New York: Timbre Books, 1984), 4.

2.   Interview with Gualtiero Marchesi by John Mariani, March 3, 1982.

3.   Unpublished interview with author.

4.   The names were concocted by Marchesi to be provocative—Flowers of Evil sautéed and negentropic spray; the implosion of semilogical turbot in the style of Umberto Eco; and the Simulacra of Random meats with a fire of "touch wood" (luck).

5.   Enoteca Pinchiorri website, http://www.enotecapinchiorri.com/econtenuti.html.

6.   Mission statement on GRI website, http://www.gruppo.com/mission.php.

7.   All remarks and quotations from speakers are from transcripts of Seminars and Roundtable Discussion of the 1983 Convention Gruppo Ristoratori Italiani (Jan. 20, 21, and 22).

### Chapter 13   A New Respect

1.   Mimi Sheraton, "A Stylish and Popular Place for Pasta," *New York Times,* March 24, 1978, http://select.nytimes.com/mem/archive/pdf?res=F00E1FFC3C5513728DDDAD0A94DB40 5B888BF1D3.

2.   Bryan Miller, "Restaurants," *New York Times,* April 15, 1988, http://www.nytimes.com/1988/ 04/15/arts/restaurants–750588.html?scp=6&sq=parioli%20romanissimo&st=cse.

3.   Interview with Lidia Bastianich by John Mariani, Feb. 22, 2010.

4.   Interview with Piero Selvaggio by John Mariani, Feb. 1, 2010.

5.   Piero Selvaggio, *Valentino Newsletter* (1999).

6.  Piero Selvaggio and Karen Stabiner, *The Valentino Cookbook* (New York: Villard, 2001), xvi.
7.  Ibid.
8.  Ibid., xvii-xviii.
9.  "Valentino, Inagiku, Moustache Café," *Gourmet,* July 1980, 14.
10. John Mariani, *Mariani's Coast-to-Coast Dining Guide* (New York: Times Books, 1986), 473.
11. Ibid., 464.

### Chapter 14   No More Excuses

1.  Marcella Hazan, *The Classic Italian Cook Book* (New York: Harper's Magazine Press, 1973), 13.
2.  Marcella Hazan, *Marcella's Italian Kitchen* (New York: Alfred A. Knopf, 1986), 8.
3.  Alain Ducasse, *Ducasse Flavors of France* (New York: Artisan, 1998), 247.
4.  Ibid.
5.  Interview with Sirio Maccioni by John Mariani, Feb. 5, 2010.
6.  Giuliano Bugialli, *The Fine Art of Italian Cooking,* 2nd ed. (New York: Clarkson Potter, 1990), xvi.
7.  Ibid., xviii.
8.  Ibid., xiii.
9.  Corti Brothers website, http://www.cortibros.biz/website/newsletters/itemsbycat.asp.

### Chapter 15   Flash in the Pan

1.  Lord Byron, *Don Juan* (1823), Canto XIII, stanza 99.
2.  "Italian Imports," *Life* (April 14, 1952), 89.
3.  Valerie Steele, *Fashion Italian Style* (New Haven, CT: Yale University Press, 2003), 57.
4.  Jack Cocks, "Suiting Up for Easy Street: Giorgio Armani defines the new shape of style," *Time* (April 5, 1982), 60.
5.  "The Italian Look," *Newsweek* (Oct. 22, 1978), 36.
6.  Interview with Alessandro Grassi by John Mariani, Jan. 12, 2010.
7.  "Fashionista," Stephen Fried website, http://www.stephenfried.com/fashionista.html.
8.  Interview with Nick Sullivan by John Mariani, Feb. 1, 2010.
9.  "*La Storia del Bagutta,*" Bagutta website, http://www.bagutta.it/english.html.
10. Interview with Nick Sullivan.
11. Marian Burros, "New Management at DDL Foodshow," *New York Times,* April 14, 1982. http://www.nytimes.com/1984/04/14/style/new-management-at-ddl-foodshow.html. Despite poor sales in New York, De Laurentiis pushed west and opened another DDL in Beverly Hills, but by spring 1984 he was forced to sell the New York operation.
12. "Second Opinion," Letters, *New York,* June 3, 1996, 7.
13. Cited in Mark Sullivan, "The Trouble with Harry's," *Vanity Fair,* Dec. 2009, http://www.vanityfair.com/culture/features/2009/12/cirpriani–200912?currentPage=2.

14. Michael Gross, "August or No, Diners Rush Bellini and Bice," *New York Times*, Aug. 22, 1987.

15. "Restaurants," *New York Times*, Oct. 23, 1987, http://www.nytimes.com/1987/10/23/arts/restaurants–923487.html?scp=1&sq=bryan%20miller%20%20%20too%20chic,%20too%20crowded&st=cse&pagewanted=2.

16. William Stadiem and Mara Gibbs, *Everybody Eats There: Inside the World's Luxury Restaurants* (New York: Artisan Books, 2007), 161.

17. Interview with Pino Luongo by John Mariani, Feb. 2, 2010.

18. Ibid.

19. Pino Luongo and Andrew Friedman, *Dirty Dishes* (New York: Bloomsbury, 2009), 134.

20. Ibid., 145.

## Chapter 16   Trattoria Mania

1. John Mariani, "Esquire's Best New Restaurants 2009," *Esquire*, Nov. 2009, 92.

2. Interview with Michael Chiarello by John Mariani, Feb. 16, 2010.

3. Ibid.

4. Ibid.

5. Melissa Kirsch, "Mezzaluna," *New York*, http://nymag.com/listings/restaurant/mezzaluna/.

6. Emily Green, "Food & Drink: Italy, the food, now open at a restaurant near you: Polenta and pizza feature on the menus of these fashionably 'Italianate' London restaurants. But each one is distinctively different, says Emily Green," *The Independent* (Dec. 5, 1992), http://www.independent.co.uk/life-style/food-and-drink/food—drink-italy.

7. Interview with Nick Vuli by John Mariani, Feb. 18, 2010.

8. Interview with Charles Schicolone, Feb. 15, 2010.

9. "Eating Out," *New York Times*, Dec. 8, 2000, http://www.nytimes.com/2000/12/08/arts/eating-out.html?scp=19&sq=carmine's&st=cse.

10. Florence Fabricant, "De Gustibus; Upper West Side's Host with the Most," *New York Times*, Dec. 5, 1990, http://www.nytimes.com/1990/12/05/garden/de-gustibus.

11. Richard David Story, "That's Italian," *New York*, Sept. 24, 1990, 30.

12. Interview with Frank Scognamillo by John Mariani, Jan. 6, 2010.

13. The River Café," Squaremeal.com. http://www.squaremeal.co.uk/restaurants/london/view/81457/The_River_Cafe.

14. Jasper Gerard, "Restaurant Reviews: River Café, London," *Telegraph*, Aug. 4, 2007. http://www.telegraph.co.uk/foodanddrink/restaurants/3338993/Restaurant-reviews-River-Cafe-London.html.

15. Alasdair Scott Sutherland, *The Spaghetti Tree* (London: Primavera Books, 2009), 215.

16. Ibid., 216.

## Chapter 17   *Salute!*

1. Frances Moore Lappé, *Diet for a Small Planet*, revised ed. (New York: Ballantine Books, 1975), xvii.

2. Jayne Hurley and Bonnie Liebman, "Xtreme Eating 2010: Pestocide," *Nutrition Action Health Newsletter,* http://www.cspinet.org/nah/articles/xtremeeating2010.html.
3. Moira Hodgson, "Taking the Fat Out of Eating," *New York Times,* March 17, 1982, http://www.nytimes.com/1982/03/17/garden/taking-the-fat-out-of-eating.html?scp=16&sq=Alfredo%20Viazzi&st=cse.
4. Frances Mayes, *Every Day in Tuscany* (New York: Broadway, 2010), 249.
5. Slow Food website, http://www.slowfood.com/about_us/eng/philosophy.lasso.
6. As Gillian Riley has written in *The Oxford Companion to Italian Food,* Slow Food "catapults some foods from the basic local subsistence fare to the luxuries of international high gastronomy."
7. Oldways website, http://www.oldwayspt.org/our-story-told-founder-k-dun-gifford.
8. Ibid.
9. Nancy Harmon Jenkins, *The Mediterranean Diet Cookbook* (New York: Bantam Books, 1994), xv.

### Chapter 18 Alta Cucina

1. Levy Restaurants website, http://www.levyrestaurants.com/Levy/AboutLevy/Restaurateurs.htm.
2. Ibid.
3. Interview with Tony Mantuano by John Mariani, Feb. 1, 2010.
4. Ibid. "We would never serve pizza and meatballs in the main dining room," said Mantuano, "because we didn't believe it fit the image of the *alta cucina* we wanted to do."
5. Interview with Michael Chiarello by John Mariani, Feb. 16, 2010.
6. Interview with Ferdinand Metz by John Mariani, Feb. 17, 2010.
7. Interview with Tony May by John Mariani, Feb. 4, 2010.
8. Ibid.
9. Florence Fabricant, "In New York, Food Fit for Italy's Princes," *New York Times,* Aug. 17, 1988, http://www.nytimes.com/1988/08/17/garden/in-new-york-food-fit-for-italy-s-princes.html?scp=11&sq=san%20domenico%20restaurant&st=cse.
10. Bryan Miller, "Restaurants: San Domenico," *New York Times,* July 22, 1988, http://www.nytimes.com/1988/07/22/arts/restaurants–595688.html?scp=15&sq=san%20domenico%20restaurant&st=cse.
11. Ibid.
12. *Larousse Gastronimique* (New York: Clarkson Potter, 2001), 626.
13. Interview with Marco Maccioni by John Mariani, Dec. 20, 2009.
14. Interview with Tony Vallone by John Mariani, March 1, 2010.
15. Menu at Tony's, Houston, Texas.

### Chapter 19 Mondo Italiano

1. Michael Steinberger, *Au Revoir to All That: Food, Wine, and the End of France* (New York: Bloomsbury USA, 2009), 221.

2.   Michael Bateman, "Food & Drink: Taste from A to Z," *The Independent,* Oct. 11, 1998, http://www.independent.co.uk/arts-entertainment/food—drink-taste-from-a—z–1177695.html.

3.   Michael Winner, "Stop the Week: Winner's Dinners," *Sunday Times* (London), June 29, 2003, http://www.timesonline.co.uk/tol/news/article1146310.ece.

4.   A. A. Gill, "Luciano," *Times* (London), Dec. 4, 2005, http://www.timesonline.co.uk/tol/life_and_style/food_and_drink/eating_out/a_a_gill/article596522.ece.

5.   Marco Pierre White website, http://www.frankies-knightsbridge.org/.

6.   Ruth Reichl, "Restaurants; A Radical Departure With Sure Footing," *New York Times,* Aug. 26, 1998, http://www.nytimes.com/1998/08/26/dining/restaurants-a-radical-departure-with-sure-footing.html?scp=40&sq=babbo%20restaurant&st=cse.

7.   Interview with Michael White by John Mariani, July 10, 2009.

8.   Ibid.

9.   Torre del Saracino website, http://www.torredelsaracino.it/Website.

10.   Rashmi Uday, "Go for Some Foodism," *Times of India,* Sept. 6, 2009, http://timesofindia.indiatimes.com/life/food/food-reviews/Go-for-some-foodism/articleshow/3603816.cms.

11.   *Gambero Rosso*—"the red prawn," after the name of a tavern in Carlo Collodi's children's story *Pinocchio*—began in 1986 as a supplement to the left wing newspaper *Il Manifesto,* then appeared on its own as a highly influential gourmet and wine guide, for a time allied with the Slow Food movement. Since 1990, it has published a comprehensive restaurant guide and has its own magazine, cooking school, and TV studio.

12.   "A Taste of January," *Gourmet,* Jan. 2009, 30.

13.   Nina Elder, "The New American Classics," *Bon Appétit,* May 2009, 84.

14.   Eric Wilson, "Kalman Ruttenstein, 69, Who Kept Bloomingdale's Chic, Dies," *New York Times,* Dec. 9, 2005, http://www.nytimes.com/2005/12/09/fashion/09ruttenstein.html?scp=1&sq=kal%20Ruttenstein%20+%20da%20silvano&st=cse.

15.   Julia Moskin, "A Dollop of Salami, Spreading From Calabria," *New York Times,* Dec. 22, 2009, http://www.nytimes.com/2009/12/23/dining/23nduja.html?scp=5&sq=nduja&st=cse.

16.   Ed Levine, ed. *Pizza: A Slice of Heaven* (New York: Universe Publishing, 2005), 10.

17.   Daniel Maurer, "Balthazar Bakery Lends a Hand at Pulino's, Now Three Weeks Away," New York Grub Street.com, Feb. 10, 2010, http://newyork.grubstreet.com/2010/02/balthazar_bakery_lends_a_hand.html.

18.   Rob Patronite, "Profile: Co.," *New York,* Dec. 30, 2008, http://nymag.com/listings/restaurant/co/.

19.   Ibid.

20.   Lilia Byock, "Tables for Two: ABC Kitchen," *New Yorker,* May 17, 2010, 20.

21.   Interview with Fortunato Nicotra by John Mariani, Feb. 17, 2010.

# Index